THE MANAGEMENT
OF
EDUCATIONAL PERSONNEL

Readings on the Administration
of Human Resources

Revised Edition

Edited by
Louis G. Romano
Richard L. Featherstone
Michigan State University

Nicholas P. Georgiady
Miamai University, Oxford, Ohio
Sister Dorita Wotiska
St. Stephen School, Principal

Library of Congress Cataloging in Publication Data
Main entry under title:

The Management of educational personnel.

   Includes bibliographical references.
   1. Teachers--Selection and appointment--Addresses,
essays, lectures. 2. Differentiated teaching staffs--
Addresses, essays, lectures. I. Romano, Louis G.
LB2835.M28 1976   658.3'7'3711   76-44378
ISBN 0-8422-0544-6

WHITEHALL COMPANY/Publishers
1200 So. Willis Avenue
Wheeling, Il. 60090

CONTENTS

Selection

PREFACE

The administration of educational personnel is an emerging field, but for the present it lacks its own body of literature and research. This situation has been due to the extremely small number of personnel directorships in our public schools. Such positions were limited to the largest school districts such as those found in cities like New York, Chicago, San Francisco and Milwaukee. Those who filled these positions were not specifically trained and their functions were limited to selecting the "right" professional for a position, which is only one element of the personnel administration process.

In the business sector, the development of personnel administration as a management function has preceded by several decades a similar development in the management of the public schools. Also, there has been a corresponding lag in the development of literature and research specifically related to personnel management in educational enterprises. Many personnel problems resulted from industrialization which brought about tremendous changes in manpower management in the private sector. Unions and collective bargaining became one of the concerns of management during the twenties and thirties while only recently in education have we experienced the emergence of collective bargaining, or as the educator prefers naming the process, "professional negotiations." At present there are still many states where there is a lack of legislation encouraging and regulating the conduct of professional negotiations.

This book of readings may be used as a text for a course in educational personnel administration, but it can also be used as a supplement to another text or as a reference tool for practicing educational personnel directors. Care was taken to include writings to complement the topics covered in several texts in educational personnel administration.

Chapter I gives the reader insights into the nature of administration. It is interesting to note that all of the writings are from the business world. Emphasis is placed on the position as a professional task -- and its future.

One of the most important tasks of the personnel director is the recruitment and selection of personnel. Chapter II is divided into sections on manpower needs, recruitment, interview, and selection. Special attention is focused on successful techniques to be used in this important process.

Once a professional has been selected, the task of induction of the individual into the organization must be resolved. This topic is discussed in Chapter III.

During the sixties, exciting staff patterns emerged which were usually considered when educators planned, included team teaching in their school organization. Chapter IV discusses various patterns of differentiated staffing while Chapter V focuses on the expectations and use of para-professionals or teacher aides.

Chapter VI includes writings in the area of assessment of teacher evaluation. Greater emphasis on teacher evaluation is found in the literature and is due to the clamor for "account-ability" by the tax-paying public.

With the emergence of professional negotiations, the editors have included several pertinent writings on this im-portant topic in Chapter VII. Because of its recentness in education, administrators and teachers must have a clearer perspective of the purposes, process and limitations of negotiation. Without this knowledge, teachers and administrators will continue to fumble along - and lose sight of their most important goal - maximizing learning for boys and girls.

Professional salaries and benefits are discussed in Chapter VIII with a look to future trends while Chapter IX covers topics related to the field of education. Without good morale, and basis human relations, the working relationships between administrators, teachers, and Boards of Education can be ad-versely affected.

Thus, the book presents a wide range of topics correlated with subjects treated in most basic texts in educational per-sonnel administration. It was also prepared to insure that students interested in this emerging field are presented with timely issues and topics relevant to the future of personnel administration.

Chapter I

The Nature of Personnel Management

The traditional personnel concepts as they have been carried on in the past are under heavy fire. Serious questions have been raised as to their appropriateness in light of a rapidly changing and increasingly competitive industrial society. The possibility of several new directions have been raised by writers in the field as alternatives to existing theories and practices. As is to be expected, whenever the specter of change is raised, there is a defense mechanism set in motion which seeks to justify present operations. However, the stresses of the times call for an objectivity which will permit unbiased examination of the changing conditions, their effects on personnel functions and a search for alternative means of carrying on these important functions.

The scientific study of the nature of change and its effects on individuals and on organizations provides significant data that are useful in identifying desirable directions and possible problem areas. It is interesting to note variations in responses according to the sizes of firms providing such responses. It is also of interest to note the degree of agreement among different executive levels and positions as regards the effects of change on personnel operations in various departments. Various threads running throughout these data are identified with matters of cost factors, effects on personnel (the humaneness factor) and trends towards and away from centralization among others. Certainly all of these deserve consideration in any analysis of changes in personnel functions.

The emergence of a host of problems, some new and some persistent from the past, has made it essential that managerial philosophy and theories of management be re-examined. Underlying much of the unrest is a concern on the part of the individual with himself and his role or relationship with the organization he is associated with. There is growing realization, for example, that rather than adapt the individual to the demands of the organization, more attention must be focused on adapting the organization to the needs, expectations and potential of the individual. A growing militancy on the part particularly of more youthful employees underscores the need for such philosophic reflection and re-evaluation. The appearance of underground newspapers and increases in drug habits among employees provide further evidence as to the need of this kind of attention. Certainly the role of the personnel manager is to be alert and attuned to such manifestations of deep-seated disturbances. This strongly suggests the advisability of training programs for supervisory personnel to permit them to fathom deviant behavior by employees, their causes and their proper handling. There

can no longer be any justification of leaving role definition to whimsical or haphazard performance.

Even the role of the personnel manager and his title
as well is being reexamined with the suggestion that it
be retitled as human resources management. The implication is that human resources are important enough to deserve the same kind of attention given to finances, technology and production, transportation, sales, etc. The
investment in people is not one that can or ought to be
denied or downgraded.

PERSONNEL MANAGEMENT — ART OR SCIENCE?

Len Peach

Let me first focus attention on the personnel manager, because in the end, it is his character, definition and interpretation of personnel management which will determine whether we call it an art or a science.

We are not as a profession universally loved. In *Up the Organisation* an ex-managing director said that the first step of any managing director should be to fire the personnel department[1]. Writing in 1955 Drucker[2] stated that the personnel administrator's job is 'partly a file clerk's job, partly a housekeeping job, partly a social worker's job and partly fire fighting' to 'head' off union trouble or settle it. He continued, 'the things the personnel administrator is typically responsible for —safety and pension plans, the suggestion system, the employment offer and union grievances—are necessary chores. They are most unpleasant chores . . . and none of these activities in itself are of such a nature as to call for more than moderate capacity in its management.' Drucker was particularly critical of the failure of personnel management to involve itself in the organization of the work and the organization of people to do the work—

'the two most important areas in the management of workers'. There are still many personnel departments at the level of Drucker's description. Limitations of resources and reporting structure may reduce the impact of a personnel department, but, for the purposes of this article, I am assuming a developed function whose objective is to influence and create an environment in which a company can recruit, develop, motivate and retain the employees it needs to fulfil its business objectives.

The developed function

It should have a policy, planning and research role in addition to providing personnel services such as recruiting, information and guidance to line managers on matters such as industrial relations and management and individual development. It is this role which will ultimately influence the environment and produce the relationships to make the most of the human resources in the enterprise. In fulfilling these responsibilities, the personnel manager is as concerned as any other functional manager with ensuring that the company's objectives are met; he is contributing as an expert in his own field, with particular responsibility for the effective and profitable use of people; he is also a catalyst or change

Len Peach is director of personnel for IBM United Kingdom Ltd.

PERSONNEL MANAGEMENT, Jan. 1972, pp. 26-29.

agent.

Inconsistent objectives

Let us look at some of the pressures on him. Not even his overall objectives are consistent. For example, retention. Whereas his objective during a period of economic boom is to retain labour, during a period of slump it will be to lose part of the labour force by natural or forced wastage.

Then there are the increasing complexities of his job. The personnel manager faced by the new Industrial Relations Act will have to add to his toolkit a knowledge of labour law to go with an awareness of the analytical techniques used in salary and benefits surveys; knowledge of government pension schemes, insurance, sickness legislation; an ability to interpret what the systems analyst is saying to him about computerized payrolls, records and information systems; a knowledge of the social sciences—industrial psychology, industrial sociology, industrial anthropology and so on; a trusteeship in the company pension scheme; an awareness of complex income tax legislation and its effect upon top management remuneration; and very probably he will also be responsible for the company's catering policy! Other influences complicating his life will be the government—whichever political party is in power—which will be oscillating between stimulating the economy, and damping down the economy, creating overfull employment or large scale unemployment, introducing new labour laws whether on unions, training, redundancy or redeployment of labour. Then there will be the trade unions and employee representatives making impossible and unrealistic claims etc. To add to this there is the 'flavour of the month' or 'the mood of the moment' in personnel management. The last two years or so this has been to 'quantify'—the figures produced must be figures in which the personnel department has faith, not underlined to meet the changing trends of fashion.

When the pressures are so many, so varied and in some cases so contradictory the application of scientific research may seem of little use. There is a need to preserve a balance between meeting the needs of shareholders, customers and employees; to be conscious of and able to influence the various power situations within a company; and to be aware of the input of government both as a legislator and as a customer. There are strong social pressures: the younger generation, the minority groups; and so on; there is a need for increasing consultation and participation; there is a need for self education. Yet resources are inevitably limited both in personnel and in other departments on whose services the personnel manager relies.

I feel that I should now attempt a definition of science and scientific method against which to judge personnel management. My preference is for that given by Stanley Beck[3]. 'Science is a body of tested objective knowledge obtained and unified in principle by inductive methods'. Scientific method implies observation, hypothesis, experiments to prove the hypothesis and the formulation of principles.

Professor Hanika, *New thinking in management*[4], defined the art or craft stage of management as that in which the skill used is passed from practitioner to apprentice. Later experience is collected, collated, analysed and systematized with the aim of formulating principles. In the course of time, Hanika continued, these principles may form an integrated structure of thought explaining phenomena and offering reasonable predictions of the outcome of given acts or decisions. The question which I am addressing is how far have we in personnel management progressed in our use of scientific method as defined by Beck and in acquiring an integrated and predictive structure of thought as stipulated by Hanika.

I have already cast doubt upon our ability to predict because of the changing pressures and the multitude of relationships with which personnel management must contend. It is a sobering thought that although the science of economics has existed for 200 years the ability of economists to predict is still in doubt. Certainly none of the economists writing in the leading financial newspapers in the United Kingdom or in the review published by the National Institute of Economic and Social Research at the end of 1969 predicted the wages explosion of 1970. The only excuse given for the economists is that 'they are dealing with humans and their institutions, both of which are inclined to do thoroughly irrational things'. If such an excuse is valid for economists then it is freely available to personnel managers.

Certainly in the last 20 years the personnel manager's techniques kit has increased considerably. The bond with the social sciences has grown and although I am not convinced that a personnel manager has to be a social or a behavioural scientist he should be capable of interpreting their work and making use of it in situations where it may lead to the improved use of human resources.

Man and machine

Using the social sciences I believe that we have made significant progress in developing understanding of motivation in the working environment. The early school of scientific management led us to believe that man was an extension of a machine. This viewpoint took no account of psychological motives or social factors and was later replaced by the human relations school which became obsessed with the material or welfare needs of employees. Now McGregor, Herzberg and Maslow have helped managers to understand how low motivation can exist side by side with high pay, benefits and good working conditions and attention of

management is now directed at the job content as well as the job context. Notice I am using the words 'understanding' and 'attention is directed'. The real test is how many of us as personnel managers are working in the field of job enlargement and job enrichment and are applying and testing, for example, Herzberg's conclusions.

Certainly Herzberg's conclusions are no panacea. Our own work in IBM indicates that the more challenge one provides in the job the more is demanded: two years after a job has been organized the job has ceased to be demanding. We once reorganized the work on our keypunch production line at our Scottish plant to create jobs which required greater skills and a longer work cycle. At first we experienced the 'pain of change' and lower production during retraining. Now we have employees who would prefer to build whole keypunches rather than the major sub-assemblies which constitute their present enriched and enlarged jobs. Herzberg's remarks that the motivating effect of a salary increase is shortlived, and that 'you get hungry again', may well apply to job enrichment, although the time span is longer. I was recently told a story which illustrates both Maslow's hierarchy of needs and the changing priorities of a personnel manager. At one of our plants which enjoys a good reputation for job enrichment, because of a falling workload a reallocation of work led to one of our employees receiving a low skill job. He immediately complained to his employee representative. 'Do you know,' he said, 'I have just been given a job which I did 17 years ago.' 'Well,' replied the representative, 'you know the alternative'. The employee said he did and returned to his work. Self actualization had receded and the importance of job security had now become paramount.

Let us now examine a number of

13

examples which show how a personnel manager can use scientific method in the identification and demonstration of existing personnel problems in his company. One of the most important applications of the social sciences is in the use and interpretation of attitude surveys. The attitude survey quantifies attitudes and helps to dispel inaccurate assumptions and beliefs held by senior managers, including personnel management, and provides information for action and motivation programmes. They have the advantage of being comprehensive and anonymous; the responses can be broken down by department, age, sex or skill; and can be used for trend measurement, problem identification and pure research. Repetition of core questions in each survey reveals trends.

Sign of weakness

The objections to attitude surveys from both managers and trade unions centre round feelings that surveys are a sign of weakness, that they know how employees feel anyway and, particularly on the management side, that it is best not to create problems by identifying problems—particularly if they are insoluble. For surveys to be successful there must be prompt and comprehensive feedback to employees and there must be an action plan including indications where and why action cannot be taken. Attitude surveys are of great value to the personnel manager in establishing the environment within the company or function and of measuring subsequent changes, and their use brings him as near as he can come to scientific assessment of human problems.

There is, of course, always a subjective element in the interpretation of a survey. As a trained historian used to Marxist and other interpretations of history I have been interested to see that evidence to support the theory to which the researcher is committed is usually found in some form in the results. However a well constructed survey will provide a number of correlated questions so that the interpretation can be thoroughly checked.

Now let us look at planning and control aspects of personnel management. The scientific method has again been applied in the field of compensation, salary and benefits. This use of inter-company surveys enables a company to establish and control against salary objectives set in a quantified form. Instead of maintaining a policy expressed in general terms —'we pay above average salaries'—it can set as a target salaries which are 'on the weighted average of the leading companies' for similar work or which 'at midpoint of the salary bracket are x per cent above the weighted average of the leading companies.' The same system can be used for benefits or perquisite programmes. This practice sounds one of the most 'scientific' but a number of areas remain for management judgment which may change the measurements substantially. First with whom does a company wish to compare—with competitiors, with companies in a similar industry, with leading companies? Which jobs does it wish to include? Having reached a decision on that, the accuracy of the information has to be ensured by visits to the contributing company to ensure that the jobs which are being compared match. Then problems may arise because of differences in the maturity of the population. A young company with a high promotion rate may find itself drawn into paying higher salaries than it need if for example its average length of service in a job grade is one year compared with an average rate in other companies of say 3 or 4 years. Since no company is willing to devote a disproportionate amount of its personnel resources to completing salary surveys, judgment has to be applied to decide whether the final salary relationship with the outside market is satisfactory.

Complex claims

Trade union claims are now being prepared in greater detail and personnel departments need to have their own salary and compensation departments preparing their own comments in an equal, if not greater depth. There is, however, a considerable scope for the application of judgment, and the negotiations with a trade union will be largely determined by the tactics of management within parameters established by their salary and benefits comparisons, and their willingness to take the commercial risks of a prolonged strike.

My comments on the scientific base for salaries would not be complete without some points on job evaluation. I have yet to meet a job evaluation system which is scientific. The method of arriving at job grading used in most companies is logical and analytical but essentially judgmental. Although job evaluation is essential to create an equitable base for the salary system, it is not scientific; nor is there a universal system of values of relationships. Most systems reinforce the company's own prejudices.

I find it surprising that the investigation of salary methods and policies seems to have been abandoned by motivational researchers. There has been little or no research into the best methods of applying salary increases to obtain maximum motivation. The emphasis placed by modern sociologists on the job content factors has removed interest from research into salary methods and procedures. I believe the timing of a salary increase is all important. I have no faith in annual reviews or reviews on fixed dates. I believe that salary increase for merit should be given when *deserved* and that fixed reviews should be avoided subject to safeguards against management forgetfulness. It is the unexpec-

ted increase and the unexpected promotion which motivates—unexpected both in time and in amount.

How much use does personnel management make of 'scientific' aids even when these are readily available? A responsibility of all personnel managers is recruitment. Notwithstanding the batteries of tests which have been developed for selection purposes during the last half century most companies still rely upon the one to one interview—'40 minutes of inspired intuition', which is used in recruiting an employee, who may be an asset or a liability for the next 30 years.

Even when scientific tests are used they are seldom used with the degree of sophistication which goes into their design. That is not to say that tests alone should constitute the only means for selection. Motivation, energy and persistence are impossible to measure. So is the social environment in which the successful candidate will work in his new job. The same comments can be made on selections for promotion within a company. We have no scientific method of measuring 'potential' and the identification of a future managing director continues to be intuitive. Current performance is the only assessable and sometimes measurable criterion.

In management development, personnel management has made progress in developing systems which influence managers to more effective performance. Again the major developments have been as a result of the lessons of social science research being applied in the working environment. A fully integrated management development programme comprising management training schemes based on actual training needs, appraisal and counselling systems concerned with the man manager relationship and the latest addition, organization development, should be the objective of every major company.

Assessment of objectives

The 'systematic' approach in management development requires not training based on the opinion of training officers but training based on the real needs of managers as established by a training needs survey. In assessment, the great advance of the last ten years has been the switch to assessment by and management by objectives. I have found it useful to insist that objectives are broken down in two major categories: job, and people. Under the 'job' heading objectives should be divided into routine or repetitive, innovation or improvement. Under the 'personnel' heading, into personnel and personal.

Organization development is still in its early stages and there is a controversy as to whether it belongs in the personnel department. Since it is concerned with organizational relationships and people behaviour which ultimately influence and in some cases determine the environment in a company, I believe it does belong in personnel. The objective of organization development is, as Burke describes it, 'not evolution, not revolution but planned change'[5]. By changing group norms we change group behaviour. Its processes may be labelled scientific but not everyone would accept this classification and certainly its success, as in psychiatry, is heavily dependent on the social skills or the 'art' of the consultant or change-agent.

Predictable aggregates of people

Another area of personnel management where scientific method can be used is manpower planning. Aggregates of people are more predictable than individuals. Typical processes — to prove my point of scientific method— are observation of, and predictions of, changes in productivity; linking with sales and production forecasts; observation of transitions from untrained to trained with appropriate amendments made of leavers; management promotions and transfers to other skills; analysis of leavers by manpower parameters of the present population; prediction of future distribution and leaving patterns and integrations with growth and shrinkage predictions to produce hiring and training requirements.

The problem of interpretation of personnel statistics is best illustrated by the history of labour turnover which exemplifies both the use of scientific personnel methods and their limitations when concerned with interpretation. When labour turnover statistics were first produced they were welcomed as indications of employee morale or management competence. Then the manpower planners pointed out and partially proved that turnover was related to the state of the economy, the industry, the skill and sex mix of the firm and its age and length of service distributions. They went further and showed how by careful recruiting you can both reduce turnover and approach an ideal age or other distribution. This form of 'science' helps but will take us only part of the way towards understanding why people leave and what should be done to encourage them to stay. Even the addition of the results of attitude surveys and the more doubtful reports of exit interviews will still leave plenty of scope for the experience and intuition or 'art' of the personnel manager.

As I indicated earlier certain influences are continuously changing the situation in which the personnel manager is operating. Economic marketing, financial and profit considerations; technical developments; the influence of government and other external bodies; the internal political climate and relationships; the social setting; cultural considerations at local, national and international level; the influence of trade unions and of course the company's priorities. This does not excuse the failure to use scientific method. It does indicate some of the difficulties of interpretation.

I have concentrated on areas where I believe that we in personnel have made most progress in attempting to introduce scientific method—motivation and attitude surveys, salary and benefit policy, manpower planning and management development—although in each of these I have claimed that interpretation and judgment still plays a significant part in the final outcome.

I know of one major British company which makes no use of scientific techniques but which has a very large number of personnel employees who are in daily contact with its employees. It is a very successful company with a magnificent industrial relations record. Its success is due to its respect for its employees which began with its founder and has permeated management ever since. Such a company is exceptional and the need is usually for scientific techniques to change or mould management. opinion and to create an environment to make the best use of its human resources. In conclusion, however scientific the approach of personnel management may be, the application ultimately remains an art.

1. Townsend, Robert. *Up the organization*. Michael Joseph (1970).
2. Drucker, Peter F., *The practice of management*. Heinemann (1955).
3. Beck, Stanley. *Simplicity of science*. Penguin.
4. Hanika, F. de P. *New thinking in management*. Lyon, Grant and Green in association with the Administrative Staff College. Henley (1958).
5. Burke, R. L. and Bennis, W. J. 'Changes in perception of self and others during human relations training.' *Human Relations Journal*. Vol II (1961).

The Professional Personnel Man in Public Education

JOHN E. KEEFE

UNDOUBTEDLY one of the greatest problems confronting education today is the area of employee relations as it relates to salary structures, personnel policies, negotiations, employee rights and privileges and related issues. In many school districts, the preponderance of these problems is presenting almost traumatic experiences by virtue of militancy, walk outs, lock outs, union elections—and resignations of key school administrators. Some school districts saw the signs on the horizon and had prepared for this new era of change, while others either failed to recognize the problem, or assumed the attitude of "it can't happen in our district." They were caught napping and are suffering as a result.

To present an analogy in the area of employee relations and employee militancy, public education today is where the Private Sector was in the middle 1940's. In short, education is 20-25 years behind schedule. As a result of World War II, there evolved a greater concern for people, the emergence of special employee relations programs, and the appearance of the professional personnel man. Personnel programs which included hospital/surgical coverage, life insurance, recreation activities, tuition loan and refund, formalized wage and salary administration, true employee performance evaluation, etc. were undertaken by the more progressive firms.

PERSONNEL JOURNAL, Mar. 1970, pp. 213-215.

Unionism and recognition drives became more prevalent and the professional personnel man emerged as an employee relations expert versus the heretofore image of employment manager or recreation specialist.

Now, the crux of the analogy. These new young personnel men were pitted against the "pros" in unionism, John L. Lewis, Walter Ruether, Michael Quill and others who had been in the labor movement many years. School administrators now confronted with adamant employees and union drives know whereof I speak. Many have been unable to cope with the present problems and have had to obtain services of professional personnel people on a consulting basis—at a very costly figure. Many school districts are now at the cross road where they have to face the problem squarely or suffer the consequences.

New terms, which were previously nebulous and found only in textbooks, are appearing in educational circles, such terms as performance appraisal, recruiting, management by objectives, program budgeting, negotiations, job analysis, salary administration, grievance procedures and performance pay, among many others.

School administration, although far behind the Private Sector in personnel programs, has an opportunity and a challenge to reduce this 25 year gap to a 5 year span. How?

Trained professional personnel people are available. As mentioned earlier, 20-25 years ago there was no such being; someone was pulled from the ranks and assigned the job of conducting a recreation program or showing new employees the ropes. But today, school districts can hire a personnel man who is both able and experienced. Anyone who is contemplating doing this should go to the Private Sector. These people have educational and teaching backgrounds and can be hired at a price which is within a school district hiring rate range. Let's proselyte from industry for a change and retrieve some of those fugitives from the educational field who are now professional personnel people.

The professional personnel man will pay off in the long run in efficiency and time and money saved. Anyone who is now conducting a semblance of a personnel program knows that a true professional is needed. An ex-principal cannot acquire in one year what the professional personnel man has learned in 10 or 15. You certainly wouldn't hire a personnel man as an Assistant Superintendent of Curriculum and Instruction! In hiring a personnel man, try to select someone with at least 8-10 years of personnel experience—don't settle for a job analyst, interviewer or training instructor with 2-3 years background. Select someone who has *large program* experience in all phases of personnel. His experience should encompass depth in the following areas:

—Employment
—Wage and Salary Administration
—Training
—Personnel Records
—Management Development & Performance Evaluation
—Organization Planning
—Employee Evaluation Programs
—Negotiations
—Employee Benefit Programs

Further, such "new" educational programs as performance pay, differentiated staffing, management by objectives are "old hat" to him and he has already gone through his period of experimentation in these fields.

Many of you are probably making the statement that "our district cannot afford a personnel man." However, in time, effort, efficiency and cost savings, a personnel man can pay for himself.

1. How much valuable time of a business

manager is spent in hiring custodians and secretaries?

2. How much time of an assistant superintendent is spent in recruiting teachers? (Some superintendents perform this function.)

3. How about your wage and salary programs? Do you have a formalized wage and salary and job evaluation program or do you operate your pay programs from a "shoe box"? Are employees properly classified? How controllable are your salaries? This is an area which the taxpayer is beginning to scrutinize. Do the pioneering yourself. Are there union threats because of pay inequities?

4. What has been done to place employment programs on a cost per hire basis? What about a formalized program to reduce employee turnover?

5. How much thought has been given to reducing absenteeism?

6. How about a program of performance evaluation to weed out sub-par employees and to reward rightfully good performance?

7. How effective is your college recruiting program—are you getting the "cream of the crop?"

8. What about manpower planning and control? Do you have most of the vacancies filled by the close of school with well qualified teachers and administrators? How about proper utilization of in-house manpower capability?

9. Are your employee benefit programs placed on a cost basis to assure proper coverage, as well as to control costs in the area of insurance programs, sick leave and other benefits. Are you getting the proper publicity and "mileage" from the many dollars spent in this area?

10. What about the important area of employee negotiations? Negotiation is a science and an art. Poor preparations and poor strategies can be costly. The professional personnel man has been trained in these areas and knows the techniques. He is skilled in the nuances of negotiating and such other important areas as contract language, counter proposals to demands, costing of economic items, contract term and termination, etc.

11. As a follow-up to negotiations, there is the crucial area of contract administration. It is meaningless to negotiate a contract or agreement if it is not successfully administered. First line supervisors—principals—must be trained in the area of handling grievances and the other provisions of the contract. There must be uniform application or there will be erosion of administrative rights.

Let's not forget the area of the non-instructional employee. This support group cannot be forgotten or ignored in the employee relations program. The same problems exist here as with the professional staff.

From experience, the writer knows that there are many professional personnel people with teaching backgrounds. Fifteen or 20 years ago, there was a natural flow of teachers to industrial personnel departments because the backgrounds were similar; namely, dealing with people, knowledge of testing programs, job information and related areas. In many universities, the Industrial Psychology/Guidance/Personnel Administration courses were all dovetailed.

Review your own situation carefully and you will find that through application of good personnel techniques, the professional personnel man will pay for himself in many ways through proper salary controls, lower recruiting costs, etc. The mere hiring of 1-2 fewer teachers will cover his salary. Further, a simple item such as reduction in employee turnover and absenteeism will pay his salary.

Let's not pursue a "nickel/dime" approach to a large dollar operation. The School Board, the community and the taxpayer should have an appreciation of the savings that can be made. Your employee relations program will be improved in consistent personnel policies, a greater concern for people and—most important of all—continuity of the education program.

The Personnel Administrator of the 1970's

ROSSALL J. JOHNSON

STATED in broad terms, personnel management as it is known today is too narrow and must be expanded to a point where the function requires that there be intervention in the day-to-day operations of an organization in order to protect the investment in human resources. In other words, a positive posture is needed.

To indicate a new role for the personnel manager, a change in name seems to be appropriate. Somewhat arbitrarily, the title of Director of Human Resources Management has been selected. This Director is not a Personnel Administrator with a new title, but an executive with training in information systems programming, budgeting, and organization theory, as well as the basis of psychology, sociology, and economics. Such a director can be thought of as a controller of human resources. There is an analogy in a way—the Controller of Finances is concerned with money aspects of an organization, while the Director of Human Resources Management is concerned with people. One should establish budgets for people and set up people reserves just as one must set up reserves of money. And finally there must be an evaluation for the use of people just as there is for money. The reason for drawing this analogy is that very few organizations give as much con-

PERSONNEL JOURNAL, Apr. 1971, pp. 298-309.

sideration to their investment in people as they do to their money investments.

It is becoming more and more apparent that the mobilization and allocation of human resources is of greater concern and import to organizations than the management of financial and physical resources. There is no dispute that a business enterprise cannot get off the ground without financial backing and that for certain types of operations there is no business without the physical resources. But the prevailing thought should be that these resources are less valuable if they are misused, and it is people who will determine the fate of these resources.

The above, of course, is obvious and has been a well-known fact of life for some time. What is not so evident and what has been given less than adequate attention is the management of the people who are working with the money and the facilities. Much attention has been given to the structuring of the organizational pyramid, but little to the impact of individual development or change on the personnel.

A survey of some seventy companies in the Chicago area revealed that the planning of human resources is done only on a short range basis. Less than ten of these companies indicated plans for projecting people requirements for more than one or two years. There was little evidence that any of these companies had the necessary information for developing a long range manpower budget.

Traditionally, the personnel department has been viewed as a staff or service department, and traditionally, its role has been to engage in activities connected with:

Employment
Training
Wage and Salaries
Labor Relations
Various Fringe Activities

Safety
First Aid
Recreation
Insurance
Cafeterias

The proposal here is not to do away with or neglect these areas but rather, to incorporate them into a model that will allow the people problems in industry to be considered in a more systematic way. This means that the area of personnel administration will be expanded and the *staff* orientation will be shifted to a control orientation.

Basically, the idea is to view people as a resource which must be managed with as much care as a corporation manages its funds. This means that there is a controller of people resources, and this also means that there is a people budget, a people audit, and control mechanisms to ensure that the people are being used as budgeted. Here the similarity stops because people are not dollars, and where dollar A equals dollar B, person A does not equal person B. The control mechanism must recognize individual rights and differences. It is at this point that the complexities of human resources management begin to become evident.

To examine this problem a simple over-all systemic approach will be introduced. Human resource management means that there is an appropriate selection of people who will implement the inputs into an organization so that the desired outputs result.

The following comments will start with the outputs, jump back to the inputs and then look at the implementation. Since basically there is a money input and a profit output, a program planning, and budget system would be appropriate.

The desired output is reaching the organization objectives. In operational terms the objectives can be stated according to activities, markets, profits, product or service, i.e., something that is operational in nature and something that the Director of Human Resources Management can interpret in terms of people requirements. The director is not taking a passive, advisory role in this planning stage, he is directing the thinking of management rather than sitting back and waiting for personnel requisitions to come in. He is not waiting, he is agitating. A key to the success of human resources management is that the attitudes of all executives be changed to expect the role of the human resources director to be control-oriented.

The director is first of all demanding *operational* objectives and then asking what talents are needed now and tomorrow so that the objectives can be met. He is also asking what changes need to be made in the organization structure now or in the future. This applies to an ongoing corporation or organization, where objectives change over a period of time. These objectives need to be clarified so that appropriate skills can be acquired, maintained, or developed. If the corporation is considering a change in objectives, the impact on the people budget should be reviewed *before* the decision is made. The emphasis on the phrase "before the decision is made" is another important point: in the past many corporations have completed a merger arrangement, shifted production facilities, opened new plants, etc., without considering the people problem. For instance, the lack of appropriate integration of the people in a number of mergers and acquisitions has been the cause of less than expected earnings and even resulted in failures to reach objectives.

The Penn Central Railroad would be an example of an organization that failed to live up to its expectations because of the lack of integration of the two organizations.

The director of human resources must be in on the initial stages of most decisions. This means that his position must be at the vice-president level, and it also means that he should be an active member of the planning committee and in frequent consultation with the president. The director must be in a position to head off the dissipation of human resources and must be able to anticipate future demands for people talents. This requires the centralization of the function of human resources management. These are budgeting problems that should be in constant control. In summary then, the output of an organization is the target, and the shifting of the objective—gradual as it may be—is a necessary part of the control information. To reach these objectives, the inputs must be appropriate.

Inputs

One of the inputs required in a corporation is, of course, people activity. As indicated, the input must be appropriate if the output target is to be met. Here, again, there should be active participation on the part of the Human Resources Management department. It is at this stage that skills are being specified.

Not only should there be budget information for today, there must also be information for next year and the year after and for the next ten years. Unlike dollars and machines, people cannot be put into the bank or stored or sold for scrap or junked. People *now* make demands for security, and when a person is separated, a charge is made to the company. The separation cost may, in part, be in monetary terms such as increased premiums on unemployment insurance, or separation pay, or it may be a cost in terms of negative reputation, so that the best workers do not apply for jobs with the corporation, or it may be a cost in terms of poor employee relations, or a cost in terms of work disruption. And it is conceivable that in the not too distant future it may be that an employee cannot be separated without government approval. With these kinds of costs and restrictions facing the corporation, the days of trial and error are limited, and corporations need to sharpen the skill of budgetary control over human resources now. It should be recognized however, that all human resources needs cannot be satisfied; thus a trade-off must be made, a trade-off in terms of efficiencies versus desired skills and knowledge.

The input is in terms of the skills needed for the output. But the determination of the needed skills is dependent not only on the output but what is available in the organization. The term *skill* has a very broad definition and means not only achievement but also potential, and it means both ability in a technical sense and in the interpersonal behavior sense. To determine what is available in an organization and what is needed requires a sophisticated information system that will allow intelligent evaluations and decisions. There is no question, for instance, that, when a human resource need arises, the present manpower inventory of an organization should be thoroughly and quickly searched and evaluated before turning to external sources.

Implementation

Up to this point there have been comments on the output and the input. The core of the problem lies in the way in which inputs of the organization are transferred into outputs.

That is, implementation is the necessary link between the two.

Keeping in mind that the concern is with an on-going organization, it must be remembered that nothing stops and that decisions are made continuously, even though the executives may choose not to make a decision, for that in itself is a decision, and the organization continues with its progress either toward the objective or off in another direction. Because implementation is on-going and because there is no stopping point, control mechanisms are needed. Just as control mechanisms are used to govern the disposition of money, so it is necessary to have a systematic allocation of human resources.

Financial budgets are based on estimates, usually of revenue and in terms of what is needed to get the job done. The human resource budget is no different except that a much longer time factor is involved. A one-year human resource budget is mandatory, while a ten-year projection is also vital to maintain high efficiency and position attitudes as well as organizational continuity.

One might question the realism of a ten-year budget. There is no doubt that such a long projection will be subject to considerable revision as time goes on, but this is true of all budgeting processes. While ten years was arbitrarily selected, for some industries an eight or twelve-year budget might be more appropriate. The basic purposes of the long-range budget are to bring about a rethinking of organizational goals, an analysis of the human resources, implications of current trends in technology and an evaluation of the present manpower inventory in terms of future requirements. If an organization is unable to establish a long-range budget, then there should be a questioning of the adequacies of the current information; probably the whole information system needs to be overhauled with new inputs supplementing or displacing old ones.

The recent economic downtrend is a case in point. While the extent of the business setback could not be predicted, the need to plan for such an eventuality should have been recognized. Many organizations are now trimming their people requirements so as to reduce costs. While some reduction in the work force may be a direct result of loss of sales, some of it was based on an edict from above: cut your personnel by 10% or 15% or some other set figure. No thought was given, no investigation was made as to the long-term impact. There was a need to cut costs, and the consequences of wholesale discharge are to be faced later. Unless an organization is on the verge of bankruptcy, such across-the-board reduction in personnel is a very costly approach to the problem. If there are excesses of personnel in various departments, it probably is not 10% in each section. Some may be overstaffed by 50% and others by 2% or 15% or even understaffed. One should ask: if a company has extra staff, why did it wait until financial problems developed before reducing the staff and why not do it in an orderly manner at the time the excesses arise? To ask the question in a different way: what have the various corporations done about the internal environment on a continuous basis so that external factors will have a reduced impact?

Is there an implication that these mass layoffs and panic cost-cutting procedures needn't have taken place? It would seem so. All too frequently management is pressured into emergency situations which may relieve the immediate crisis, but which, over an extended period, year in and year out, may cause heavy losses.

It is imperative that the human resources be controlled and that control be centralized so that consistency and flexibility are not lost.

The human resources budget requires considerable information, and the gathering processes and interpreting of this information require the efforts of many people. This is not a nose counting operation; it is a planning, programming, and budgeting procedure that is stated in terms of the work requirement, when it is to be done, and what kinds of skills are required. But its complexities are many. Perhaps a broad outline of some of the information will indicate the job to be done.

There are at least seven areas where information is needed for the implementation of effective control and use of the human resources. They are:

1. Evolution of the Organization

An organization goes through an evolutionary process from its inception to a period of rapid growth, to a plateau, to a decline or another growth period. Each step in the evolutionary process means changes in personnel, changes in the decision making process, changes in information system or, broadly speaking, changes in the organization structure and procedures.

For instance, in a new organization the main thrust may be on selling of ideas and objectives and in establishing role relationships. Later, the selling of objectives may be routine and the roles may be well coordinated. Those who are the specialists in the management of human resources should be observing to see that the appropriate changes in thrust come about because of the evolutionary processes and that the organization adjusts to the changes in emphasis.

There are any number of examples of organizations which entered a market with specific quality of goods or services only to find that later, when an attempt was made to change the quality in order to be more competitive, some people in the organization evidently didn't understand the need to change with time and refused to adjust. Or perhaps the owner-manager makes decisions today with 5,000 employees in the same manner as he did when there were only 50. The human resources manager needs to stand to one side and observe this evolutionary process so that he may make the appropriate recommendations and decisions.

2. Flow of People

What are the causes of the flow of people through the organization and in and out of the organization? Death, illness, retirement, obsolescence, involuntary separation, advancement and transfer, and voluntary separation. How many of these can be predicted? Perhaps all except the last one—voluntary separation—and even this may be predicted at times.

Actuary figures will not pinpoint the specific individual who will die, but it will indicate how many probably will die before reaching retirement and how many will be incapacitated by illness. Do companies make use of this available information in estimating manpower needs in five years or ten years? Everyone knows when his boss is going to reach retirement age, but is good use made of retirement information when forecasting people needs? Few companies use such information.

Obsolescence is a tough one, but in some cases the signs are quite obvious if one is trained to look for them. Here the director of human resources and his staff can make a unique contribution since it should be part of their job to anticipate obsolescence before it arrives. Those employees with obsolete skills should be alerted to the condition well before the fact. Such timing allows for planned retraining or planned early retirement. When pinpointed early a valuable employee (valu-

33

able in terms of attitudes and reliability) may be transferred to another job.

Discharge—defined here as leaving the organization at the request of the organization—involuntary. It may be because of unacceptable performance or because of reduction of work-force, etc. Within certain time constraints this can be anticipated, but over an extended period of time it is an unanticipated change unless a pattern can be established. While it is acknowledged that there will be some involuntary separations, in most organizations there are far too many. Here is an area where the human resources department can be useful in reducing turnover.

Voluntary separation is frequently the cause of an unpredictable void in an organization. This is a costly type of separation because it not only leads to less efficient operations, but frequently results in the vacancy being quickly filled by an unqualified person who must be trained on the job by an individual who is not completely acquainted with the job.

There have been studies on the probability of an individual advancing in the organization and how long he can expect to remain in any one position. This type of information can be useful in career planning for selected individuals, and it can be helpful in determining problem areas in the developing system. Blind alleys in the flow of personnel can be opened up and favored avenues for advancement can be re-examined. Undesirable voluntary separations can be reduced by regulating the avenues to advancement.

3. Role Establishment

Role Establishment refers to a process where individuals understand role relationships so that behavior may be predicted more accurately. There may be a difference, for instance, in view of the role of an engineer.

He may look upon himself as a professional person and, therefore, behaves in a "professional manner," while the production manager sees the engineer's role as that of "any other employee" and refuses to accept the professional role behavior. While this type of information does not directly affect the number of people in a budget, it does allow for the full utilization of those in the work force. This, then, is a new and important dimension that is part of the job of the people budget director—the human resources manager. He must be observant of those potential points of friction that will reduce the efficiency of the organization. This leads directly into the area of interrelationships.

4. Interrelationships

Manpower requirements are increased or decreased according to effectiveness of interrelationships. These relationships can be at the interpersonal level or interdepartmental or interdivisional level. For the sake of brevity, these can be classified as intra-organizational relationships. In the past, the effectiveness of such relationships was dealt with at the local level. However, the inefficiencies and frictions and even sabotage that results from inappropriate intra-organizational relationships are too expensive to tolerate over extended periods of time. If the human resources are to be utilized efficiently and the budget is to be held to minimum requirements, the director of human resources must pinpoint inappropriate relationships. This is especially important at the levels above the interpersonal level. It may mean a direct intervention by the director of human resources, but hopefully, a correction will be encouraged from within. In effect, the director has taken on the role of change agent.

5. Change and Time

Change frequently causes people to feel

threatened. The director of human resources can reduce the feelings of insecurity if he is able to anticipate change and send out the appropriate information or establish programs to meet the changing conditions.

A time factor is involved because most changes can be anticipated. The need is to identify those things which are going to disturb people—perhaps a new automatic machine, a different technique in packaging, a computerized operation, or the dropping of a line of goods. All of these have a lead time before the change becomes a reality, and it is during this time that action should take place to relieve anxieties.

6. *Evaluation and Reward*

Evaluation should be considered an ongoing process at different levels. The job of the director of human resources management is to see that it is a continuous process and that the various levels are evaluated. While productivity may be one factor in evaluation, the organizational effectiveness of a group of people should also be included. At the individual level, some form of equity theory should be incorporated so that the relationships between perceived contribution and reward can be balanced with "actual" contribution and reward. Much more information must be processed more efficiently so that evaluations have greater validity and acceptance and thus, rewards may be more equitable.

7. *Will to Work*

Considerable research work has been carried out in the areas of the measurement of attitudes and the elucidation of motivating factors To date there has been only limited success in pinpointing causes for poor work performance. Close supervision has been found to have caused both high and low productivity. The authoritarian leader has been shown to be more efficient, while the democratic leader has happier subordinates. On the other hand, there have been unhappy but efficient subordinates under a democratic leader. The director of human resources must be in the main stream of information flow so that he can make an analysis and recommendations on the will to work.

Centralized Control and Auditing

Considerable stress has been placed on control of human resources in the implementation comments. The term "control" is one of the words that is frowned upon by rights groups because it implies using workers as puppets. Here the term "control" is used to imply that people are operating in an organization with set objectives and that their talents are utilized to meet these objectives. At the same time, the organization has obligations to the individual in terms of compensation, job satisfaction, etc. Supposedly, there is a mutual advantage which can only be attained when controls are instituted.

Organizations are dynamic systems where the characteristics are continually changing. Because of the dynamic aspects, fixed rules and regulations, fixed policies and procedures, as well as the organization structure are outdated rather quickly. Some one person should be responsible for noting the conditions which have an impact on the human resources and then "recommend" changes that should be made.

The term "recommend" may imply a passive role, but the intent here is to indicate that the changes recommended will be adopted in most instances because the director is responsible for the management of the human resources.

It is the thesis here that the total human

resources be controlled through a central point via the vehicle of the human resources programming, planning, and budgeting. In addition, it is recommended that the director of human resources management be given a major role in guiding the structuring of the organization and control of the people aspects.

There is a fine line to be walked by the director of human resources in this dominant role, for it is all too easy for him to undermine superior-subordinate relationships. There is no intention of disrupting the rapport of supervisors with subordinates. It is anticipated that the control mechanisms would strengthen the ties by the very fact that there is consistency, there is planning, there is increased flow of pertinent information, and there is more appropriate selection and training of supervisors. The director of human resources is one man with a staff, and he is in no position to know of or contend with all of the interpersonal contacts. This is not his function. His job is to see to it that through the placement of people, the flow of information, and the development programs, dysfunctional interpersonal and intra-organizational interactions are reduced. The supervisor is still the key to appropriate management of the human resources.

The inputs of people into an organizational effort are so critical that they must be controlled in a positive way and from a central point. It is no longer an acceptable practice to allow the supervisors, department heads, or division vice presidents to set independent policy or make independent decisions concerning the disposition of people.

While the trend is toward decentralization in industry, the purse strings in financial management are held in the home office. The management of human resources should be under even greater control because of the

38

long range implications. Not only should the human resources "purse strings" be centralized, but some basic policies should be adhered to in all parts of the organization.

Human Resources Audit

The audit of human resources management should be an integral and on-going function of the centralized control mechanism. This type of audit opens up a new facet to the control of the use of people. Some examples of the function may clarify the position.

First, there is the routine part which checks budgeted personnel against actual. As indicated before, this is not a numbers game but an audit of talents, skills, and potential. The computer can be very useful in maintaining a continuous audit of this type. There is also the evaluation of new employees in terms of the ability to handle the position they have been hired to fill, and also in terms of potential to be useful employees five years from now and ten years from now.

There are more complex issues to audit. For instance, the effectiveness of an organization is determined in part by an understanding by everyone of the objectives and goals. When there are multiple goals or objectives, there is a need to weight them. Question: Do all employees weight them the same? How do you motivate people toward the same goals or objectives and at the same time, how do you get them to give the same weights?

Simple example:

What are the objectives of the fire department?
1. To put out fires
2. To reduce property damage
3. To save lives
4. To prevent fires

Do all firemen weight these the same? Which has the top priority?

The area of interpersonal or intra-organizational conflict should be subjected to audit. One should start with the assumption that not all conflict can be avoided and also that some conflict may be desirable. The problem then comes down to judging what is desirable and/or unavoidable conflict. While the fine differences may not be definable, there are conflicts which are so gross that there is no question but that the conflict is detrimental to the organization. It is these situations where the director of human resources can use his office to reduce or eliminate the friction.

An example:

A group of computer experts may be so intent on changing over an accounting department's procedures that they encounter a united resistance and their efforts are nullified. Two factions now are at odds: the computer group and the accounting department. The expertise of the director of human resources should be used to effect a "cease-fire" so that changes can be brought about to reduce conflict.

The above example is one of those instances where the director of human resources should not wait to be called in, but should be instrumental in initiating action. His position is that these are human resources that belong to the company and the misuse of them must be eliminated.

The basis for human resources decisions should also be incorporated into the audit process. The guiding question is: are the people decisions based on an open or closed system of information? "Closed system of information" means that only a limited amount of information within the organization is available as a basis for the decision. "Open system" means that both internal and external sources of unrestricted information are referred to. Generally speaking, the tendency is to use the closed system, and frequently this is acceptable. But when the open system should be used and is not used, some very poor decisions can result.

An example:

Take a situation where a supervisor comes to work intoxicated and as a result creates a number of embarrassing incidents. The policy is quite clear in this company on dealing with inebriated employees. (1) The employee shall immediately be sent home. (2) The employee should not report back to work until a disposition has been made of his case and the penalty established. (3) Reporting for work in an intoxicated condition is considered sufficient grounds for immediate discharge.

A closed system approach could easily occur in the above situation, and in all probability the supervisor would be discharged. An open system approach might reveal that the supervisor:

1. Had been with the company for thirty years with no record of intoxication.
2. Is two years away from retirement.
3. Is physically deteriorating to the point where he is approaching senility.
4. A tragedy in his personal life had occurred prior to the date of his offense.

Now, after additional information is available, one might ask if a decision other than discharge should be made. Although the above type of incident may be appropriately handled right now in many organizations, there is a nagging question of, "Do we catch all of the closed system type of decisions which should have been based on an open

41

system type of information?" It is up to the director of human resources management to audit this and to see that adequate information is used as a basis for people decisions.

To sum it up, the role of the personnel director must be expanded; his image must be changed. The staff position of personnel director as an advisor to line personnel should be set aside and in its place there should be a director of human resources who guards the people investment through centralized control and inspection. The director of human resources management must report directly to the chief executive officer and be a party to all planning from the beginning.

The chief occupation of the director of human resources, then, is to:

1. Establish and manage a human resources planning, programming, and budgeting mechanism and auditing system.
2. Review and revise the information system so that adequate decision information is available.
3. Identify critical people areas and critical people problems.
4. Interpret events and situations in terms of impact on human resources.
5. Analyze the effectiveness of the organization today, recommend action, and plan for tomorrow.

Such a director needs to have expertise in the planning, programming, budgeting systems approach, and he must be capable of establishing an appropriate information system and control mechanism. Basic to the job is a working knowledge of organization theory, psychology, sociology, and economics. A professional with these qualifications is a necessity. Conditions of the 1970's will not allow anything else.

YARDSTICKS FOR MEASURING PERSONNEL DEPARTMENTS

George S. Odiorne

Dramatic changes in technology have produced a world of technical and professional employees that differs drastically from the early days of personnel in the 1920's and beyond. Because the composition of the work force is changing, the work of personnel and industrial relations departments is changing.

In 1920, almost half our employees were blue collar. Today, blue-collar workers make up somewhere over 20%. In 1920, the research bill in the United States was less than $100 million dollars. In 1967, it will run in excess of $23 billions. In 1920, approximately 150 firms had research departments. Today, over 16,000 firms have research programs or departments.

In 1920, the industry of the United States was primarily a national industry which engaged in foreign trade. Today great international divisions operate foreign enterprises manned by foreign nations operating on American investment and along the lines of American technology and American management principles.

In 1920, staff positions such as market researcher, operations researcher, personnel researcher, organization planner and the like were non existent. Today they are common.

Since 1920 we have seen the creation of entire new business staff professions such as accountants, computer programmers, quality control and reliability experts and industrial engineers. Mechanization has been supplanted by automation in both factory and office. Larger accumulations of capital, more stable money systems, the gains

PERSONNEL ADMINISTRATOR, 1967, Vol. 12, pp. 1-6.

of creative chemistry, electronics, atomic energy and the rising influence of government in the employment relationship have all changed the personnel job.

Such changes call for new yardsticks for personnel departments. How can you evaluate whether or not your personnel administration staff is adequate, its activities germane, its effectiveness high?

At present we find five major yardsticks which are being used to audit and evaluate personnel departments. They include the following:

1. You might audit yourself by comparing your personnel programs with those of other companies, especially the successful ones.

2. You might base your audit on some source of authority, such as consultant norms, behavioral science findings, or simply use a personnel textbook as a guide.

3. You might rely upon some ratios or averages, such as ratios of personnel staff to total employees.

4. You might use a compliance audit, to measure whether the activities of managers and staff in personnel management comply with policies, procedures and rules, using what I would call the internal audit approach.

5. Finally, and my own personal recommendation — you might manage the personnel department by objectives and use a systems type of audit.

My general plan is to discuss each. Since you already know my bias in favor of the last method, you will note that I will employ an abstraction ladder technique to destroy the first four approaches. This will leave the final systems approach as the recommended method for auditing your own personnel activities.

Not simply based on speculative or pipe-smoke cogitation, the recommendations are based on actual field attempts at experimental installations of such a system, with some tangible evidence in such substantial places as Ford, Honeywell, General Mills, Aetna and other similar firms to confirm its value in practice.

I would not be candid if I did not admit that not every facet of this approach is without some controversial aspects. I freely predict that it is the method which will be increasingly accepted. In our seminars at the Bureau of Industrial Relations we have adopted a unifying theme which runs through the hundreds of seminars which were attended by 10,000 managers last year. Much of my confidence lies in the favorable response which we at the Bureau have received to our approach to the personnel and industrial relations job.

After discussing the shortcomings of other approaches, I should like to outline the major facets of what we rather immodestly refer to as the Michigan approach.

Let's look at each audit system in turn:

1. **Copying other companies.** It is pretty natural and not without some merit that we should try to imitate the successful. If we learn that GE, IBM, RCA, Dupont or General Foods is practicing a certain kind of personnel technique, it is not surprising that we tend to imitate them. They are successful in the overall results which their companies achieve. We presume that copying individual programs is to increase the likelihood of achieving similar overall results from their experience for our own.

Yet, the model which calls for imitating the best isn't without dangers. We may imitate the wrong things. We might copy some irrelevancies rather than the fundamental germ of the idea. We may copy something which was designed to meet a specific local problem within the model firm, but which doesn't suit the needs of our own firm and its problems. Even worse, we may imitate those things which a few isolated individuals, whose low work pressure permits them to appear most frequently at conventions as speakers, declare to be their company practice. But, which the great bulk of their managers have never practiced, nor do they intend to ever try.

Many personnel and training men fall into the self-deluding habit of describing their own desires and plans to outsiders in terms that would create the impression that their firms are smoothly operating monolithic machines which have none of the real-life problems and obstreperous people which you and I always seem to encounter in our own shops.

Learning from another's experience is valuable if you can learn all of the details of that experience. Short of that, constructing new programs based on copy-cat thinking might mean borrowing the other fellows' troubles along with his gains.

2. **Basing your audit on some outside authority.** A second method of devising yardsticks for evaluating your personnel department is to find an expert authority and adopt his criteria.

a. **The search for experts** who will do our thinking and decision making for us often starts with a checklist. A list of all the personnel functions and a rating scale of how well each is done usually comprises the basic audit instrument. This list can come from a textbook, from a manual, or from some commonly applied audit. The University of Minnesota's Triple Audit would be one such example, or the Industrial Relations Counselors Procedure another. There are many such lists, many of which are constructed by copying from the others.

b. **Consultant's observations** comprise another type of expert or authoritative rating. The consultant has visited and worked for numerous firms. He has a well stocked memory drum of personnel practices he has seen elsewhere. He will tell you how your personnel program stacks up against the others he has seen. He may also tell you how to correct any shortcomings.

c. **Behavior science research.** One of the most amazing sources of expert knowledge in recent years are the findings of behavioral science against which present practices are rated. Such norms as Theory X or Theory Y, Managerial Grid, and Autocratic-Democratic scales would be examples of norms and values which are proposed by academic research types as tests of personnel administration effectiveness. The X guys are bad, the Y types are the good guys, and so on.

The common ingredient to all such standards for personnel departments is that they are general in scope and are applied to specific departments, located in specific companies, at a specific time. Not without some uses in obtaining ballpark estimates of how you compare with others, such authoritative guides are a poor beginning point for measuring personnel effectiveness. As ultimate criteria they have many shortcomings.

3. **Measuring your department against an average.** Closely related to the others is the practice of counting things and rating the findings against some averages. The ratio of personnel people to other employees, the ratio of professional staff to clerical staff, the ratio of managers to workers, or the ratio of offers to acceptances in college recruiting are common terms in personnel department evaluation efforts. This can be calculated in dollars to results ratios, percentages of total workforce ratios. Negroes, females, impending retirements, t u r n o v e r, absenteeism, are examples of averages we use. In the use of personnel statistics, the use of averages of one kind or another is commonplace. Frequently, it is enlightening and useful.

Some limitations do exist here. Such statistics only have meaning as internal control devices, not as evidences of success or failure. When the statistics for your firm are matched against the averages for all firms, or even for leading firms, you may be committing a blooper in logic. To some, the use of averages or statistics is mistaken for managing by objectives. While we may use such data in setting and evaluating performance against targets, there is more to managing by objectives.

4. Measuring compliance against policy, procedure, rules. The fourth approach to evaluating the performance of personnel departments is that of auditing compliance with policies, procedures and regulations out in the work force and sales office. Increasing in frequency, the trend seems to be toward turning the dirty job of conducting such inspections over to the internal auditing department. The steps in preparing such audits goes about as follows:

a. The personnel department in cooperation with the internal auditor takes out the policy and procedure manuals on employment, selection, testing, grievance handling, time off with pay, leaves of absence and all of the other areas of concern, and converts it into a checklist.

b. From some commonly available checklists they add others and compile it all into an internal auditor's guide to policing the line organization on behalf of the personnel department.

c. The internal auditor, along with the regular duties of checking revenue and expense procedures, also probes into personnel practices and issues a compliance or non-compliance report. The personnel department is thus removed from the unpleasant task of being policemen. When the report is unfavorable, they are then properly sympathetic and helpful in correcting the deficiencies.

As a kind of manipulative system, it helps protect the good guy image of the personnel department. As one personnel manager put it to me:

It's really a wonderful plan. The auditors are all viewed as snoopers and SOB's anyhow.

The main advantage of the system is that it takes the personnel department out of the role of controller and turns it into a service and advice department, which is a softer and more pleasant image. The disadvantage is that it turns over to the controller some personnel functions and may not be as cleverly concealed as we suppose. The general manager who gets a favorable financial audit, but is clobbered because he has varied from a personnel policy for good reason, will hardly welcome innovative suggestions from the personnel people. It also implies that exact and slavish conformity to every personnel regulation and rule is to be placed in the same category as a violation of the rules for handling cash receivables, inventories, billings, and purchase orders. There is a difference between personnel practices respecting people and accounting practices regarding control of cash. Each in its way has some useful purpose. Auditing people for their management of cash is nothing more than removing temptation — a biblical kind of work. Intervening between manager and subordinate by strict definition of every detail of that relationship is hardly biblical, or even human.

5. **The objectives approach to auditing personnel departments.** My own preference, based on close observation of each of them, is the fifth approach to auditing the personnel department. To wit: Did it set sound objectives? How well did it achieve the objectives which it set for itself? Measuring results against objectives for personnel departments offers the best chance for integrating the personnel department into the parent organization which created and sustains it.

Yet, an anomalous situation exists in many firms. The personnel, management development and the training departments have been leaders in espousing management by objectives for other managers, but have been amazingly reluctant at installing the same system in their own shop. The reasons given often include such evasions as "our work is too intangible and can't be measured." This invites two immediate questions:

1. How can you be so insistent that everyone else do something which you yourself evade?

2. If your output is so vague that it can't be described or measured, what would the company be missing if it were eliminated?

The plain facts are: Many personnel departments are being managed by objectives. They do it and find it exciting and helpful. They are more successful than those which do not manage by objectives.

What is success for a personnel department? Personnel departments don't produce tangible products. They produce intangible softwares. These intangible softwares are made and sold for a captive market consisting of line departments and other staff departments, plus top management. By applying management by objectives to your personnel department, you are able to use a marketing approach to personnel department administration.

A marketing approach to personnel administration? The beginning point for managing the personnel function by objectives is to determine that we are in the business of making and selling certain kinds of products for a captive market. What is this captive market? It consists of those departments which produce and sell the hardware or are themselves staff departments to these same producers and sellers.

The purposes of **the firm** are to make and sell such things as automobiles, chemicals, soap or cereals. Or, to produce and sell some kind of consumer services which will be sold such as insurance protection, investment advice, or education.

The purposes of its own captive departments such as personnel, public relations, traffic, legal and the like, are to help the hardware departments succeed or to help the top management of the firm manage the organization.

It is the loss of insight into its own purposes which gets personnel departments into low repute inside its own firm, or leads to its being crippled in size, budget, and effectiveness.

It is precisely in this regard that the four criteria for auditing personnel departments can contribute to its lower effectiveness rather than raising its effectiveness. Outside authorities, behavioral sciences, practices of other firms, ratios, compliance with policy and consultants have value only to the extent that they impel the personnel department in your organization toward the objectives of your customers. The demand for personnel services is a derrived demand. Personnel functions are like an organ which depend upon the entire organism for its sustenance. At the same time, it comprises a part of the organism and strengthens it by performing a vital function.

What are the stages in setting sound objectives for the personnel department? Since the personnel department is primarily a producer of softwares, it must research its markets and find out what its customer, the primary producing departments, need, want or will buy. This requires that line objectives be reasonably clear. In too many cases the line departments are unclear on where they are going and the personnel department is trying to help them get there.

If operating departments are not clear on objectives, the personnel department has a challenge — to train them in setting objectives, and in selecting people by objectives, appraising performance against objectives and administering salaries by objectives.

With these primary department objectives, the personnel department has the basis for establishing its own targets. As an intangible softwares department, it works at an organization-wide level. And, it should be working on five-year plans, with one-year objectives and commitments to them.

At the beginning of each year, every staff member in the personnel department should be required to make a commitment to his immediate superior, with respect to three kinds of responsibilities. They should reflect what this staff member intends to contribute on his job during that period, with perhaps some quarterly indicators and measuring points noted in advance.

These three kinds of objectives should include, in ascending order of importance, the following kinds of goals:

A. **Regular routine chores.** In this category he states those regular, ordinary recurring responsibilities for which he accepts responsibilities. The outcome here should be stated in terms of average expected outcome but should always include a range of high and low expectations as well. The importance of stating objectives of this kind in a range cannot be overestimated.

No personnel man worth his salt would reasonably expect that he can predict exactly how many college graduates or computer programmers he will hire during the coming year. He could state the range of expected successes and failures. This is more than a ballpark guess because it is based on present levels in stating the average expected. The lower level of expectation is the figure below which he must inform the boss in time to take action, if he fails. The highest expected outcome states the most optimistic possibility and would indicate superior performance.

It is always a mistake to set targets for a single outcome in regular duties. Even more foolish are those managers who simply take last year's outcome and add two percent.

The first major mistake in setting personnel objectives is to set a single target rather than a range of possible outcomes. The second is to give a man a single responsibility area upon which his entire performance will be measured. Such areas of routine responsibility should be stated to permit **trade-offs of one outcome for another.**

You could get all the college recruits you need if you could have an unlimited budget for recruiting. Budget compliance must be a trade-off responsibility with head count of campus hires. You could operate with no grievances for a whole year but labor costs would go through the roof. You must trade off certain numbers of grievances in order to keep labor costs down. Grievance levels often are trade-offs for labor cost levels. The number of regular responsibilities must include the trade-offs of cost, quantity, quality, service and time pressures.

b. **Problem solving objectives.** The second major category of objectives for personnel departments begins where the regular routine responsibilities leave off. They consist of immediate and on-the-spot problems which exist in the organization that the personnel department must solve. Usually they are found in the indicators for the routine responsibility. An indicator running below minimum acceptable levels is a problem. A problem very specifically stated is the best kind of objective possible. Every staffer in your personnel department should be identified as responsible for some problem or problems upon which he will work. This doesn't mean he will solve two problems per year. He may solve only part of one or he may solve a dozen. The key point here is that he has two or more in front of him at all times. They are before him with a known order of priority and an agreement with his boss that they are important. Also, what priorities exist for their solution.

c. **Innovative goals.** T h e hardest of all to measure but probably the area of greatest contribution for personnel departments is that of innovating, introducing changes or raising the quality of employee relations to higher levels than before. This may mean introducing new ideas from the outside which will enhance the performance of the customer departments. It means keeping abreast of new developments which might contribute to such growth. It means making orderly feasibility studies of their application to your business. It means intelligent and aggressive action in installing new programs and making them work.

This trio of categories, routine, problem solving and innovative, comprises an ascending scale of excellence in personnel work. It also comprises an ascending scale of need fulfillment for the people involved, whether you prefer Maslow's hierarchy of needs, or Herzberg's motivation and maintenance factors.

More important, it attunes the personnel program, budget, and staff toward the needs of the parent organization, not to some theoretical, unrelated checklist of audit items. The personnel departments make available only those items of advice, service, or control which its market research among its customers shows that they need, have asked for, or can be sold.

Should personnel departments sell their wares to other departments? The personnel man can take the position that selling isn't part of his job description otherwise he'd have joined the sales department or marketing staff. Such beliefs lead to these standards errors of the frustrated personnel staff man:

He sees the line manager as an enemy who seeks to frustrate him — an obstacle on the path to professional success — rather than as a customer whose needs must be met and around which his wares must be shaped.

He relies too heavily on faith in top management backing to knock down the barriers to his programs.

When line managers won't buy

his wares, he cites this as proof of their autocratic nature, incompetence or uncooperative nature. He creates a special island empire and either abandons the project or goes it without line help. Often the personnel department has ogre images which they have attached to some of the most influential managers.

To survive, he measures his success more and more in intra-departmental terms: The number of programs installed. Trainees covered. Forms approved or processed. Man hours devoted to each project and similar sympomatic measures.

Ultimately, he is a likely candidate to start searching for more felicitous grounds, a more enlightened management climate or more progressive company where all obstacles to his plans will be removed.

Strategies for success: Know your client and design your product catalog to suit his needs.

Be ready for opportunities.

Produce tangible results early in the game.

Build major projects on prior success.

A NOTE ON PROCEDURE

A final note may be in order on procedure for getting started. A system which has worked for me, and for many firms with whom I have worked, is to supplement individual goals conferences between boss and subordinate with departmental meetings. In these meetings, the major department heads each presents his statements of objectives and plan for achieving these objectives to his colleagues and his boss in a group presentation.

At the end of the first year, a repeat of this meeting can be held with an additional agenda item. "Here were my objectives for the year past and here are my results. Now, here are my objectives for next year." The supportive effects and the elimination of duplication and overlap is helped greatly.

There is also a strong motivation effect in such sessions as well. The subordinate who might attempt to set unreasonable goals, either unrealistically high or unacceptably low in their range, will be hesitant to present such estimates to his peers who have an opportunity to question his reason for his particular goal statements.

The possibilities of mutual aid are also enhanced and the unity of effort resulting from such interchanges is high. Getting out of the office with your key subordinates for a couple of days to discuss specific purposes and objectives can remake your department. It can also increase your contribution to your organization as well as your acceptance. Such a plan comprises the best audit of your own personnel department possible.

Chapter II

The Effective Recruitment and Selection
of Personnel

In this chapter a variety of topics are dealt with as they relate to matters of recruitment and selection of personnel in various lines of endeavor including business, industry and education. In a sluggish economy accompanied by a rise in unemployment, the first to suffer are the poor and unskilled. This is an outgrowth of a concomitant decline in on-the-job training since a glutted labor market immediately excludes those with limited skills from qualifying for the fewer jobs available. To offset this, the suggestion is made that programs of classroom training be instituted to provide publicly funded assistance in job skills acquisition since private employers find it less necessary to hire and train disadvantaged, untrained workers. The advantages of such a policy are identified with the value to the individual of his greater self-fulfillment and the avoidance for the community of a heavier burden in welfare costs among other values.

The critical importance of the interview function in the recruitment and selection process is set forth in descriptions of several widely varying approaches to screening candidates and their appropriate job placements. While this is applicable to many fields of endeavor, it is particularly true in education today where a surplus of candidates in numerous educational job categories permits a selectivity on the part of employing school boards and other educational agencies. To afford proper exercise of the option of selection, it is imperative that criteria for selection be carefully determined and applied. Several suggestions for this are made citing examples of questions to be asked, qualities to be examined and other factors to be assessed and evaluated in arriving at selection decisions and assignments.

The matter of personnel recruitment is also examined in several articles. Since the recruitment process is directly related to the effectiveness of the recruiting official, his qualities are an important factor in the success of any program. Also deserving attention, as pointed out in several articles, are the application instrument or form as a source of information about the applicant useful to the recruiter in making his important decisions, a full knowledge of the needs of the employing concern or agency both present and long range with their implications for candidate selections, and the involvement in the interview and selection process of not only the interviewing personnel official but also those personnel with whom the successful candidate will work. The result should be a more valid and reliable decision on the most worthy and appropriate candidates for the jobs being staffed.

A further aspect of the selection process and certainly an important one is the attention necessary for the early identification of candidates with potential for ultimate management or leadership responsibilities. Several approaches are discussed for accomplishing this citing models for study. The importance of a systematic approach to this task is underscored.

Discussion is also centered on the value to recruiters as to the perceptions and expectations of first year teachers with regard to employing school districts. What teachers look for and perceive to be important in a job and a community ought to be known to recruiting officials.

As part of the rapidly changing social scene, hierarchial authority is being moved aside by the emerging authority represented by various "power" groups. In education, this can be viewed in the changing nature of the role of the school principal and the method of his selection. Signs point to the possibility that the principalship as it is now structured, may be on its way out. In its place will come two distinct and separate positions. One will be that of the staff instructional leader and the other, the school building manager. The latter would be the representative of the superintendent and the staff instructional leader would be chosen by the "power" represented by staff of the individual building. Examination of the growingly complex nature of the present singular role of the principal provides considerable support for this possibility.

A commonly accepted practice of accepting at face value the references provided by a previous employer is questioned as to its efficacy. The validity and reliability of such references have been shown to be deficient in enough cases to raise the serious question of their value to an employer. Suggestions for dealing with this condition are offered following an analysis of the weaknesses frequently found in such statements examined in research studies.

As if the previously stated problems and trends are not enough to make the task of the personnel director a difficult if not impossible one, there are a number of other pressures brought to bear on him by often well-meaning but misguided individuals seeking to attain a specific end. The net result is a further obfuscation of the already difficult problem of making personnel selection decisions rational and consistent with sound principles of personnel management and operation.

TEACHER SURPLUS *AND* TEACHER SHORTAGE

William S. Graybeal

The casual reader of educational literature may be perplexed by the seeming conflict in pronouncements about the current status of supply of and demand for public school teachers. Some observers, including the Research Division of the National Education Association, have reported that there is now a surplus of qualified teachers for most assignments, an adequate supply in several assignment areas, and shortages in a few others. Other observers, again including the NEA Research Division, have reported a continuation of teacher shortages this year; that a large shortage of teachers would exist if the public schools met minimum standards of quality in programs and staffing. The primary difference in these conclusions results from a difference in the assumptions underlying the estimate of the demand for qualified teachers.

The NEA announcement of *surpluses* reflects the comparison of the supply of qualified teachers with the numbers of teachers who *actually will* be employed for a given school year. The difference between the number of applicants and the number of positions being filled gives a picture of actual employment opportunities awaiting new graduates prepared to teach and former teachers desiring to reenter teaching. This estimate of the demand for teachers includes the new teachers needed for positions related to school enrollments and for replacement of teachers leaving active employment.

The announcement of continuing teacher *shortages* is based on the comparison of the supply of qualified teachers with the numbers of teachers who *should be* employed in a given school session to attain a specified standard of educational quality at that time. This is a theoretical estimate — the shortage does not reflect the number of actual

PHI DELTA KAPPAN, Oct. 1971, pp. 82-85.

positions which will be filled as quickly as qualified applicants are available. It is useful, however, for long-term planning and evaluation. Comparison of the estimated supply with this estimate of the demand provides an indication of the possible impact of current teacher supply upon continued progress in improvement of education.

If the projected standard of quality in education is realistic in likelihood of attainment, continuing growth in the supply of new teachers accompanied by relatively small growth in school enrollments will provide sufficient staff to meet this standard in the foreseeable future.

The existence of a practical limit to the amount of financial support likely to be directed to public education should be recognized. Otherwise the projected standards of minimum quality in education programs and staffing are only speculative, since it is unlikely that they will ever be attained. Long-term planning is not meaningful if it is based on the assumption that there will always be sufficient teaching positions created to provide employment for all interested people who meet minimum qualifications for entering teaching.

The projection of an attainable standard of minimum quality in educational programs and staffing does provide, however, a long-term goal toward which such progress and the adequacy of present and future supply may be evaluated accurately. The results of this evaluation provide information useful to institutions as they plan for future enrollments and programs. It will also be extremely valuable to college freshmen as they attempt to select programs leading to employment after their graduation three or four years from now.

The NEA report of a teacher oversupply two years ago resulted from the observation of 1) an *actual* surplus of qualified applicants for open positions, and 2) the outlook that unless present trends are changed, the supply of qualified applicants will also exceed the quality-based level of demand within the near future. For the first time in recent history the five-year outlook is for *actual* surpluses which, if accumulated, would provide more teachers than needed to attain a standard of minimum quality.

Because this sharp change in the future supply of qualified teachers calls for serious thought and action in adjusting some of the factors influencing teacher supply and demand, the NEA has established a task force which is reviewing the implications of the teacher manpower situation. The task force will provide direction to NEA efforts to accomplish more complete utilization of available teacher manpower, assist unemployed teachers, and guard against possible deleterious outcomes of a teacher surplus.

There is no question that the supply of graduates prepared to teach also is inadequate for the number of teaching-related jobs which *should be* created. Large numbers of additional jobs should be created to assure day-care services for pre-school children, to improve recreational and educational experiences for people in every age group of the population from pre-school to "golden age," and to assist large numbers of people now underparticipating in the benefits of American life (culturally different; physically, mentally, and emotionally disadvantaged; socially maladjusted; etc.). If society were to allocate sufficient resources to create enough of these additional jobs, the personnel requirements would likely exceed the estimated future surpluses of teachers. However, the present-day teacher education programs may not provide the best preparation for these teaching-related occupations. It might be more efficient to create the needed jobs in these areas and then to organize programs to prepare people for each of these areas as a specialty. This would relate their preparation directly to their future assignments and would encourage them to enter these occupations directly rather than to accept such assignments as a second choice because of difficulties in finding a teaching position.

The following paragraphs summarize the considerations underlying the NEA Research Division's estimates of teacher supply and demand. Details about these estimates and the specific figures are given in the annual NEA Research Division report, *Teacher Supply and Demand in Public Schools.* The projections and the considerations underlying them are reported in the October *NEA Research Bulletin.*

The Supply

In addition to currently employed staff, the present supply of teachers comprises former teachers who have interrupted their careers; college graduates completing preparation to enter teaching positions for the first time; graduates who have postponed entry into teaching; former teachers desiring to return to teaching from supervisory, administrative, or supporting positions; and those ready to enter teaching as a second career.

Of the public school teachers employed in 1965-66, 87.4% were employed as teachers the preceding year, 8.5% were attending college or university full time, 1.6% were engaged in home-making or child-rearing on a full-time basis, 1.1% were working in a nonteaching occupation, and the remainder were in military service, unemployed and seeking work, or in other classifications. These estimates were obtained during a period of general teacher shortage and may not be accurate for a period in which the supply is equal to the demand for new teachers. Some of those attending college or university full time the preceding year were experienced teachers who had interrupted their careers to acquire advanced preparation. However, it is clear that the majority of new teachers (persons employed for a given school year who were not employed as teachers anywhere the preceding school year) came from the graduating classes of colleges and universities.

National estimates of the new supply of college and university graduates completing preparation to teach for the first time with minimum certification requirements have been reported annually by the NEA Research Division for 24 years. The numbers of graduates prepared to teach have represented from 26.7% (in 1950) to 36.2% (in 1971) of all graduates receiving the bachelor's and first professional degree.

NEA Research Division projections for the 1970's are for teacher education graduates to be 37% of the projected numbers of graduates receiving the bachelor's and first professional degree. Unless there is a considerable change in the emphasis given to teacher education, it seems likely that future numbers of graduates prepared to teach will continue to grow at about the same rate as the total number of college graduates.

Reflecting the growth in total number of college graduates, the supply of graduates prepared to teach in 1971 (305,711) is more than twice as large as was observed in 1961 (129,188). Projections of college and university graduates show that by 1978 the annual number of graduates prepared to teach (397,000) will be three times as large as the number in 1961.

Not all teacher-education graduates normally enter teaching immediately following graduation. Even in times of critical shortage, more than one-fourth of these prospective teachers postpone entering or decide not to enter teaching during the year following their graduation. Thus we estimate the number of beginning teachers available for entry (supply) in any period in terms of the percent of all teacher education graduates *known* to have entered teaching immediately following their graduation during a period of teacher shortage. Active interest in employment as teachers is projected to be 83.3% of graduates prepared for the elementary level and 69.2% of those prepared for the secondary level.

The annual supply of qualified graduates available for teaching positions was between 65,000 and 90,000 in the 1950's; it increased to 198,000 in the 1960's; it reached 217,750 in 1970; it is projected to grow from 229,053 in 1971 to 266,000 in 1975; it could continue to grow from 277,000 in 1976 to 308,000 in 1979. These projections show the annual supply of beginning teachers in the 1970's to be between two and three times as large as the annual supply of 80,000 to 90,000 observed during the late 1950's.

The supply of qualified persons in the pool of unemployed teachers during a given school session is difficult to estimate accurately. The 1960 U.S. Bureau of the Census reported 304,460 persons as elementary- and secondary-school teachers not gainfully employed at the time of the census. These were people who had completed at least four years of college. An assumption that this group contains the 20-year accumulation of about 1.5% of the teaching staff employed in the public schools provides an estimate that 439,000 persons were in this pool in 1971. This source of supply will continue to grow by at least 2,000 persons each year, reflecting the growth in the total teaching staff during the past 20 years.

The number of reentering teachers employed in 1960 was 18.3% of the persons estimated to be in this pool. Because the year 1960 was in a period of

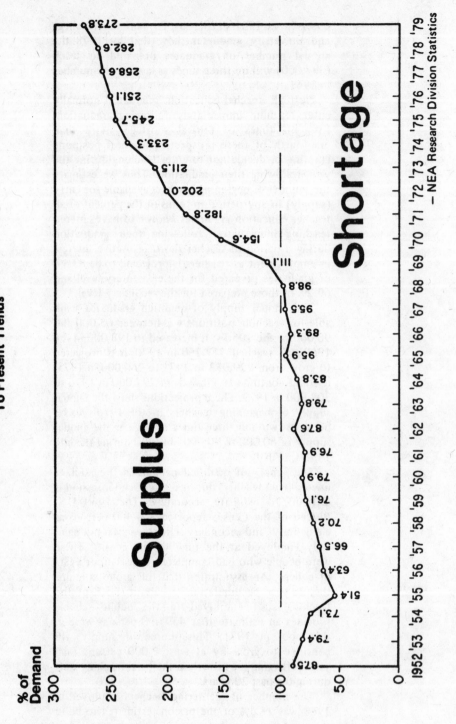

FIGURE I
Supply of Beginning Teachers as Percent
Of Normal Demand, 1952 to 1979, According
To Present Trends

— NEA Research Division Statistics

general teacher shortage, this rate of entry may provide an estimate of the supply from this source if attractive positions were available. It would have meant the employment of 80,400 former teachers this fall, about 16,900 more than the number actually employed.

Estimates of Normal Demand

The demand for new teachers to replace those leaving through normal turnover is estimated to be about 8% of the total number of teachers each year. This is derived from two studies by the U.S. Office of Education and from a series of sample surveys conducted by the NEA Research Division. Because these estimates were derived during a period of improvements in educational quality, projections using these estimates are likely to reflect a continuation of the rate of these improvements.

The numbers of experienced teachers reentering teaching after at least one year away from it have been about 3% of the total number of teachers employed the preceding year.

Normal demand, therefore, to replace teachers leaving the profession is estimated to be about 8% of the total number of teachers, with reentering teachers filling three-eighths and beginning teachers filling the remaining five-eighths of these positions.

The number of teachers needed to handle enrollment growth was projected on the basis of recent trends of improvement in the pupil-teacher ratio. Because the estimated demand for reentering teachers is based on turnover, the demand for teachers to handle enrollment growth is treated as demand for beginning teachers.

The demand for new (beginning and reentering) teachers for replacement and enrollment change is the *actual* demand for teachers for a given year. The distribution of this actual demand among subject areas and grade levels is estimated by applying the distribution of the numbers of new teachers reported to have been employed the preceding year (23 states are currently able to report this information).

Because the number of births each year began to decline in 1962 and continued to decline each year until 1969, the enrollment potential for public schools in the 1970's will not increase significantly.

61

The projected growth in the total number of public school teachers between 1971 and 1979 (24,000 positions) will not be as large as the growth in teachers employed in *any one* of the 10 years immediately prior to 1970 (average annual growth of 64,200 positions). As a result, the major source of demand for new teachers during the 1970's will not be increased enrollments but improvements in staffing quality and replacement of teachers in normal turnover. The total annual demand for beginning teachers after 1971 will be between 108,000 and 115,900 through 1979, less than half as large as the projected supply in each of these years (average annual supply of 271,200 between 1972 and 1979).

Quality-Based Estimates

The estimated demand for new teachers to attain minimum quality in educational programs and staffing comprises the normal demand described above plus the new teachers needed to reduce the number of oversize classes, to replace teachers having substandard qualifications, to enlarge school offerings and programs for pupils not now being served (kindergarten, special education, courses not offered because of shortage of qualified teachers), and to replace teachers misassigned for a major portion of their time. Precise standards for these components, however, have not been announced and validated.

During the period of teacher shortage, NEA Research Division estimates were based on the following standards for class size and minimum educational qualifications for teaching: The maximum acceptable teacher load has been 34 pupils per class in elementary grades or a teaching load of 199 pupils per day in secondary grades. The minimum acceptable educational qualification has been the bachelor's degree. An acceptable sign of progress toward providing special education programs has been the number of teachers needed to serve half of the children requiring but not currently having special education services in a single year.

In periods of widespread teacher shortage there was little question that these were standards for rock-bottom *minimum* quality in education programs and staffing. It was accepted that each component of these standards was more than justified and that needs were much greater than the levels projected. However, in these years there were not sufficient numbers of qualified teachers to fill even the normal vacancies. In the current period of teacher surplus, with an adequate supply of qualified teachers available for most assignments, additional research and evaluation should guide decisions about the relative effectiveness of establishing a higher minimum acceptable level of quality in each of these areas. However, it should be remembered that current economic, financial, and employment trends do not suggest attainment of even the former standard for minimum quality in the immediate future, much less an improved standard.

Attainment of these minimum standards in the fall of 1971 would have required 351,200 beginning teachers, 122,100 more than the supply. But the accumulated surpluses of beginning teachers in the fall of 1969 and the fall of 1970 included 96,900 persons. This number is almost equal to the number of beginning teachers needed in 1971 to attain the minimum levels of educational quality. These facts show that unless the annual supply of beginning teachers is reduced for years following 1971, or unless the quality of educational programs and services is improved to levels above these minimum standards, the period of teacher surplus would begin in the fall of 1972 even though these minimum standards of quality are achieved.

The class size component of this minimum standard probably has least professional acceptance. A very desirable revision – maximum class size of 24 in elementary grades and maximum teaching load of 124 in secondary grades – would be a professionally more acceptable *minimum* standard. Further reduction would also be desirable to meet a professionally acceptable standard for most effective instruction.

Achievement of such a revised minimum standard (based on class size maximums listed above) would have required the employment of 729,900 beginning teachers in the fall of 1971, 500,800 more than the number available at that time. This revised standard would have required the addition of 565,800 teaching positions, an increase of 27.7% over the total number of teachers in public schools in 1971.

The number of beginning teachers needed to attain this revised standard of minimum quality is approximately equal to the projected surpluses of beginning teachers between 1970 and 1974 (573,100) persons. Our present course will provide adequate potential staff to attain this revised standard of minimum quality in 1974, at which time the projected continuing growth in teacher supply would create a period of teacher surpluses beginning with that year.

Present trends are for future annual supplies of beginning teachers to be considerably larger than normal demand. The present margin is sufficient for supplying the increased numbers of beginning teachers which will be needed if the rates of school improvements are increased. The likelihood of an increasingly abundant supply of beginning teachers in the future gives reason for the profession to direct attention to two goals: 1) increasing the demand for beginning teachers through rapid improvements in educational quality, and 2) selectively decreasing the future numbers of graduates prepared to teach. In view of the prospect of a surplus, it should be remembered that there will continue to be a need for at least 100,000 beginning teachers annually for the next decade.

Recruitment of Teachers— A Need for Reevaluation

PAUL FITZGERALD

ALTHOUGH most superintendents believe that recruitment of teachers is one of their most important functions, a great deal of effort, time and money is usually not put into this highly important task. When it is considered that the decision to hire a teacher begins the process in which hundreds of children are directly affected, usually for a number of years, then the recruitment process deserves scrutiny by every school board member and administrator within a school system.

Most school districts today are attempting to upgrade their inservice training programs. Until such programs demonstrate improvement in the quality of education, the decision about whom to hire remains paramount. The conclusion that a great deal more could be done in this vital area was drawn from a study analyzing the recruitment of elementary and secondary teachers in twenty-five randomly selected Iowa school districts.

Many different aspects were examined in this analysis of recruitment. Seven cost variables were used to calculate expense per teacher recruited—advertising, travel, telephone, interviewing candidates, staff meetings, office expense, and secretarial expense. These represented both direct and indirect expenses incurred while recruitment took place. In addition, recruitment analyses were also made

PERSONNEL JOURNAL, Apr. 1970, pp. 312-314.

in the following categories:

1. Comparative costs between education and industry.
2. Methods used in recruitment.
3. Written school board policies and financial allocations to recruitment.

It was found that the average cost per teacher hired amounted to $146. In determining this cost, other aspects were investigated. One of these was recruitment cost in relationship to the size of the school districts. The cost differences among districts were not great when this factor was considered. As indicated, the average cost per teacher hired was $146, whereas, in the largest school districts, those having more than 10,000 pupils, the cost dropped to $110. The smallest school districts, those having less than 700 pupils, had to expend $160 per teacher hired. This difference may be attributed to the fact that some of the cost factors, especially travel expense by school personnel, did not change a great deal whether the administrator recruited five or fifty teachers.

In another analysis, a cost comparison was made between the hiring of experienced and inexperienced teachers. It was found that it did cost more to hire the experienced teacher. Per hire cost for an experienced teacher was $182 compared to $107 for an inexperienced teacher. Part of the cost difference was due to the great amount of correspondence that had to be handled by the administrator. This was a direct result of the popular method in Iowa of advertising for teachers in newspapers. Also, the expense of interview time at the district office was involved in hiring an experienced teacher.

It was also determined by the investigation that there was not a significant cost difference for the recruitment of teachers in different subject areas. The subject areas were divided into high and low demand, as determined by interviews of superintendents, an analysis of teacher vacancies as listed in a statewide newspaper, and data from the National Education Association. The results showed that the cost to hire a teacher in the high demand category was $166 as compared with $122 in the low demand subject areas. The reason for the similarity in cost was that in some of the low demand subject areas, the hiring of a coach was involved. This usually demanded the interviewing of many more candidates, with greater expense as a result.

The cost facts can be compared with results of methods of recruitment as reported by the superintendents. The most common methods used were advertisements in the newspaper and college placement bureaus. Both of these required more office work and less travel or direct contact with prospective teachers by superintendents. In fact, two of the primary cost factors in recruitment were routine office expense and secretarial expense. Since these were significant costs, one might assume that extensive recruitment effort was not made outside the district. The smaller schools did not seem to have either the money or the personnel to allow much latitude in the recruitment effort.

Also, the recruitment costs for staff meetings was not a major area of expense. Staff meetings were held on a very irregular basis. It would seem that if recruitment is important enough, long range planning would be appropriate throughout the year. Also the lack of written school board policies and budgets for recruitment in many school districts indicated that it is relegated to a second place status. Thus, the amount of resources expended for recruitment, both financial and human, does not seem to be in proportion to the importance of the task of attracting quality teachers.

It is especially interesting to compare recruitment costs and efforts between education and business. When the per hire cost of $146 for education was compared to the financial effort put forth by business and industry, there was an enormous difference. The recruitment cost in business, which was obtained from fourteen corporations listed on the New York Stock Exchange, amounted to $1822 per professional hired. In many instances, business firms paid visitation expense to the person in addition to moving expense. Few districts paid either of these expenses. Common cost factors were used by most of the corporations. The $1822 figure was based on the following costs:

1. Advertising.
2. Recruiter's salary and travel expense.
3. Employer agency fees.
4. Applicant's plant visit expense (including wife's travel).
5. Relocation expense.

Efforts can be made by school administrators which would greatly improve the recruitment process. Administrators in smaller districts are at a distinct disadvantage because of the lack of specialists in such areas as curriculum, finance, and personnel. Because he must serve in so many capacities, the chief administrator cannot devote the needed time to recruitment. Thus, it is logical that a planned cooperative effort on a county or area basis could be of assistance to all involved. This might take the form of combining the teacher vacancies of a number of districts. In their recruiting travels and correspondence, administrators could be of invaluable assistance to one another with this type of cooperation.

If there is cooperation between school districts, an added benefit should be scheduled staff meetings specifically concerned with recruitment. The meetings should consider recruitment in relation to present and proposed building facilities and curricula needs.

One problem of recruitment in education that is not shared by industry is the payment of travel expense to prospective recruits. Many teachers cannot afford to pay such expenses themselves. In order to attract quality teachers, at least partial payment for visitation expenses should be considered. A plan that might warrant consideration would be one that pays part or full expenses to teachers who eventually sign a contract in the district.

Because of a lack of over-all direction in many districts, specific school board policies for recruitment of teachers should be adopted by the board of education. These might include personnel responsibilities for recruitment. Also, the over-all budget limitations, including an analysis of the cost factors, should be considered. Cost factors might include secretarial, telephone, materials, and teacher visitation. In addition, the framework for the methods used in recruitment could be explained. These policies would give direction to recruitment in a district. They should allow enough flexibility for recruitment personnel to operate in many situations.

It is apparent that recruitment has not been a well planned and efficient operation within many school districts. A great deal of time or effort is not put into this task although the results of recruitment will eventually determine to a great extent the quality of education received by the students. Thus, a reexamination of the policies and procedures of recruitment is a necessary step for the improvement in the quality of a staff.

In Search of an Administrator

Gary Johnson

Regardless of your type of organization, its success will depend, in large part, upon how good your administrators are. Whether it is an aerospace company, a retail store, or a college or university, there will be little difference in this dependence. I do not mean to imply that the administrators are necessarily the most *important* persons in an organization— obviously, in a college or university, the faculty is most important; in an aerospace company, the scientist is most important; in a retail store, the salesman is most important. However, the role of an administrator and you should not expect to find all in such a way as to give the individuals most important to the organization an opportunity to display their skills to the best advantage. For this reason, good administrators are most essential if the organization is to function successfully.

When you go in search of an administrator, you should set your aims as high as possible—commensurate with the salary and the opportunities your organization can offer him. All the same, there are *many* qualities comprising the personality of a good administrator and you should not expect to find all of them developed to the highest potential in the person you hire or promote. In searching for an administrator, you must evaluate your *needs* carefully so that you hire someone who is correctly qualified for the job you have. Always evaluate the individual by his administrative abilities, not solely by the performance of the administrative unit for which he

MANAGEMENT OF PERSONNEL QUARTERLY, Winter 1970, pp. 17-20.

is responsible. It is possible for an administrative operation to be reasonably successful and for the administrator who supervises that operation to be a very poor administrator. The following two examples will explain this differentiation.

- An administrator in a University business operation was an aggressive, driving woman who maintained extremely tight control over her subordinates. She described their job areas distinctly and expected them to operate efficiently within the prescribed area. She allowed them to suggest innovations within the operation, but these innovations were only to be implemented after she approved them. Although she had no patience with incompetent individuals in other offices and did not hesitate to advise them of this, she was very patient in working with people who were new or for whom her area was a new learning experience. She was skilled in determining those situations in which she could drive and those in which she must very carefully lead. She was knowledgeable in her own area of responsibility. Her operation ran quite smoothly, her subordinates respected and liked her as a supervisor and, if she were not universally loved within the entire organization, she was universally respected.

This woman was an excellent administrator, and her operation functioned well.

- A supervisor of a sizeable service department in a large industrial organization was almost totally incapable of making any decision and, once a decision had been made, he was susceptible to pressures to change the decision. Fortunately for him, 1) he was related to the owner of the business, 2) he had the ability and/or good fortune to employ excellent subordinates, and 3) he recognized his own weaknesses as an administrator. The kindest thing to be said of this man as an administrator was that his operation functioned best during his vacation time. His personal secretary had all of the attributes of a Marine drill instructor and his three immediate subordinates were bright, aggressive men. Without (to my knowledge) any direct discussions between his secretary and his immediate subordinates, the man was isolated to the maximum degree possible from others within the organization. His subordinates handled all the day-to-day department operations and made recommendations regarding policy or procedural changes. His secretary rerouted telephone calls and mail to the appropriate subordinate so the decisions were made. The supervisor was advised so that if he wished to make any changes in the decisions he could—but he didn't. Naturally, with his personality, he found it as difficult to overrule a subordinate as he did to disagree with others in the organization. Essentially, the man relegated himself to a figurehead and maintained his activities, insofar as the department operations were concerned, to a minimum. As a result, the unit for which he was responsible was a reasonably successful one from an administrative point of view. Most of the time when it was unsuccessful, it was because, for one reason or another, he had become involved directly in a problem.

It is important to detect this kind of situation—an organization which functions well administratively, but an individual responsible for the organization who is not a good administrator—when you are searching for an administrator and evaluating references. A really good administrator will be able to sell himself quite easily but, unfortunately, a very poor administrator with a good staff may also do an excellent job of selling his supposed qualifications.

What constitutes a good administrator in your specific organization may not be exactly the person who would fit best into another organizational structure. However, if an administrator is good, he can adapt and do a better than adequate job in almost any administrative situation except those, perhaps, requiring technical skills which must be learned. Even in those cases, if there is a period allowed for this learning process, most good administrators should be able to meet the requirements of the job.

To conclude satisfactorily your search for a good administrator, you should establish a model of some of the major qualifications for a good administrator. The following model naturally includes my own personal bias but, also, it includes my reflection on those qualities which seem to be common to a high degree in most administrators. (The following use of the pronoun *he* is strictly idiomatic. I do not mean to imply that women cannot be good administrators—they can.)

One of the primary qualifications is that he be *intelligent*. I do not think it is possible for a stupid person or even an individual with mediocre intelligence to become an effective administrator. The good administrator must deal with other intelligent individuals and highly complex situations, and identify discrete priority groupings quickly and correctly. Naturally, an administrator should be very *knowledgeable* in his own special field but it also is important that this knowledge extend both into ancillary and unrelated fields of interest; the good administrator must reflect the ideals of the renaissance man—to be knowledgeable in many subjects. It is helpful if an administrator is a quick, clever person but this is not essential, merely helpful. A methodical and unimaginative individual can be a successful administrator in certain areas but the individual with *imagination* who can innovate—the individual with that undefined extra quality which we sometimes call style or flair—that is the individual who is not only a good administrator but makes working within your organization a pleasure. All of these qualities are tied very closely to the individual's native ability and the training and personality development he has received. None of these qualities will be apparent to you or to others with whom he works unless he is *articulate*. By articulate, I mean possessing the ability to express himself well verbally and in writing. Except in the most specialized circumstances, unless an individual has developed a high degree of verbal and written skills, it is very difficult for him to be classified as a good administrator. Many fortunate individuals speak and write well as one of their native talents, for others, learning to communicate verbally or in writing is an agonizing experience. Unless you want to take the time and risk of training an individual to speak well or to write well, you must automatically disqualify the inarticulate individual.

Since one of the primary on-going functions of an administrator is working with people, certain personality traits or qualities are exceptionally important for a good administrator to possess. Again, your own special situation will dictate the specific qualities and to what degree these qualities are required. Because an administrator is constantly faced with pressure situations—pressures of meeting deadlines, pressures of working with people, pressures of interaction in the organization—one of the requisite qualifications you must look for in an administrator is a sense of humor—he will need it. *Sense of humor* does not mean the practical joker, traveling salesman stereotype to which we have become accustomed on the American comic scene; rather, *sense of humor* refers to a state of mind that allows an individual to smile and occasionally laugh at his own foibles and those of others, a state of mind that relieves the pressures on both himself and others in a way not possible for the man who is essentially humorless. It is not that a humorless individual cannot succeed as a good administrator—he can—it is just more difficult for him and for those around him. Inherent in desirable personality qualities of a good administrator is *honesty* in his dealings with people. (Honesty does not *necessarily* imply a strict morality, but certainly, it *is* refreshing to find an administrator with a deeply developed sense of morality.) However, the honesty to which I refer concerns itself more with a direct, open approach to problems and dealings with people. It is not necessary for an individual to be direct and blunt for the sake of directness alone; there are times when the utmost tact and diplomacy must be employed by an administrator and he must be aware of those times. But in most day-to-day dealings, it is easier for the administrator to be very direct (and at times blunt) in his interpersonal relationships with others. The overwhelming majority of people would much rather know exactly what they have to be told (even if they don't like it) rather than wonder just what it was the individual with whom they were talking meant. It is essential that a good administrator interact well with people both inside the organization and outside the organization. This, however, is a trainable trait susceptible to continuing development.

Another area which can be of critical importance is how an administrator works with his personal subordinates; if he has a one-man office, it may be less than a crucial problem. Otherwise, this can be a very serious problem—both for him and for you. It is sufficient to say that the skills and abilities which the administrator needs in working with individuals outside of his own office should be applied equally in dealings with subordinates inside his office. He should particularly maintain a high degree of *personal detachment* and objectivity; he must be *interested* in his organization and in the people who work for him but, if he becomes personally involved with their problems or allows himself the luxury of playing favorites, his effectiveness as an administrator is reduced. A good administrator is *socially conscious* by definition. However, one who tries to weld his subordinates to him both professionally and socially is not only asking for trouble (—he usually gets it—) but he destroys the degree of objectivity necessary for a supervisor in working with his subordinates. He must demonstrate complete *self-control* and self-discipline when interacting with his own staff and with others outside his staff. It is important to consider this point carefully. When speaking of self-control, we cannot regard a show of temper as a loss of self-control and self-discipline—not necessarily, at least. If the administrator "loses his temper," he has lost his self-discipline and his control of the situation in question. However, a controlled display of temper (perhaps temperament might be a better word), when properly used by an administrator, can be extremely effective. A reputation for a volatile temper can enhance an administrator's reputation— however, a reputation for temper *tantrums* can destroy an administrator's reputation. You cannot gauge self-control and self-discipline in terms of an individual's personality traits, only in terms of how he controls and uses these personality traits.

Certainly, the mark of a good administrator is his *adaptability* to new and changing environments.

However, it is a definite mistake for an administrator to develop a chameleon syndrome and attempt to be all things to all men—he can't be. The really good administrator is not remembered for the times that he said "yes"—anyone can say "yes." He is remembered and appreciated for the times when he said "no," regardless of the pressures, and held firm in his decision because he knew he was correct. Yet, an administrator must be willing to admit when he *was* wrong; if he assumes an attitude of fairness in his dealings with others, he will usually find a reciprocal attitude—but he won't always expect this. An administrator should be respected (if he isn't respected, there are many problems for him); however, he should not expect to be universally loved. Almost all of the examples of good administrators that I can identify as universally loved by everyone in their organization were (or are) religious leaders. And, while many administrators are accused of messianic tendencies, I would strongly urge you to disqualify anyone in your search for an administrator who has this attitude.

An administrative habit pattern which has been overrated in recent years is *organization*—many consider that only an organized administrator is a good administrator. This is not true—an organized administrator commands a more efficient use of his own time and that of others but an administrator cannot automatically be classified as good or bad because he is not always well-organized. The seemingly disorganized administrator can be a very effective and hard-driving administrator. I must admit to a personal prejudice for a highly organized administrator but this reflects a personal bias, not an evaluation of qualities which should be included in our model for an administrator.

In constructing our search model for an administrator, we must give careful consideration to the power triumvirate—*ambition, aggressiveness* and *self-confidence*. It is theoretically possible for an administrator to be successful without one of these three characteristics but, except in the most specialized situations, it is doubtful whether an administrator could be successful lacking any *two* of these three characteristics. I label these characteristics as the power triumvirate since, in my mind, they represent the self-generating power plant for the individual administrator. Much has been published and dramatized in recent years regarding the negative aspects of ambition, aggressiveness, and self-confidence; this publication has resulted in a considerable popularization of the phrase "power corrupts and absolute power corrupts absolutely." The ambitious, aggressive individual brimming with self-confidence often is characterized as the villain in society who falls victim in the final act—either to his own lust for power or else to the clear-eyed, self-effacing, idealistic hero. As is the case with most dramatizations, the negative aspects of the power triumvirate characteristics are portrayed in an unrealistic, one-dimensional manner. *Any* characteristic can become a negative characteristic. We can all conjure up the memory of some individual who corrupted what is normally accepted as a "good" characteristic to the point that it became either socially unacceptable or nauseatingly boring. As with all personality traits and characteristics, the power triumvirate must be directed with restraint commensurate with the individual situation. An administrator must be superbly self-confident of his abilities, but only to the extent that he is not blinded into believing that he lacks any flaws. An administrator should be aggressive, to the extent that the individual situation demands it—this will mean a variation in the degree of aggressiveness used in various situations. An administrator should be ambitious, but only to the extent of his abilities and the situations which develop (or which he himself develops). If the administrator loses control of one of these characteristics, then his personal power plant becomes very akin to a nuclear power plant with proper controls removed—a menace to himself and to all around him.

The last, and in my estimation, the most important quality of a good administrator is the proper instincts. Whether or not this represents a highly refined, specialized development of the survival instinct in man, I do not know; I only know that those instincts which protect and preserve a good administrator are not instincts which can be trained—he must be born with them. As with any other native talents, these instincts must be developed and nurtured or else they will atrophy. It is difficult to describe how to identify such instincts when you are searching for a good administrator. His performance on a previous job is an indication, but perhaps the best indicator is his performance for you. Any clever person may fake the instincts for a brief period—no one can fake them for an extended period in a continuing job situation. To this extent, you must depend on your *own* instincts in evaluating an individual, or else defer a final decision until after the individual has worked on the job for a period of time. This may mean that you will have to admit to an error in judgement on your part if you have not hired a man with the proper instincts, but you must be willing to do this.

This model may be of assistance to you in setting priorities for the special situation that attends your search for an administrator. However, in any situation, the ultimate mark of a good administrator is that he makes things work within the organization and sees that they work well. For your search, you need 1) a thorough knowledge of the needs of your own organization, 2) a careful evaluation of the administrators that you consider and 3) in all honesty, you need that unfathomable factor called luck. Good administrators can be found, whether they are the experienced, suave, sure administrators with years of job experience or the bright, aggressive, young men with the right instincts and years of experience yet ahead of them.

Toward More Productive Interviewing

ROBERT A. MARTIN

M OST supervisors consider interviewing to be an essential step in the employment process. Yet, one wonders whether those supervisors receive interview comments which are properly focused on the more valid and meaningful employment screening criteria. Very often, in the writer's experience, hiring decisions are based upon a few relatively meaningless numbers—typing speed, number of years of experience, grade point average, SAT scores, salary on previous job. Too often those numbers are assumed to possess, by both employment interviewers and supervisors, magical screening virtue. Specific numbers tend to develop an inviolate sanctity; their precision is usually assumed. Yet all of the many correlation studies would indicate that the assumptions are invalid.

The difficulty may be that too many interviewers focus too finely on a few relatively meaningless statistics and detailed descriptions of specific abilities, and too many supervisors seize upon those statistics and descriptions as inviolate screening criteria. The result is that many perfectly satisfactory applicants are turned aside and, conversely, many are hired who shouldn't be.

In order to attack this focusing problem we consolidated the combined thinking of forty supervisors, who had participated extensively

PERSONNEL JOURNAL, May 1971, pp. 359-363.

in employment interviewing, and eight full time recruiters. The supervisors had acquired considerable experience with many different classifications—from janitors to division managers. The forty-eight participants were assigned to two Interview Seminars of equal sizes. Three two-hour meetings were scheduled for each group.

The first session was devoted to soliciting from the participants as many employment screening criteria as would come to mind. No effort was made to rate the criteria according to importance. All were encouraged to volunteer criteria, no matter how trivial they might have appeared to others. The criteria were:

Scholastic performance	Extra-curricular activities
General intelligence	Responsibility
Energy	Quality of schools
Compatibility with others	Ability to communicate
Relevant experience	Line, staff, or project type
Appearance	Achievement/security
Initiative	oriented
Goals	Reasons for job changes
Personality	Marital status
Flexibility	Integrity
Breadth of interest	Job openings
Draft status	References
Honesty	Security clearance level
Present location	Number of dependents
Past salary	Attitude
Competency	Motivation
Age	Maturity
Race	Discipline
Sex	Self confidence
Physical condition	Mannerisms
Leadership potential	Habits
Job change frequency	Hobbies
Patents/Publications	Morals
Degree level	Creativity
Health	Memory
Progress	

The number and variety of the criteria made a visible impression on the participants. After a great deal of discussion and argument, they gradually reached the conclusion that to place almost exclusive emphasis upon one or two numbers—typing speed, grade point average—would be doing a serious disservice to the applicants. Innumerable criteria are involved in making the totality—the entity of the applicant. That awakened realization could be considered a minor breakthrough.

Next, the two groups were asked to select the ten most important criteria from the above list. After much argument and soul searching, the two independently derived lists emerged as follows:

(Ranked in order of importance)

Group I	Group II
1. General intelligence	Basic capability for job
2. Ability to communicate	References
	Productivity
3. Maturely directed energy	Motivation
	Compatibility
4. Ambition	Experience
5. Specific professional competence	Communication
	Salary
6. Integrity	Sincerity
7. Attitude/personality	Personal background
8. Creativity	
9. Growth potential	
10. References	

With a little stretching of the imagination a basic similarity can be seen to exist between the two lists. Thus, it was not too difficult to merge the two, and even consolidate the lists into only six basic criteria.

After a great deal of discussion, it was decided that the best way to portray the approximate importance of each of the six basic criteria would be to use the triangular format with the area of each trapezoidal section indicating its relative importance.

The result is perhaps more significant than it looks. It is suggested that if the interviewing guide is used as described below, more qualified applicants will be accepted for employment and fewer unsuitable people will be hired simply because they possess a few very specialized skills—which are usually very easy to acquire—but who lack the basic abilities and attitudes which more normally ensure success.

Interviewing can be separated into two basic phases. Phase I will consider the basic employment screening criteria possessed by the applicant, and their relative importance,

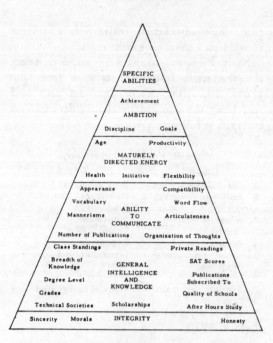

SPECIFIC ABILITIES

Achievement

AMBITION

Discipline · Goals

Age · Productivity

MATURELY DIRECTED ENERGY

Health · Initiative · Flexibility

Appearance · Compatibility

Vocabulary · Word Flow

Mannerisms · ABILITY TO COMMUNICATE · Articulateness

Number of Publications · Organization of Thoughts

Class Standings · Private Readings

Breadth of Knowledge · SAT Scores

GENERAL INTELLIGENCE AND KNOWLEDGE

Degree Level · Publications Subscribed To

Grades · Quality of Schools

Technical Societies · Scholarships · After Hours Study

Sincerity · Morals · INTEGRITY · Honesty

FIGURE I.
Employment Screening Criteria, and Their Relative Importance

and Phase II will deal with some attitudes of the applicant as they relate to the managerial and philosophical environment associated with the job.

We start with Integrity. Fortunately, the vast majority of people are reasonably honest, so the base upon which we should build our interview is usually a solid one. After that, it gets more interesting.

The most important criterion to consider for the vast majority of all hires is "General Intelligence and Knowledge." So important is this one criterion that during times of a sellers' market affirmative hire decisions should be made when the applicants are well endowed with "General Intelligence and Knowledge" but with only a modicum of the other criteria. Applicants who have the appropriate level of general intelligence and the proper breadth and depth of knowledge, within a broad field, can be easily and quickly trained for a surprisingly wide variety of

Phase I

82

assignments. In many cases they can bring fresh and imaginative approaches to problem areas in which they never had detailed experience.

Two examples may illustrate the importance and validity of assigning so much weight to the "general intelligence and knowledge" criterion.

One of the happiest and most challenged new hires in our company involved a woman in her late fifties who suddenly became a widow after many years as a housewife. She had a sixth grade education and an IQ of about eighty. She was a friendly and warm hearted person without known, saleable skills. When she applied for a job, though, there did happen to be a position for which, if she had been screened according to whether or not she had the specific experience involved, she would have been rejected. This being an extremely simple example, the job in question involved selling doughnuts and coffee in the morning from a small table at the gate of a large aerospace firm. The woman put her whole heart and soul into the job. She quickly learned the names of her customers, their preferences—glazed, sugar, chocolate, coffee, cinnamon, or plain doughnuts; black, creamed and/or sweetened coffee. She discovered that sales varied by the days of the week and according to the weather. She worked with such joy and dedication at her job—and was so obviously challenged—that she could predict almost exactly how many and what variety of doughnuts would be sold each day. She could even predict the number which would break. Not being saleable she would feed them to the birds. After seven years on the job, she retired when she reached sixty five. Her general intelligence and knowledge were ideal for the job.

Two of our most successful Engineering Recruiters had never interviewed anyone prior to their hire. But because of their extensive general knowledge and high intelligence, and their exceptional ability to communicate —they both read widely and well—they were able to quickly become productive. If specific experience had been insisted upon, we would have been deprived of their contributions. Actually, their very lack of specific experience turned out to be an advantage. They boldly questioned the established ways of recruiting and, by so doing, inspired helpful innovations.

The interviewer can learn to estimate the degree to which general intelligence and knowledge are possessed by questions relating to schooling, readings, hobbies, extra curricular activities, after hours studies, IQ and SAT scores, grades, variety of courses taken, etc. Many questions should be asked. Judgments should not be made on only four or five clues, nor should undue emphasis be placed on the single criterion, grades.

If, in the judgment of the experienced interviewer, the applicant possesses the appropriate level of "general intelligence and knowledge" within the broad field of endeavor or profession involved, and if the urgency of the opening requires, a hire, no-hire recommendation may be made without further ado! (Of course, this is not to suggest that a person who rates "zero" in all the other screening criteria would be a worthwhile hire. One has to start with the assumption that a respectable amount of each criterion is possessed—the more the better, of course.)

Knowledge, without any ability to communicate, is the same as no knowledge. Yet an exceptional ability to communicate faulty knowledge could create serious problems. Therefore, the possession of the appropriate level of general intelligence and knowledge can be considered as more important than the ability to communicate. Hence, the smaller trapezoidal area of the latter.

Communication is accomplished not only through words, but also through appearance and mannerisms. Most of us would have difficulty in listening attentively to an unpleasant or unkempt person. Factors for the interviewer to consider would be word flow, vocabulary, verbal organization, poise, number of publications, efficiency in the use of words, the ability to focus on the heart of the problem. A good feel can be obtained for the applicant's proficiency in this area simply by engaging him in an informal bull session on any wide range of topics of mutual interest. Many times such discussions make interviewing very enjoyable.

A bull in a china shop has a great amount of energy, but he is not maturely directed, by the standards of most shop owners. Hence the importance attached to *maturely* directed energy. It has been said that inspiration is ninety per cent perspiration. It is conceivable that a person with a tremendous amount of energy, but with limited intelligence and knowledge can accomplish comparable results. But since quality and speed are more normally associated with general intelligence and knowledge, energy has to be considered of lesser importance. A feel for the energy level of the applicant can be obtained by inquiring about his activities, his rest requirements and his accomplishments, and by observing his actions.

Few of us will be lucky enough to achieve without ambition. It is, more normally, essential for success. Yet, it is not always necessary to seek out only the ambitious man. There is room at the very top for only one. Consequently, it is sometimes necessary to screen out the potentially impatient ones.

Comments on specific abilities will be omitted, simply because it is the purpose of this article to de-emphasize that screening factor.

The Second Phase

Basic attitudes, personalities and personal philosophies are relatively immutable characteristics. Serious mismatches in employment may occur if careful attempts are not made to unearth the modes of operating that all of us possess in varying combinations and with varying intensities. For purposes of illustration and analysis the modes will be described in terms of basic dichotomies.

For example, an obvious mode of operating, expressed as a dichotomy, is *intellectual vs. manual*. Some engineers have strong preferences for theory and analysis; others like laboratory hardware and field testing. Most craftsmen are justifiably proud of their manipulative dexterity. Some people are comfortable in either mode. But in any case, probing questions must be asked in order to determine the preferences and, of equal importance, the intensity of those preferences.

Another dichotomy to investigate is *interpersonal vs. solitary*. Some people are miserable unless they're continually embroiled in volatile groups; others can't stand being interrupted. Hobbies, outside interests, specific sports, direct questions and family size could provide clues.

There is the *future vs. present* dichotomy. Some people are visionaries who delight in speculating about the future. They excel as market strategists, planners, forecasters. They are concerned with the evolutionary trends in technologies. They are bored and impatient with the present and would be unhappy with a position as an auditor, for example, even though they may have been trained as accountants.

Other dichotomies could include:

planning vs. doing
oral vs. written
leading vs. following
staff vs. line
research and development vs. manufacturing
systems vs. components
"broad brush" vs. detail

achievement vs. security oriented
large vs. small companies
technical vs. business.

Such dichotomies, and others, should be considered for all job applicants. Of course, with many of them, intensive questioning will not be necessary, but it is vital for the interviewer to have them in mind.

The main thrust of this article is the attempt to persuade interviewers to deemphasize the few relatively insignificant employment screening criteria, traditionally accepted as inviolate, and concentrate, rather, on the several more basic values which more truly represent the entity of the applicant.

Specific numbers, specifically test scores and grades, which, unfortunately, exude an aura of authenticity, should be avoided.

On the other hand broader, more subjective values should be stressed. The interviewer should be prepared to probe both the applicant and his references in order to be able to judge the critical values of general intelligence and knowledge, communications skills, energy and ambition and the basic dichotomies—line vs. staff, loner vs. mixer, system vs. component, leader vs. follower, detail vs. system, etc.

In a sense, this article suggests that the interviewer should deemphasize the job description. Most such descriptions are loaded with restricting detail and, if observed to the letter, would greatly increase the employment problem. Many specific skills are easily learnable, provided they are related to the proper level of general intelligence and knowledge.

There is no easy "ten step guide to instant interviewing ability." Interviewers should always be aware that a trifling amount of knowledge is a very dangerous thing—especially when dealing with the lives of others. To reject applicants simply because they have responded, "I don't know," to a couple of questions (the interviewer proudly jumps to the conclusion that they're not sure of themselves) or because they've had three jobs in three years (they're irresponsible job hoppers, "of course,") or because they express an interest in one specialty (they're too narrow and, "of course," specific interests are not transferable to other fields.)

All such factors are clues, but minor clues. Dozens of them constitute an entity. Consider the entity!

Improvements in
The Selection Interview

ROBERT E. CARLSON

PAUL W. THAYER

EUGENE C. MAYFIELD

and

DONALD A. PETERSON

THE effectiveness and utility of the selection interview has again been seriously questioned as a result of several comprehensive reviews of the research literature.[1] Not one of these classic summary reviews of the interview research literature arrived at conclusions that could be classed as optimistic when viewed from an applied standpoint. Yet none of this is new information. As early as 1915, the validity of the selection interview was empirically questioned.[2] Despite the fact that it is common knowledge that the selection interview probably contributes little in the way of validity to the selection decision, it continues to be used. It is clear that no amount of additional evidence on the lack of validity will alter the role of the interview in selection. Future research should obviously be directed at understanding the mechanism of the interview and improving interview technology. As Schwab has stated, "Companies are not likely to abandon the use of the employment interview, nor is it necessarily desirable that they do so. But it is grossly premature to sit back comfortably and assume that employment interviews are satisfactory. It is even too early to dash off unsupported recommendations for their improvement. A great deal of research work remains, research which companies must be willing to sponsor before we can count the interview as a prime weapon in our selection arsenal."[3] This was essentially the conclusion that the Life Insurance Agency Management Association reached some six years ago. In addition, the life insurance industry, through LIAMA, took action and sponsored basic research on the selection interview.

The research reported here is an attempt to improve the use of the selection interview in the life insurance industry. The role of the interview in selection presented a particularly difficult problem for the life insurance industry where each agency manager is responsible for many of the traditional personnel management functions. In addition, these agencies are scattered across the U. S. and Canada and make centralizing the selection process diffi-

[1] See, for example,

R. Wagner, "The Employment Interview: A Critical Summary," *Personnel Psychology*, Vol. 2 (1949), pp. 17-46.

G. W. England and D. G. Paterson, "Selection and Placement—The Past Ten Years," in H. G. Henneman, Jr., et al. (Editors), *Employment Relations Research: A Summary and Appraisal*, New York: Harper, 1960, pp. 43-72.

E. C. Mayfield, "The Selection Interview: A Reevaluation of Published Research." *Personnel Psychology*, Vol. 17 (1964), pp. 239-260.

L. Ulrich and D. Trumbo, "The Selection Interview Since 1949," *Psychological Bulletin*, Vol. 63 (1965), pp. 100-116.

[2] W. D. Scott, "The Scientific Selection of Salesmen," *Advertising and Selling*, Vol. 25 (1915), pp. 5-6 and 94-96.

[3] D. P. Schwab, "Why Interview? A Critique," *Personnel Journal*, Vol. 48, No. 2 (1969), p. 129.

PERSONNEL JOURNAL, Apr. 1971, pp. 268-275, 317.

cult. In order to strengthen the role of the selection interview in each manager's selection system, LIAMA has been doing basic research on the selection interview for the past six years.

The research reported here is part of a long-run research program concerned with how interviewers make employment decisions. Its purpose is to try to determine the limits of an interviewer's capability in extending his judgment into the future. This summary covers the early studies in a program of research to develop interim tools and the training necessary to make the selection interview a useful selection instrument.

The first step in the interview research program was to observe and record numerous interviews, to interview in depth the interviewers on their decision process, to conduct group decision conferences where the interviewers discussed their perception of their decision process for a given taped interview, and to examine the published research on the selection interview. Based upon this information, a model of the selection interview was constructed that specified as many of the influences operating during the interview as could be determined. Initially, there appeared to be four main classes of influences operating to affect/limit the decision of the interviewer. They were:

• The physical and psychological properties of the interviewee

• The physical and psychological properties of the interviewer

• The situation/environment in which the interviewer works

• The task or type of judgment the interviewer must make

The research strategy has been to systematically manipulate and control the variables specified in the model, trying to eliminate variables that do not have any influence, trying to assess the magnitude of those variables that have an influence, and adding variables that other research has shown to be promising. The first section of this article will describe some of the research findings; the second section will describe some of the materials that have been developed; and the third section will describe the interviewer training that has been developed.

What Are Some Findings?

Structured vs. Unstructured Interviews

One question that has often been asked is, "What kind of interview is best?" What interview style—structured, where the interviewer follows a set procedure; or unstructured, where the interviewer has no set procedure and where he follows the interviewee's lead—results in more effective decisions? In this study, live interviews were used. Each interviewee was interviewed three times. Interviewers used the following three types of interviewing strategies: structured, where the interviewer asked questions only from an interview guide; semistructured, where the interviewer followed an interview guide, but could ask questions about any other areas he wished; and unstructured, where the interviewer had no interview guide and could do as he wished. The basic question involved was the consistency with which people interviewing the same interviewee could agree with each other. If the interviewers' judgments were not consistent—one interviewer saying the applicant was good and the other saying he was bad—no valid prediction of job performance could be made from interview data. Agreement among interviewers is essential if one is to say that the procedure used has the potential for validity.

The results indicated that only the structured interview generated information that enabled interviewers to agree with each other. Under structured conditions, the interviewer knew what to ask and what to do with the information he received. Moreover, the interviewer applied the same frame of reference to each applicant, since he covered the same areas for each. In the less-structured interviews, the managers received additional information, but it seemed to be unorganized and made their evaluation task more difficult. Thus, a highly-structured interview has the greatest potential for valid selection.[4]

[4] R. E. Carlson, D. P. Schwab, and H. G. Henneman III. "Agreement Among Selection Interview Styles," *Journal of Industrial Psychology*, Vol. 5, No. 1 (1970), pp. 8-17.

Effect of Interviewer Experience

In the past it had been assumed that one way to become an effective interviewer was through experience. In fact, it has been hypothesized that interviewers who have had the same amount of experience would evaluate a job applicant similarly.[5] To determine whether this was indeed the case, a study was done that involved managers who had conducted differing numbers of interviews over the same time period. Managers were then compared who had similar as well as differing concentrations of interviewing experience. It was found that when evaluating the same recruits, interviewers with similar experiences did not agree with each other to any greater degree than did interviewers with differing experiences. It was concluded that interviewers benefit very little from day-to-day interviewing experience and apparently the conditions necessary for learning are not present in the day-to-day interviewer's job situation.[6] This implied that systematic training is needed, with some feedback mechanism built into the selection procedure, to enable interviewers to learn from their experiences; the job performance predictions made by the interviewer must be compared with how the recruit actually performs on the job.

Situational Pressures

One of the situational variables studied was how pressure for results affected the evaluation of a new recruit. One large group of managers was told to assume that they were behind their recruiting quota, that it was October, and that the home office had just called. Another group was ahead of quota; for a third group, no quota situation existed. All three groups of managers evaluated descriptions of the same job applicants. It was found that being behind recruiting quota impaired the judgment of those managers. They evaluated the same recruits as actually having

greater potential and said they would hire more of them than did the other two groups of managers.[7]

One more highly significant question was raised: Are all managers, regardless of experience, equally vulnerable to this kind of pressure? Managers were asked how frequently they conducted interviews. Regardless of how long the person had been a manager, those who had had a high rate of interviewing experience—many interviews in a given period of time—were less susceptible to pressures than were those with a low interviewing rate. The interviewers with less interviewing experience relied more on subjective information and reached a decision with less information. It was concluded that one way to overcome this problem of lack of concentrated interviewing experience was through the general use of a standardized interview procedure and intensive training in its use.

Standard of Comparison

Another condition studied was the standards managers applied in evaluating recruits. It was found, for example, that if a manager evaluated a candidate who was just average after evaluating three or four very unfavorable candidates in a row, the average one would be evaluated very favorably.[8] When managers were evaluating more than one recruit at a time, they used other recruits as a standard.[9] Each recruit was compared to all other recruits. Thus, managers did not have an absolute standard—who they thought looked good was partly determined by the persons with whom they were comparing the recruit. This indicated that some system was necessary to aid a manager in evaluating a recruit. The same system should be applicable to each recruit. This implied that some standardized evaluation system was necessary to reduce the large amount of information de-

5 P. M. Rowe, "Individual Differences in Assessment Decisions," Unpublished doctoral thesis, McGill University, 1960.

6 R. E. Carlson, "Selection Interview Decisions: The Effect of Interviewer Experience, Relative Quota Situation, and Applicant Sample on Interviewer Decisions," *Personnel Psychology*, Vol. 20 (1967), pp. 259-280.

7 Ibid.

8 R. E. Carlson, "Effects of Applicant Sample on Ratings of Valid Information in an Employment Setting," *Journal of Applied Psychology*, Vol. 54 (1970), pp. 217-222.

9 R. E. Carlson, "Selection Interview Decisions: The Effect of Mode of Applicant Presentation on Some Outcome Measures," *Personnel Psychology*, Vol. 21 (1968), pp. 193-207.

veloped from an interview to a manageable number of constant dimensions.

Effect of Appearance

Some of the early studies utilized photographs to try to determine how much of an effect appearance had on the manager's decision. A favorably rated photograph was paired with a favorably rated personal history description and also with an unfavorably rated personal history. It was found that appearance had its greatest effect on the interviewer's final rating when it complemented the personal history information.[10] Even when appearance and personal history information were the same (both favorable or both unfavorable), the personal history information was given twice as much weight as appearance. However, the relationship is not a simple one and only emphasized the need for a more complete system to aid the manager in selection decision-making.

Effect of Interview Information on Valid Test Results

In many selection situations, valid selection tests are used in conjunction with the interview data in arriving at a selection decision. Two recent studies have investigated how the emphasis placed on valid test results (*Aptitude Index Battery*) is altered by the more subjective interview data. Managers do place great emphasis on the AIB knowing that the score does generate a valid prediction.

However, how much weight is given to the score depends on other conditions; e. g., a low-scoring applicant is judged better if preceded by a number of poor applicants, unfavorable information is given much greater weight if it is uncovered just prior to ending the interview, etc. This finding suggested that what is needed is some system that places the interview information and other selection information in their proper perspective.[11]

[10] R. E. Carlson, "The Relative Influence of Appearance and Factual Written Information on an Interviewer's Final Rating," *Journal of Applied Psychology*, Vol. 51 (1967), pp. 461-468.

[11] R. E. Carlson, "The Effect of Interview Information in Altering Valid Impressions," *Journal of Applied Psychology*, In Press.

Interview Accuracy

A recent study tried to determine how accurately managers can recall what an applicant says during an interview. Prior to the interview the managers were given the interview guide, pencils, and paper, and were told to perform as if *they* were conducting the interview. A 20-minute video tape of a selection interview was played for a group of 40 managers. Following the video tape presentation, the managers were given a 20-question test. All questions were straightforward and factual. Some managers missed none, while some missed as many as 15 out of 20 items. The average number was 10 wrong. In a short 20-minute interview, half the managers could not report accurately on the information produced during the interview! On the other hand, those managers who had been following the interview guide and taking notes were quite accurate on the test; note-taking in conjunction with a guide appears to be essential.

Given that interviewers differed in the accuracy with which they were able to report what they heard, the next question appeared to be "How does this affect their evaluation?" In general it was found that those interviewers who were least accurate in their recollections rated the interviewee higher and with less variability, while the more accurate interviewers rated the interviewee average or lower and with greater variability. Thus, those interviewers who did not have the factual information at their disposal assumed that the interview was generally favorable and rated the interviewee more favorable in all areas. Those interviewers who were able to reproduce more of the factual information rated the interviewee lower and recognized his intra-individual differences by using more of the rating scale. This implied that the less accurate interviewers selected a "halo strategy" when evaluating the interviewee, while the more accurate interviewers used an individual differences strategy. Whether this is peculiar to the individual interviewer or due to the fact that the interviewer did or didn't have accurate information at his disposal is, of course, unanswerable from this data.

Can Interviewers Predict?

The ultimate purpose of the selection interview is to collect factual and attitudinal information that will enable the interviewer to make accurate and valid job behavior predictions for the interviewee. The interviewer does this by recording the factual information for an applicant, evaluating the meaning of the information in terms of what the interviewee will be able to do on the job in question, and extending these evaluations into the future in the form of job behavior predictions. The question is, "How reliably can a group of interviewers make predictions for a given interviewee?" Without high inter-interviewer agreement, the potential for interview validity is limited to a few interviewers and cannot be found in the interview process itself.

In this study, a combination of movies and audio tapes were played simulating an interview. In addition, each of the 42 manager-interviewers was given a detailed written summary of the interview. The total interview lasted almost three hours and covered the interviewee's work history, work experience, education and military experience, life insurance holdings, attitude toward the life insurance career, family life, financial soundness, social life and social mobility, and future goals and aspirations. After hearing and seeing the interview and after studying a 20-page written summary, each interviewer was asked to make a decision either to continue the selection process or to terminate negotiations. In addition, each interviewer was asked to make a list of all the factual information he considered while making his decision. Also, the interviewer was to rate the interviewee in 31 different areas. The ratings were descriptive of the interviewee's past accomplishments, such as his job success pattern, the quantity and quality of his education, his family situation, financial knowledge and soundness, etc. Finally, the interviewers were asked to make job behavior predictions in 28 different job specific activities such as, Could he use the telephone for business purposes? Could he make cold calls? Would he keep records? Would he take direction? What about his market?

The interviewers agreed quite well with each other on which facts they reportedly considered in making their employment decision. Almost 70 percent of the factual statements were recorded by all the interviewers. The remaining 30 percent of the factual statements were specific to interviewers. This tended to confirm a hypothesis of Mayfield and Carlson where they postulate that the stereotypes held by interviewers consist of general as well as specific content.[12] It was concluded that interviewers do record and use similar factual information with agreement.

The interviewers agreed less well with each other on the evaluation or value placed on the facts. The median inter-interviewer correlation was .62, with a low of .07 and a high of .82. This means that the interviewers still agreed reasonably well on the evaluation—good vs. bad—quality of the information they received. They would make similar selection-rejection decisions.

The job behavior predictions of the interviewers, however, were not nearly as high in agreement. The median inter-interviewer correlation was .33 with a low of —.21 and a high of .67. This means that the interviewers do not agree with each other on how well the interviewee will perform the job of a life insurance agent in 28 different areas. In addition, those predictions that required the interviewer to extend his judgment further into the future had significantly greater inter-interviewer variability than did those predictions that could be verified in a shorter period of time. Thus, interviewers can agree more with each other's predictions if the job behavior is of a more immediate nature.

These findings imply that although interviewers probably use much the same information in making a decision, they will evaluate it somewhat differently. Furthermore, the interviewers are not able to agree on how well the individual will perform on the job.

Thus, it was concluded that interviewers evaluate essentially similar things in an appli-

---

[12] E. C. Mayfield and R. E. Carlson, "Selection Interview Decisions: First Results from a Long-Term Research Project," *Personnel Psychology*, Vol. 19 (1966), pp. 41-53.

cant; they agree reasonably well whether an applicant's past record is good or bad, but they cannot agree on good or bad for what. Yet here, and only here, is where the clinical function of the interviewer is difficult to replace with a scoring system. In being able to make accurate and valid job behavior predictions, the interview can pay for itself in terms of planning an applicant's early job training and as a mechanism whereby a supervisor can learn early how to manage an applicant. In order for the interviewer to be able to make accurate and valid job behavior predictions, it follows that he must have a feedback system whereby he can learn from his past experiences. Only through accurate feedback in language similar to the behavior predictions can the interviewer learn to make job behavior predictions. The results further imply that the interviewer must be equipped with a complete selection system that coordinates all the selection steps and provides the interviewer with as relevant and complete information as possible when he makes job behavior predictions.

Conclusions

These early studies in LIAMA's interview research program provided little in the way of optimism for the traditional approach to the selection interview. However, this research did indicate specific areas where improvements in selection and interview technology could be made. It did indicate where interim improvements could be tried and evaluated while the long-term research on the interview continued.

Two major applied implications may be derived from the interview research to date. First, the selection interview should be made an integral part of an over-all selection procedure, and to accomplish this, new and additional materials are needed. The new materials should include a broad-gauge, comprehensive, structured interview guide; standardized evaluation and prediction forms that aid the interviewer in summarizing information from all steps in the selection process; and an evaluation system that provides feedback to the interviewer in language similar to the preemployment job behavior predictions

he must make. The second major applied implication is that an intensive training program for interviewers is necessary if interviewers are to initially learn enough in common to increase the probability of obtaining general validity from the selection interview. Thus, the early studies have provided specific information that has been used to change the way selection is carried out in the insurance industry.

Implementation: Development of a Selection Process

As a result of and based upon the early interview research, LIAMA constructed the *Agent Selection Kit.* This is a complete agent selection procedure to be used by agency branch managers and general agents in the field. Selection begins when the agency head secures the name of a prospective recruit and ends when the new agent has been selling for six months or when negotiations or employment is terminated. Because research demonstrated the necessity of formally taking into consideration each step in the selection process, each step in the procedure is carefully placed to maximize the potential of succeeding and following steps. The *Agent Selection Kit* introduced the following new ideas to the insurance industry:

(1) *Selection should more properly be viewed as manpower development.* The *Agent Selection Kit* is a completely integrated process, more properly described as manpower development; it goes beyond just selection. The assumption is that if industry is really going to have an appreciable effect on the manpower problem, it will have to think of recruiting, selection, training, and supervision as parts of a total manpower development process and not as entities by themselves. Quantity and quality of recruiting have an impact on selection—selection affects training—training capabilities, in turn, should affect selection. Unless viewed as a continuous, dependent process, maximum use cannot be made of the information the tools provide. If viewed as a complete process, the information gained from each step is carried forward to make future steps and the final decision

more powerful.

(2) *Organizational differences must be taken into consideration in selection.* Because the *Agent Selection Kit* is a complete selection process, it can be modified to meet company and agency differences. By clearly spelling out the philosophy and principles behind the steps in the *Agent Selection Kit*, the company and the agency head are able to evaluate what is being gained or lost by altering the steps in selection. Further, because the agency head is forced to make job behavior predictions, he can begin to consider each recruit in terms of his particular agency needs, style, and strengths. Agency differences as well as individual differences enter into the employment decision in a systematic manner.

(3) *A career with any company should be entered into based on realistic job expectations.*[13] The company should know what the job recruit expects from his association with the company. Under such a condition, the manager can make a manpower development decision that properly considers selection, early training, motivation, and supervision practices of the applicant in question. The job recruit should know what the company expects of him, how the company is going to help him accomplish these goals, and the difficulties and benefits he may encounter in undertaking the job. With such knowledge, the recruit can make more than a job decision. He can make a career decision. The creation of realistic expectations further implies that the employment decision be one of "mutual consent." Professional management of the future will not be able to rely on a slanted job presentation to attract recruits to a career in hopes that one or two applicants will succeed. Manpower development decisions will replace selection decisions. The *Agent Selection Kit* is built around the concept of "mutual consent" with respect to a career decision. There are already indications that the recruit of the future will respond to a "mutual exploration" theme, where together he and the manager will examine the individual's future

13 Life Insurance Agency Management Association, *"Realistic" Job Expectations and Survival*, Research Report 1964-2 (File 432).

in an industry. The *Agent Selection Kit* provides a systematic fact-finding procedure that appeals to the recruit.

(4) *The selection interview should proceed according to a highly-structured format.* The *Agent Selection Kit* contains two self-contained structured interview guides. The first interview guide is to be used with applicants who have had extensive prior work history and concentrates on this work experience. The alternate interview guide is to be used with applicants just completing their education or military experiences and without any work experience. In addition, both interview guides cover the recruit's education, military experience, attitude toward insurance and toward the insurance agent's job, family commitments, finances, social mobility, social life, and future goals and aspirations. The interview guides present the initial series of questions and several alternative probes. Experience and pretesting have indicated that recruits are receptive to a structured approach and that interviewers can learn to use the guides after brief, but intensive, training.

(5) *Employment decisions should be based on predictions of future job behavior.* The *Agent Selection Kit* considers decision-making from the point of view of a prediction of future behavior, rather than from vague, over-all impressions of potential or character. The manager manages the agent's activity, use of the telephone, record-keeping, prospecting, etc. The *Agent Selection Kit* enables the manager to make predictions about such job behaviors.

(6) *The manager should be able to learn from and correct his selection system.* The *Agent Selection Kit* procedure contains a built-in "feedback system" that enables the manager to learn from and correct his selection process. LIAMA interview research has shown that managers do not learn from the traditional approach to selection interviewing. To correct this, the *Agent Selection Kit* includes an Agent Performance Rating Form that the manager uses to compare to his final decision ratings. Discrepancies between his prediction and results point to areas in his

selection and early training process that need extra effort.

Implementation: Training in Selection and Interviewing

To ensure at least uniform initial introduction to the material, LIAMA designed a three-day skill-building workshop. Three general training objectives and 16 specific behavioral objectives served as guides in setting up the training program. The first general goal was to develop in each trainee *knowledge* of selection and interview techniques; the second goal was to create favorable *attitudes* in the managers toward selection and self-confidence in their ability to conduct a technically good selection interview; and third, to develop *skill* in actually using the selection and interview materials. As a result of participating in the training, the agency heads are to actually be better at selection and interviewing than they were prior to training, to know they are better, and to be able to immediately use the new material with some skill. Thus, the goals of the training are to change attitudes as well as to develop knowledge and skill. These specifications dictated that the workshops be built around small-sized classes, class participation, and practice with standardized case material and controlled feedback.

To accomplish the goals of the training program, the first step in the workshop is to help the agency manager to understand and accept the principles behind the steps in the selection process. This helps to make the trainees receptive to discarding their current approach to selection and to accepting the new approach. Once the agency head accepts the logic of the principles on which the *Agent Selection Kit* is based, the next step is to get the trainee to recognize and question how he is currently conducting his selection process. This is accomplished through the use of edited tapes that demonstrate some of the effects of violating the selection principles. At the end of this first phase of the training, the agency heads are receptive to a new procedure and are aware of what a good procedure should contain.

The skill training that follows is designed to make the agency head more proficient in the use of the interview and evaluation procedures. The interview technique training includes taped examples, practice, and critique. The final evaluation practice sessions are extremely important to agency heads. Here the manager is asked to combine information from all the selection methods he has utilized —the interview, reference checks, credit reports, interview with the wife, precontract training, etc. The manager practices making job behavior predictions in areas such as use of the telephone, night work, markets, prospecting activities, etc. For the first time, managers recognize that they will not be managing the recruit's character or how impressive he looks, but rather they recognize that they must manage his work activities. Managers begin to recognize that selection should try to predict the recruit's performance in these activities.

During the workshops, the participants' attitudes swing from skepticism to receptivity, from impatience with the training detail to complete acceptance. These swings in attitude are built into the schedule, since early experimental workshops showed that they were necessary to modify and solidify managers' attitudes.

The managers leave their workshop with greater knowledge, with a skill that is well along in development, and with much greater self-confidence in their selection and early training procedure that they can put into practice immediately.

The Future

The *Agent Selection Kit* was introduced to LIAMA's 300-plus member companies in 1969. By mid-1970, 40 major life insurance companies had introduced it to their general agents and managers. Obviously, at this time it is much too early to evaluate its effectiveness. However, it is currently being evaluated as part of LIAMA's research program on the selection interview. In addition, it also provides a natural field setting for further pure research on the selection interview. Thus, LIAMA's research on the interview is an example of pure research generating an improved product, which, in turn, furthers the pure research effort.

Employees Going and Coming

The Application Form

By ROBERT HERSHEY

IN A WORLD OF CHANGE, one thing at least is static: It is difficult to distinguish between the employment applications of today and those of 50 years ago, except, perhaps, for a few quaint anachronistic questions such as "Do you use tobacco or intoxicating liquors?" True, some firms have experimented with weighted application blanks, but an examination of employment applications in current use turns up a monotonous similarity in the kinds of items included in such forms. In the past 20 years, personnel men and specialists in applied psychology have generated research that has resulted in improved techniques in recruitment, selection, testing, wage and salary administration, and training, but significant revisions of employment applications, with the exceptions of deletions or rephrasings to meet Equal Employment Opportunity Commission requirements, are virtually nonexistent.

It could be argued that the reason for this is that there is no further room for improvements—that current application forms are providing all the essential data needed,

PERSONNEL, Jan.-Feb. 1971, pp. 36-39.

such as last position, dates of employment, salary history, reason for leaving previous positions, and so forth. This may be the case, but it is more likely that because we have not expected more from employment applications, we have not made any effort to expand their range of usefulness.

Instead of limiting the employment application to its traditional purpose of a factual summation, why not capitalize on its unique characteristic of being our first contact with the job prospect? Could the form be designed to provide attitudinal information that can be explored during the interview? This seems feasible, but then one wonders whether applicants would be truthful in answering projective questions, that is, questions that require the applicant to "project" his attitudes. Would he be more or less truthful than when he is dealing with nonattitudinal information? Some answers emerge from the experience described here.

A Range of Viewpoints

In 1951, when the Maspeth Division of the Bulova Watch Company was established, it was the author's hunch that the inclusion of an unstructured question on the application blank might reveal important personal information that could be quickly developed during the course of the employment interview. In 1955, we tabulated and analyzed the answers that were given in order to evaluate just how useful such a question was. Specifically, it was "What special or personal facts do you feel the company should know about you?"

All told, 784 applications of hired applicants were examined for a response to the question. Of these, 96, or 12.2 percent, of the applicants hired answered the question; the rest left the space blank. The replies fell into nine categories. An example of each follows:

1. Skill. "I have a good knowledge of machinery."
2. Health. "I have a fused knee from an accident in 1948."
3. Accomplishment. "I was a Marine teletype operator."
4. Self-praise. "I learn fast and am a steady worker."
5. Unflattering. "I was arrested two years ago."
6. Flattering. "I wish to obtain employment in a highly rated company such as yours."
7. Sympathy. "I have my mother and brother to support."
8. Interest. "I am interested in machine work."
9. Desire for something material. "I'd like steady employment."

Our next step was to attempt to verify the accuracy of these responses. In so doing, it became apparent that the categories of flattery, sympathy, interest, and desire for something material were either unverifiable or too difficult or time-consuming to attempt verification.

The table below details the accuracies found in the other five categories.

The veracity of the responses was determined by reference to personnel and production records in cases where the variable was measurable. For example, if someone stated, "I am rarely absent," his attendance record card was examined. For statements such as "I am a fast learner," the employee's foreman was consulted. The statement was accepted only if the employee was rated above average in speed of learning on a three-point scale (above average, average, below average).

Do Job Applicants Lie?

Before evaluating the truthfulness of job applicants in completing an employment application containing projective questions, we should have as a frame of reference a measure of their truthfulness in responses to the traditional application. A sampling of 100 applications in Bulova's currently active file showed that 24 percent of returned reference checks had discrepancies in either dates of employment, job title, past salary, or reason for leaving last position. Only discrepancies of two or more months' service and deviations of five or more dollars per weekly salary were considered discrepancies in this survey:

REFERENCE CHECK DISCREPANCIES

Category	Percentage
Dates of previous employment	13
Salaries in previous jobs	7
Job titles of previous jobs	2
Reason for leaving previous jobs	2
Total	24%

ACCURACY OF SELF-APPRAISAL RESPONSES

	Skill	Health	Accomplishments	Self-praise	Unflattering	Total Responses
Number of responses	7	16	13	36	1	73
Percent of responses	9.6	21.9	17.8	49.3	1.3	
Inaccuracies	1	0	0	7	0	
Percent of accuracies	86	100	100	80.5	100	

99

What are the implications of the fact that 24 percent of the factual data on the employment application was inaccurate and only 11 percent of the attitudinal data was inaccurate? Paradoxically, there was more lying in the areas that are more easily verifiable, by reference checking. Considering how much the applicant had at stake at the time of application, one must be somewhat impressed with the truthfulness of those who answered the attitudinal question. It appears, therefore, that if a battery of subjective questions were included in employment applications, they would be answered with a higher degree of accuracy than the usual objective, factual questions.

Although the Bulova Maspeth Division experiment began in 1951, a perusal of the approximately 30 representative company employment applications in the 1967 *AMA Book of Employment Forms* reveals that only three applications have even one nondirective type of question: "State why you believe you would be a success selling"; "What do you like best (least) about this (previous) job?"; "Give any other information that you consider would complete the picture of your background." However, not a single application includes a *battery* of attitude-probing questions.

For companies that want to extend the usefulness of the applica-tion blank beyond its traditional coverage, here are some unstructured questions that could be made a supplement to their existing employment forms:

- What makes you angry?
- Are you generally lucky? Why?
- When was the happiest time of your life?
- What was the worst thing that ever happened to you?
- What kind of person are you?
- What do you like most about yourself?
- What do you like least about yourself?
- What was the best job you ever had? Why?
- What was the worst job you every had? Why?
- What special or personal fact should the company know about you?
- What's your philosophy of work?
- What would you like to change about yourself?

The creative personnel man can formulate other, similar questions of this kind. The hope is that the job applicant will have revealed some personal attitudes before the interview commences that will be helpful in the interview itself and later, too, both in placement and in appraisal procedures.

Selection by Objectives: A Function of the Management by Objectives Philosophy

Edwin L. Miller

WHY is it that many administrators and personnel selection boards are not able to recognize a highly qualified individual when he sits across the table or when his qualification record is being evaluated? Why is it that selection and promotion decisions all too often are based on idiosyncracy, hunch, managerial stereotype, and favoritism? Part of the answer lies in the decisionmaker's failure in three important functions: (1) to identify the criteria of job success; (2) to gather effectively information which is predictive of job success or failure; and (3) to evaluate the information that is obtained.

This article deals with these deficiencies. The approach suggested here is selection by objectives. It stresses an objective results method of selection which can be used in hiring people from outside the organization or for promoting from within. The intent of this article is to present an approach to more effective selection of personnel, not to judge the merits or demerits of current techniques.

Selection by Objectives

Selection by objectives is a product of management by objectives, an approach to managing which is having a forceful impact on managerial thinking and practice in both public and private sectors. Peter Drucker, one of the foremost authorities on the concept of management by objectives, points out in his book, *The Practice of Management* (Harper, 1954), that:

> Objectives are needed in every area where performance and results directly and vitally affect the survival and prosperity of the business. These are the areas which are affected by every management decision and which therefore have to be considered in every management decision. They decide what it means correctly to manage the business. They spell out what results that business must aim at and what is needed to work effectively toward these targets.

Selection by objectives embodies this philosophy. Management must spell out the objectives of the job to be filled. It must state the goals rather than the job characteristics and skills that the typical job description stresses. It must then gather evidence of the results each candidate has achieved in past jobs. (This step emphasizes the measurement of the candidate's achievements.) Management then compares and evaluates achievements of each candidate relative to the results for which the job to be filled is aiming.

Organizations do not exist in a vacuum; their needs and goals frequently change

PUBLIC PERSONNEL REVIEW, Apr. 1968, pp. 92-96.

101

for any number of different reasons. Change may be purposeful and arbitrarily initiated by those in charge. Changes in conditions outside the organization or the relative importance of functions within it may require action by top management to bring it up to date. For example, at one point in time, the objective of a department may be expanded service; therefore what is important to success is acquisition of new clients. After the achievement of expanded service, efficient handling of client claims may become the most critical function.

Job performance criteria will differ as the needs and goals of the organization change. Heed this caveat: job titles may remain unchanged, but there is no guarantee that the job content and job performance criteria of today will be the same next month, much less next year. Unfortunately, many administrators fail to recognize this dynamic quality of organizations and jobs, and consequently many personnel staffing decisions are doomed to failure from the start.

Selection by objectives takes cognizance of changing organization needs and goals, and accordingly of changes in job content and performance criteria. Before an organization can select by objectives, it must establish what the objectives for the position actually are. Thus management is forced to think about the job and its goals in terms of today and tomorrow rather than yesterday.

Selection by objectives follows George Odiorne's three part breakdown of job goals (in *Management by Objectives*, Pitman, 1965): routine duties, problemsolving goals, and innovative or creative goals. (1) The routine duties are those repetitive commonplace activities generally spelled out in the job description. (2) Problemsolving goals are concerned with problems arising from changes in the environment, or change in user demand for a service caused by unforeseeable forces. (3) Creative goals are the goals of innovating: that is, creating new methods or introducing changes for the better into the organization. These categories of job objectives represent an ascending order of complexity in management achievement.

Developing the Objectives

Before an administrator or manager can begin to select by objectives, he must determine the objectives. It is common knowledge that a job is apt to be described differently by the person occupying the position than by the person supervising it. Thus it seems particularly rewarding to draw upon the opinions of both the supervisees and the supervisor. From the parochial viewpoint, the views of present job incumbents—if they are available—should be solicited. From the more crucial and catholic perspective, the manager must be asked to classify the objectives. It is he who will supervise the subordinate in the job; it is he who will coach the subordinate; it is he who will appraise the subordinate; it is he who will recommend the subordinate for promotion.

The Critical Evidence

Once the job goals have been classified with respect to the three major categories, the selection process must attempt to uncover evidence in each candidate's history relevant to his probable operation on each level. The assumption is that the routine or regular duties are a "must" requirement. Jobs higher in the managerial hierarchy are more heavily weighted with problemsolving and innovative responsibilities. Therefore, the supervisor must, as he moves into more responsible positions of authority, demonstrate his problemsolving and creative abilities.

For promotion from within, selecting by objectives stimulates managers to begin gathering evidence about each subordinate's ability to achieve results in the critical areas of more responsible jobs. Being a sound performer in a particular job does not necessarily qualify one for promotion to a higher position. All too often an individual is promoted only on the basis of seniority, productivity, or patronage. Little or no consideration is given to whether the candidate's qualifications are called for in the higher job, or whether he has the capacity to achieve the results expected. Selection by objectives is aimed at correcting this type of error in personnel staffing decisions. Once the list of job objectives has been spelled out, the administrator is in a much more powerful position to evaluate accurately the candidate and his qualifications by seeking evidence about achievements in past jobs or in those areas considered to be critical for success in the job to be filled. Flexibility and comprehensiveness are the hallmarks of the evidence-gathering phase of selection by objectives. Foremost, the administrator will consciously strive to gather information that is predictive of job success or failure, and evaluate the information systematically. Effective interviews are a likely product of this approach to selection, because questioning will be slanted toward seeking specific evidence of results in both kind and amount. If psychological tests are utilized, critical questions are apt to arise concerning their administration, validity, and contribution to effective selection. It is quite likely that selection by objectives will stimulate a fresh look at the selection process, and a much more creative implementation of such instruments and techniques. Complacency has no place in this approach!

An Example of "Selection by Objectives" in Practice:
Sample Guidelines for Evaluating Maintenance Supervisor Candidates

Major Areas of Responsibility	Job Objectives	Indicative Past Achievements
1. Cost control	Reduce maintenance, construction, and repair costs by at least five per cent during the next year.	What costs results has he achieved? How did his costs vary? Has he remained within his budget? Did he come up with any cost reduction suggestions? Has he submitted any improvement ideas on costs?
2. Maintenance, repair, and service of equipment, buildings, and facilities	Maintain all buildings and facilities in best operating conditions. Must establish service and maintenance schedule for repairing and servicing shop equipment.	What sections or activities of a maintenance department has he led? Has he ever set up a servicing and maintenance schedule for shop and operating equipment? Has he ever been responsible for maintaining buildings and facilities in the best state of repair? How did he go about doing this?
3. Meet construction and repair deadlines	Must allocate resources to complete projects on schedule.	What type of a record has he made with respect to deadlines met, cost of construction, and quality of workmanship? Has he stayed within his budget figures? How did he go about meeting deadlines?
4. Employee relations	Develop cooperation and team spirit among subordinates, and get along with building trades unions and their officials.	What was the turnover record when he assumed charge of his section or function Did it change? Was this because of his influence? What was the grievance rate? What was the absenteeism? How has it changed? How did he get along with other section heads and his subordinates?
5. Training	Must provide guidance and instruction to subordinates to insure full utilization of available skills. Assist in resolving complex problems involving methods and techniques.	Has he ever been involved in training nonsupervisory personnel? What sorts of training has he directed? How many of his former trainees are performing effectively? How many have subsequently been promoted? How many have since been released or transferred from maintenance activities?
6. Safety	Improve upon accident record in the department. Reduce lost time accidents by at least two per cent within the next year.	What was the safety record in terms of frequency and severity when he took over his section? What direction did the safety record go? What techniques or programs has he instituted to improve upon the safety record? Have they worked?

The accompanying table presents a sample listing of the responsibilities and job objectives for a maintenance supervisor, and the measures designed to plumb past achievements believed to be related to obtaining the job objectives. Because the position of maintenance supervisor has more routine duties than it has problemsolving or innovative activities, these job objectives become the selection criteria. It should be noted that the types of data collected give evidence of the candidate's likelihood of performing the job successfully. Other positions, particularly at higher levels, emphasize the requirements of problemsolving and ultimately innovation, and these requirements become the selection criteria. Quite naturally, evidence pertaining to past achievements will be sought about the candidate's problemsolving and innovative abilities.

It is apparent that when the candidate is being evaluated on past achievements in terms of results, the evaluator or evaluators must be familiar with the objectives of the job being filled. It cannot be overstressed that the list of job objectives be relevant and current rather than irrelevant and outdated. Given the job objectives, the evaluator *must* seek evidence of past results in terms of kind and amount. Hence this approach to selection is dynamic rather than static. Furthermore, it offers a more penetrating means for evaluating the candidate's qualifications in light of the job objectives.

An Example

This approach to selection was recently introduced in a government agency plagued by disastrously poor personnel staffing decisions. The evaluation board had only the haziest notions about the objectives of the job to be filled and about the qualifications of the candidates. Job descriptions, which were frequently out-of-date, and qualification records, which described each candidate in the most general and laudatory terms, were the official information upon which the staffing decisions were to be made. Actually the decisions of the evaluation board were made upon the basis of the candidate's length of service and his personal familiarity with and acceptability to the board members: that is, whether the board members knew him and liked him.

To overcome this obvious weakness in the selection process, the agency now insists that job objectives be identified, and the performance of the candidate be appraised or evaluated in the following terms:

What results did the candidate actually achieve during his tenure in his present position? Give a year by year summary. How many of these results were directly attributable to the candidate; how many were jointly achieved with others?

The replies were matched with an intensive examination of the objectives of the vacant position. The result has been a drastic change in the way personnel staffing decisions are made, and while it is still early to be certain, preliminary reports indicate a sharpening of performance of newly-placed persons.

Unexpected results have occurred in two additional areas. First, there are several indications that numerous members of management have been seriously reexamining their own approaches to managing, and that a movement toward a result-oriented style of management has begun.

Second, management has obtained an indirect measurement of the effectiveness of its management development and training program. This particular agency had an excellent training program on paper; but discovered that candidates being considered for still more responsible positions had received little preparatory training. As a consequence, the entire training and development program is being reevaluated in light of its contribution to the development of the individual, and his preparation for more responsible management jobs.

An Aid, Not a Panacea

Hiring and promotion policy practice is badly in need of serious reexamination. Effectiveness and success of an organization, be it in the public or private sectors, rest upon the identification and selection of top-flight personnel. Whim, ignorance, and personal prejudices have no place in the effective managerial selection process.

Those individuals who make the personnel staffing decisions must know how to gather information which is predictive of job success or failure, and they must know how to evaluate the information that is obtained.

Selection by objectives is not a panacea, but it may help those who are responsible for selecting personnel to improve upon the quality and accuracy of their decisions.

CHAPTER III

The Induction of Staff

The purpose of the induction process is to assist the new staff member to become an effective working member of the total staff as quickly and efficiently as possible. In the business world, it is reported that in many instances a new employee is a deficit to a firm because he is still in the "learning" stage in the first year. In the education world the beginning teacher as we have come to know him has the heaviest work load of any member of your staff, and the efforts of beginners is done under stress conditions. Therefore, it can be concluded that in both "worlds" new staff are not functioning effectively.

It is obvious that there is a need for a carefully planned induction or orientation program in our schools. Probst presents an outlined program for supervisors to initiate which might do much to simplify the transition from college to classroom for the novice teacher. Such a program would allow the supervisor to return to the role of teacher, and let him work intensively with the beginning teacher in an unthreatening situation.

The concern of induction of employees has been a problem in the education world for many years. Edelfelt points out the need for adequate inservice education that meets the teachers needs through development of national consortium agencies, etc. with a stake in inservice education. Within the next decade, the thrust of inservice programs will be toward renewal, self-renewal.

Whatever steps are taken in the induction, it behooves the educator to create programs where more professional people are involved in the planning and where a major emphasis is upon purposeful learning for all students.

Palmatier offers key guidelines used by top innovators who are successful change agents in an educational system. Without serving the felt needs of the staff person, the induction, orientation, or in-service education becomes an exercise in futility.

From Student to Teacher
The Supervisor's Role

ROBERT E. PROBST*

THE transition from the role of student to that of teacher is traumatic at best, devastating at worst. Yet it need not be such an unnerving time if arrangements are made to ease the college graduate gently into his new position. Student teaching is one practice designed to smooth the transition, and in many cases it does so effectively; but there is more that might be done, especially by the public school systems.

Preschool orientation for new teachers is often a good example of an opportunity missed. Too frequently, the orientation consists of little more than brief—or even worse, lengthy—speeches of welcome or exhortation, and perhaps a day or two to arrange rooms and meet principals and faculty. Such an orientation does little to help prepare the new teacher to deal with the students or the curriculum. He is left to chart his own course through textbooks and curriculum guides as best he can, with little opportunity, or time, to seek additional help.

The person in possibly the best position to offer help to the novice is the subject area supervisor. The supervisor, presumably an experienced and skillful teacher with knowledge of both the students and the curriculum, and with skill in dealing with teachers, should be able to provide both knowledge and encouragement. He may find, in fact, that his commitment to the improvement of

teaching is best fulfilled through work with new teachers. The young, inexperienced teacher, not yet set in his ways, might well be willing to accept, and even to seek, advice and assistance and thus may be the supervisor's greatest hope for effecting change in the educational system. The receptivity that we would hope for in the novice would simplify the supervisor's task. There are, however, other factors that complicate it.

Difficulties Faced

One of the major difficulties is that the supervisor seldom has time to work as intensively with the beginning teacher as he might wish. The school year opens with a rash of meetings and a long list of obligations and duties that frequently keep supervisors far from the classroom during the first week of school. Under these circumstances, the young teacher is very much on his own. He may have the help of the department chairman and other teachers, but the supervisor's impact on him during this period is likely to be negligible.

If the supervisor does manage to avoid some of the meetings and get into the classroom early in the year, he faces problems of a different sort. He can now work with the teacher, but conditions militate against success. First of all, the teacher is working hard

EDUCATIONAL LEADERSHIP, Vol. 30, No. 5, Feb. 1973, pp. 464-467.

to develop rapport with the students and to earn their respect. To work too closely with the new teacher at this point may be to jeopardize these efforts and risk embarrassing him. Obviously, some observations are expected, even by students, but the frequent visits necessary to effect change in a teacher's methods are likely to unnerve the teacher in front of the people whose confidence he desperately needs. Not all young teachers are made uneasy by the supervisor's visits, of course, but unfortunately those most in need of assistance are often the ones most uncomfortable when the assistance is offered.

The situation is further complicated by the uncertainties that attend any group activity; so the supervisor, should he attempt something like demonstration teaching, risks poor results even if his lesson is good and the class responds well. If the lesson is successful, then the teacher is likely to be embarrassed by the comparison with his own efforts. The supervisor has come into the class, taken over and done well, and then the class returns to the hands of the beginner who may not be able to match the performance of the more experienced educator.

Should the lesson be unsuccessful, then the supervisor has embarrassed himself and perhaps lost the confidence of the teacher. And the lesson might very well fail, since the supervisor is in a new situation, teaching a class he does not know, a class that is in the process of adjusting to someone else's manner and style. Either success or failure might equally well be attributed to his novelty. In either case, his rapport with the teacher may be damaged, and the teacher's respect for himself and the supervisor may be diminished.

We should also consider the possibility that the supervisor may no longer be the skillful teacher he was, or should have been, before moving into administration. Several years out of the classroom can dull the skills a great deal. Should he try going back into the class as a teacher, he may find the students quite unlike those he faced two to ten years ago, and may discover that his methods are no longer as successful as they once had been.

So the supervisor must face several problems when he deals with the new teacher: first, the difficulty of finding time to work with the teacher; second, the awkwardness of working extensively in the teacher's classroom; and third, the possibility that his own teaching skills may have grown rusty in the years of administration. If the supervisor hopes to provide much assistance during the time when student becomes teacher, he must find some way of solving these three problems. One possible solution may lie in a summer workshop designed specifically to bring supervisor and new teachers together in the classroom.

The Supervisor Contributes

The workshop would involve actual work in the classroom for about four weeks during late summer. The supervisor would assume responsibility for planning a unit of instruction, and would plan specific lessons and conduct classes for perhaps the first week, while the new teachers observe. After the class, supervisor and teachers would meet to analyze the lesson. All aspects of the lesson would be discussed: the subject matter, the instructional strategies, the activities in which students participated, the response of students to various techniques, the relationship of the lesson to the one preceding and the one to follow. The supervisor would, in other words, be teaching both students and teachers, spending perhaps an hour in the classroom during the morning, and an hour or two consulting with teachers in the afternoon.

As the course progresses, the supervisor would gradually turn the class over to the teachers. He may do this in any of several ways—perhaps by first having them conduct discussions in small groups for part of the period, then slowly allowing them to assume full responsibility for planning and running the class. Again, the teaching would be subjected to discussion by all the participants. Presumably, the threatening aspect of the analysis would be diminished since the supervisor himself had willingly undergone such analysis first. During the first part of the workshop his teaching had been examined and criticized and he had, again presumably, served as a model of good-natured receptivity for others to emulate.

As the course moves from the first week to the last, more and more of the work would fall upon the teachers, so that by the end of the session they would be doing all the teaching and much of the planning. The unit, of course, would have been outlined in advance by the supervisor—the teachers would be unable to participate in the long-range planning. The supervisor would plan all of the first lessons—but by the second week, at least, the teachers may begin to assist him in planning lessons that he will teach. Soon, perhaps by the third week, the roles should reverse, and the supervisor should assist the teachers in planning lessons that they will present. By the fourth week, the teachers would be doing all the planning and teaching, and probably all the analysis of lessons.

A summer program of this sort could contribute much to the solution of the supervisor's problems in helping new teachers. It would, for instance, allow the supervisor to keep his hand in at teaching. He would have a month of it each year—not much, perhaps, but more than most supervisors now have. It would enable him to get to know all the new teachers. He would be working closely with them for a month, observing their teaching, learning some of their weaknesses and some of their strengths, and yet he would not be dealing with them in a threatening situation. Moreover, they would be used to having him and other teachers in the classroom, so they would more likely be receptive to visits later in the year. The relationship between the supervisor and the teacher could become very strong during this session.

The teachers would also have the opportunity to meet other new teachers and to grow accustomed to sharing ideas. They might consequently be less inclined to isolate themselves in their own classrooms later on. They could also become more sensitive to the students they may expect to meet when they begin their regular schedule, and this alone may be valuable enough to justify the pro-

gram. It is very difficult for a teacher who develops poor relationships with the class at the beginning of the year to recover. In such a program as this one, however, he has an opportunity to make mistakes in August and then to begin again, with a new group of students, in September. He does not have to suffer the consequences of his mistakes for a full year.

The summer session would also provide the school system, after several years of operation, with a good strong core of teachers, prepared not just by the colleges in the general methods of teaching, but also by the supervisor in the details of the system's own curriculum. Such a program could do much to achieve unity of purpose within a school system.

There would be problems, of course. One is money. The school system would have to decide whether the benefits to be derived from the program would be worth the expense of an extra month's salary for the new teachers. In comparison to the extensive training programs in some industries or businesses, however, this month-long workshop is laughably small.

The system would also have to obtain students. The program could be justified as either remedial training for students who had difficulties during the previous year, or as enrichment. The summer school operated at Duke University for the purpose of training Master of Arts in Teaching candidates is such an enrichment program and seems to have no trouble attracting students, although no credit is offered and there is no reward beyond the activity itself. In any case, the supervisor could design the unit so that it would be suitable for some group of students from the community.

A third problem might be created by the number of teachers involved in such an activity. If a school system hires 30 or 40 new English teachers each year, the supervisor of English will not be able to deal with each one as closely as he would have to in order to make the program successful. If the system is large enough to hire that many new teachers, however, it is large enough to require two or three assistant supervisors who could help with the program. If there are no assistants, the supervisor might find several superior teachers who could be persuaded to assist him.

A program such as the one outlined here might do much to simplify the transition from college to classroom, and might at the same time improve the supervisor's relationship with the novice teacher. It would return the supervisor periodically to the role of teacher, and allow him to work intensively with new teachers in an unthreatening situation. It could yield lasting benefits for his schools. ☐

Inservice Education of Teachers: Priority for the Next Decade

ROY A. EDELFELT

The inservice education of teachers will be the major focus in teacher education for the next decade: this is a prediction that I propose to justify; and I believe it will prove accurate because of the condition of the teaching profession, the state of education, the plight of teacher education, and the will of the public. The circumstances:

Inservice—Neglected Stepchild

Inservice education has been the neglected stepchild of teacher training. Most resources and effort in teacher education have gone to preservice preparation. For the last four decades, this concentration of resources and effort was defensible in order to assure that teachers were adequately prepared prior to service. Now, however, preservice goals have been largely accomplished. Almost all beginning teachers must complete a baccalaureate program that includes a practicum in student teaching and other laboratory experiences. Nearly 99 percent of the teachers currently in service have at least a bachelor's degree and a license to teach. Meanwhile, inservice education for teachers remains a wasteland of evening, Saturday, and summer courses or workshops mandated by school districts and state departments of education. Inservice education takes place almost entirely on the teacher's time and in advanced collegiate study at the teacher's expense. It is required for a standard teaching certificate or for advancement on a local district's salary schedule. It is planned and executed by educators other than teachers. Too often it is taught in a manner that violates almost every principle of good teaching. Perhaps most important, too little of its emphasis has been on improving teacher performance.

Point one, then, is that inservice education has been inadequate. It has not met teacher needs. It has been pursued as an adjunct to a full-time job. It has been required by superordinates largely without consultation with teachers. And it has not served the major purposes of improving professional performance.

JOURNAL OF TEACHER EDUCATION, Summer, 1974, Vol. XXV, No. 3, pp. 250-252.

Despite all its shortcomings, teachers apparently still want inservice education. For example, in a 1973-74 NEA assessment of teachers' needs in 20 widely different local associations, inservice education was one of three needs that surfaced in every instance. Teachers want to continue to improve; they want to be current. The data also confirmed that they want changes and improvements in inservice education so that it more adequately meets their needs.

Effect of Surplus on Inservice

At present, the supply of teachers more than matches the number of job openings. In this tight market there is less teacher turnover and hence greater stability in the teaching force. Hopefully then, the effects of inservice education should not be dissipated the way they were when large numbers of teachers joined and left local faculties each year. There is now a chance for continuity, for building a faculty over a longer term, and for capitalizing on what is learned in inservice education.

Now, college professors and administrators have begun to realize the potential market in programs of inservice education. Undergraduate enrollments are declining. In 1973, for the first time, the number of college graduates in teacher education decreased. The problem is and will be how to continue tenured college faculty unless new demands for their services can be found. This may be the most compelling reason for the growing collegiate interest in committing more resources and people to inservice education. For many colleges, it is a matter of survival. Whether teachers can negotiate new approaches, more appropriate emphases, and greater flexibility in inservice education, given these circumstances, is yet to be seen.

School-College Partnerships

Colleges and universities are becoming more receptive to working with public school teachers on inservice education. New relationships between professors and teachers have developed from school-college partnerships in preservice education. In many situations there have been incidental benefits for inservice teachers; they have learned better how to perform their own tasks as they have grappled with helping the prospective teacher. Gradually, too, professors have benefitted by finding a testing ground for theory and real situations for research.

Professionalization of Teaching

Some professors already are committed to a greater and more productive focus on inservice education. They see the limits of preservice teacher education. They understand the value of involving teachers in their own professional development and recognize the importance of dealing with actual teaching problems in advanced study. The most insightful among them also realize that the professionalization of teaching will require a more gradual induction into service, a bridging of the gap between preservice training and inservice practice. The supervised, on-the-job training periods of other professions are essential to teaching if it is to be fully professionalized.

Professional Governance

Teacher organizations now have power to influence and negotiate policy and conditions of inservice education. In addition, teacher organizations have spearheaded efforts to achieve legally sanctioned professional governance of the profession, including control over standards of preparation for, entry into, and practice of teaching. Establishing professional standards commissions promises a better balance of power within the profession and fixes responsibility for monitoring the profession with educators. The result should be not only more equitable decisions in the profession, but also better accountability to the public.

These developments — negotiations and professional governance—are important for inservice education because they provide mechanisms for dealing with problems of inservice education and a forum for devising more effective programs. But the essential collaboration among the various parties— teacher organizations, colleges and universities, government agencies, and local adminstrators— won't be easy. Each party has vested interests. There are also legitimate differences of opinion. For example, teachers want a voice in determining the content and process of staff development programs because they know most directly the problems teachers face. Teacher educators believe they should devise and control graduate training because it is their area of expertise. School district administrators feel they know what teachers need because they oversee the total school program. School boards assume that improving or maintaining professional competence is largely the responsibility of the individual teacher and is part of what they buy in hiring professional services. Per-

haps these statements are arbitrarily oversimplified, but they reflect opinions widely held by people in each category and illustrate the differing viewpoints that must be reconciled.

Redefining Inservice Teacher Education

Ultimately, agreement or compromise may be facilitated if the concept of inservice education is clarified and defined. Inservice education obviously takes more than one form. In its traditional and most widely practiced form, it is conceived as personal professional development, formalized into courses at the graduate level that lead to advanced degrees and credentials, job promotion, and added competence for the individual. This concept assumes that the teacher is an individual entrepreneur moving independently along in his or her own career.

Many Alternate Approaches

There are other possible concepts, however. For example, one can conceive of inservice education as a faculty effort, assuming that professionals who function together to attain specified educational goals and programs for students can also engage in personal and group development together, to get at both the collective and individual problems teachers face. There is some experience and research to substantiate the view that improving a group's effort is more effective when members of a group are dealt with together in a context, rather than when each individual gets inservice training separately. The success of such an approach can be evaluated in terms of the improvements in school programs that can be traced directly to inservice training.

Collective improvement can be analyzed so that it is possible to deal with the individual teacher's performance in his or her current assignment. Individual teacher achievement is then demonstrated by improved performance in accomplishing certain specific tasks—e.g., teaching reading, directing a discussion, or questioning as an instructional technique—that contribute to the total school program.

Time and space do not permit illustrating further how the teacher center concept, minicourses, protocol materials, inservice packages and modules, and other experiments in inservice education

113

are developing.* These represent yet other concepts of inservice education and deserve attention in separate articles. And the implications of performance- or competency-based teacher education and the impact of further professionalization of teaching on inservice education also need more discussion.

The point in citing alternate approaches is that there are several valid concepts of inservice education, and that it will take more than one concept to satisfy the vested interests of all parties involved. Beginning by helping each party find at least some satisfaction may ameliorate some of the conflict in views and could establish some working relationships that might last.

Need for Continuing General Education

Perhaps parenthetical but also basic is a concern for the continuing general education of the teacher. The teacher's public image is that of a well-educated person. Yet inservice training has neglected the kind of learning that would support this image. Preservice preparation can only provide a foundation in the education of a "cultured" person. That foundation must be built on thorough inservice education. This need is particularly important because so many teachers come from social classes in which culture in its deeper meaning and higher development is not prevalent.

The teacher's need in general education, of course, is not limited to culture and artistic things. The teacher must also be current in economics, political science, sociology, psychology, social criticism, and almost all other aspects of living and being. There is, then, a need among teachers for general education that continues career long—and which now is largely ignored.

Questions for the Future of Inservice

I have tried to present some of the circumstances and thoughts about inservice teacher education that are in play now and that will influence the future. To draw conclusions would be premature. But it may be helpful to raise some questions that need resolution as we begin to deal with the future:

1. What are the purposes of inservice education?
2. How will inservice programs be determined and by whom?
3. Who will control or govern inservice education?
4. How will inservice education be paid for?
5. Will or should inservice education become part of the teacher's job and be conducted on the employer's time?
6. What should the reward system be for inservice education?
7. What is the appropriate place for formal graduate study and for other forms of inservice education? Should various forms of inservice education have different requirements, standards, acknowledgments, and rewards?
8. To what extent should inservice education be related to proficiency, or be based on performance or competency goals?
9. To what extent should inservice programs satisfy local needs and to what extent should they meet more universal and generalized requirements?
10. Should inservice education be related to continuing employment, tenure, higher levels of certification, or continuing certification?
11. To what extent should inservice education be the individual teacher's responsibility—intrinsically motivated—and to what extent externally required and therefore extrinsically motivated?
12. How should inservice education be evaluated and by whom?
13. To what extent must the relationship between pre- and in-service teacher education be considered as opposed to dealing with inservice education separately?
14. What are appropriate roles in inservice education for state departments, the U.S. Office of Education, colleges and universities, teacher organizations, local school districts, regional laboratories, professional societies, and other interested agencies?
15. Who should initiate action on inservice education?

None of these questions can be dealt with singly. The problems of standards, procedures, insituation or agency role, finance, control, and governance, etc., are all interrelated parts of inservice education. So, as steps are taken in the next decade to reform inservice education, care should also be taken to avoid a piecemeal or patchwork job.

Although programs of inservice education can and should never be uniform, more collaboration is required to plan direction, establish policy, promote programs and research, and evaluate outcomes. Needed is a national consortium of agencies, institutions, and groups with a stake in inservice education to assume such responsibilities and to disseminate information to the entire teaching profession. That, it seems to me, is an urgent priority that may be the first and essential step in making the reform of inservice education the accomplishment of the next decade.

Portland's In-Service Involves All Professional Personnel

VERA M. LARSON

TRADITIONALLY, the education profession has seemed to accept three basic notions: first, that the education of a teacher is in two parts, that which comes before he receives his first certificate (preservice), and that which comes afterward (in-service); second, that each of these two experiences is different in nature, the first essentially theoretical, the second practical; and third, that other professionals know best what the individual teacher needs. Therefore, influenced by certification regulations, NCATE standards, college requirements, federal and state legislation, and community pressure, the future teacher's education is planned for him first by college personnel and later by school administrators.

Fortunately, the pressures now being exerted on our schools are forcing us to change our approach to teacher education. If teachers are to be able to cope with the complexities of today, then more than lip service must be given to the concept that a teacher is always in the process of "becoming." The education of a teacher is a continuing process and not one which ought to be divided into two distinct parts. But more than that, the focus must be on the real issue, "What will be the payoff for children?" What value is education for the teacher if it does not result in purposeful, relevant learning for students?

What follows is a brief description of how one school district is attempting to involve the entire staff in an in-service program designed to help the teacher individually and the district as a whole in the process of self-renewal.

For many years, the Portland public schools have supported an extensive in-service program for teachers. In the past, the program was developed and implemented by a central office staff of curriculum specialists. Now, the District has underway a program which seeks to involve all personnel in the planning and implementing of in-service projects which respond to the identified needs of schools and teachers. The survival of the system itself may very well depend on the degree to which this approach succeeds.

EDUCATIONAL LEADERSHIP, Mar. 1974, pp. 502-505.

115

Five Elements Are Needed

The feasibility of such an approach to teacher education depends on at least five basic elements. They are: (a) an administrative staff and a board of education which view in-service education as a top priority; (b) an organizational plan which makes it possible for in-service projects to develop "on site"; (c) coordination in planning so that in-service activities are focused on identified goals; (d) available resources such as institutions of higher learning, and support from business and professional organizations; (e) a quality professional staff. Each of these elements and how it affects the plan for total involvement of the staff in the continuing education of the teacher will be considered separately.

1. *For many years, in-service education has had top priority in Portland.*

The board of education and the administrative staff have consistently allocated a generous portion of each year's budget for in-service education. The interest of the board members in teacher education can be underscored by mentioning that in 1968 they initiated a Professional Growth Incentive Salary Program which makes it possible for teachers to move from one salary level to another by working within a planned program of study. Relevance to the improvement of the teacher's classroom instruction is the criterion on which applicability of credits for salary purposes is based.

During the period from 1966 to 1970, substantial allocations of the staff development budget were given to schools as discretionary money to be utilized as each staff saw fit in terms of curriculum development and improvement of instruction. Although a comprehensive district-wide in-service program was planned and implemented by the supervisory staff, encouragement was given to projects developed by faculties, by groups of teachers, and by individuals. This emphasis was based on the premise that the most effective in-service activities are those which are planned and implemented by the learners.

In 1970, Robert Blanchard, Superintendent of Schools, moved the district closer to total involvement of personnel in all aspects of education by decentralizing the district. The major purpose was to place decision making as near as possible to those affected by the decisions. This, combined with a program planning and budgeting system, has had an impact on planning for change in curriculum and instruction and the attendant in-service needs for all personnel.

2. *The present organizational plan of the district encourages involvement.*

The district is divided into three areas, each of which serves approximately 22,000 students. Each area is headed by an administrative team, one of whom has the major responsibility for curriculum and instruction as well as staff development. He coordinates the work of committees of teachers and administrators which make recommendations for the area as a whole. In turn, each building staff is encouraged to develop curriculum, plan for its implementation, and identify in-service activities which respond to the unique needs of the students and faculty of that school. Buildings with large staffs, such as high schools, have identified one teacher who serves as building coordinator for planning and implementing building in-service projects.

This mode of operation sounds simple, clear-cut, and functional, as described here; but the frustrations, discomfort, discouragement, and misunderstandings are indescribable. The redefining of roles and relationships is a painful process, and we have not been spared the pain. One major problem which soon became apparent was the lack of coordination, continuity, and purpose of planning.

3. *The need to establish goals and priorities became an overriding issue.*

Accordingly, in February of 1973, committees of teachers, administrators, and laymen began a careful assessment of the most crucial problems facing the district. The board of education had clearly enunciated the philosophy of the district in respect to ending racial isolation in Portland public schools by instituting an administrative transfer policy. As implementation of this policy began, teachers and administrators found there were difficulties in coping with children who come with different value systems from unfamiliar cultural backgrounds. Requests came for help with classroom management and for assistance in how to teach the disadvantaged.

State and federal policies in regard to integration, compensatory education, achieving racial balance of the staff, equal educational opportunities for the handicapped, career education, and graduation requirements were some of the realities with which we were faced.

Repeated loss of tax measures for curriculum and instruction as well as for renovation of antiquated school plants indicated a need for more and better communication with the public, especially on the part of administrators. Expressed concern from teachers, especially those from special disciplines, pointed up the need for development of new skills and knowledge if they were to be able to cope with the reality of today.

Accordingly, at the district level, the following priorities were identified: (a) *desegregation,* which is an umbrella for many components such as human relations, communication skills, teaching the disadvantaged learner, the need for changes in school organization and curriculum content, and methodology for a multi-ethnic society; (b) *administrator effectiveness,* which generates from the need to cope with an entirely new set of circumstances than those for which most administrators have been trained; (c) *retraining* of tenure teachers who, because of declining enrollments and changes in student interests, have no classes; for example, foreign language teachers; (d) *special groups* of teachers whose number is small and who need to combine efforts; for example, music teachers.

Personnel in each of the three areas, having assisted in the identification of district priorities, took these to their respective areas for consideration. Lay advisory committees, teacher advisory committees, and administrator advisory committees studied these priorities in terms of special area concerns and from that point, recommendations for area priorities were made. The area priorities, so established, support those identified by the district, but they focus more definitively on the teaching of basic skills, orientation to instructional media, goal-based instruction, career education as an integral part of the total instructional program, classroom management, individualizing instruction, and group process skills.

Each building staff is in the process of planning on-site in-service projects in terms of the priorities identified by them for their school, making certain that district and area goals are being met. It is hoped that the individual teacher will do the same kind of analysis of teaching strengths and weaknesses and that he will, either individually or with a group, pursue a program of study which meets his unique needs in relation to building, area, and district priorities.

4. *The availability of resources is a necessary component of any viable in-service program.*

The proximity to the district of 11 colleges and universities provides a wealth of personnel and assistance for cooperative ventures in continuing education. The joint appointment of personnel with Portland State University, for example, has contributed materially to meaningful, functional in-service education for the staff. The Portland Area Complex for Education Program is designed to combine the expertise of Portland State University professors and teachers in the Portland area. The Northwest Regional Educational Laboratory, located in Portland, provides another valuable resource.

Portland public schools have traditionally had the support of the business and professional community. The Multnomah County Dental Association and the Multnomah County Medical Association have played major roles in the development of curriculum materials and in the planning and the teaching of in-service classes. An example of community involvement was the recent coordination by a team of educators of the efforts of resource personnel which included judges, attorneys, police officers, and juvenile court conselors in conducting a class to aid teachers in the effective utilization of a handbook for juveniles, entitled, *Youth Faces the Law.* Leaders in business and industry have provided leadership in developing programs for incorporating career education in the total instructional program.

5. *Portland public schools have long been recognized as having a quality professional staff.*

Grants of money are awarded to districts which have demonstrated educational leadership, and Portland public schools have been the recipient of many such awards from Ford Foundation grants for education of the gifted, to a Carnegie Institute grant for teacher in-service education, to various federal grants for the training of minority teachers as well as for developing programs for teaching the disadvantaged. The most significant indication of quality, however, is that in spite of the various and sundry problems plaguing schools today, including the adversary role of teacher organizations in relation to boards of education, the Portland staff contributes generously of time and energy in a cooperative effort aimed toward dealing positively with critical problems faced by the schools.

Currently, the major thrust of the in-service program, based on identified goals and priorities, is toward renewal. Conflicts and pressures indicate the need for far-reaching changes, all of which have implications for curriculum and instruction. If the teacher is to be able to cope with a rapidly changing set of demands and circumstances, there must be an opportunity for self-renewal. If the school district as an organization is to survive, there must be a plan for renewal.

This demands a staff of highly-trained individuals who know how to function productively as they deal with urgent issues and problems. We believe that we are making progress toward this goal, for we sense a spirit of quiet determination permeating the district which is replacing the discouragement which once was extremely visible. We believe that this is due, in part at least, to the fact that we have a sense of direction, that more and more people are actively involved in planning, that the quality and the scope of the involvement continue to grow, and that the major emphasis is turning toward in-service education directly focused on purposeful learning for boys and girls. □

How Teachers Can Innovate And Still Keep Their Jobs

LARRY L. PALMATIER

In every school there probably is at least one teacher who is known as an innovator. Possibly several others feel the urge to try new ways. You may be one who labels herself or himself either an innovator or a would-be innovator. Perhaps you desire to see schools become more open, where students have more choices. Maybe you have ideas for parent involvement, a bilingual program, alternative school models, student leadership training, simulation games, human relations training, new teaching methods, student teaching supervision, reading, or life-experience curricula. You can become a change agent.

Change, however, is more easily conceived than implemented. Any teacher who has ever tried to do anything different, especially alone, knows the difficulties an individual may encounter from administrators, from other teachers in the school, and even from his or her own students. Change rarely is self-contained like the classrooms from which it originates. It usually affects others in the school, even if they are not directly involved.

Why Resistance to Change

Why do some people oppose change? Kurt Lewin, famous social psychologist, had a simple theory about this. He called it "the field-force theory," and he noted that if there were no institutional resistance to change, there would be no stability [1]. Individuals would not tolerate the accelerated pace of change in their work lives if every new fad or idea were immediately introduced and widely practiced.

Why does change in schools seem particularly difficult? The most fundamental fear of many school administrators and teachers is that control over students will be eroded. Most change efforts are seen as attempts to undermine established school discipline. Thus, having an orientation to-

JOURNAL OF TEACHER EDUCATION, Spr. 1975,

pp. 60-62.

ward change is not valued. In fact, the opposite is true. School norms emphasize conformity of all the faculty, counselors, and administrators to the way things are, not the way they could be. There is a psychological need to have everyone do the same, teach the same, go in the same direction. It is believed that if things do not change, stability and order will be attained.

Resistance to change from students is a direct result of years of conditioning. They learn passivity and dependence. They find comfort in structure for its very predictability. When a teacher tries something qualitatively different, students become insecure and may offer direct and indirect opposition.

The Successful Innovator

Some teachers, however, are successful change agents. How does one innovate and still keep one's job? The teacher's chances of success are enhanced if she or he carefully plans strategies for meeting the inevitable resistance from colleagues, administrators, and his or her own students. Let us look at what can be done.

An innovator can be defined *ideally* as a person who—

1. is personally integrated
2. is an effective teacher
3. has a positive self-image
4. has adult friends who respect her or him (preferably from among the school faculty)
5. is open to new ideas
6. responds objectively to the need for change
7. implements sound new practices.

Ten Guidelines

Depending upon how extensively one wishes to deviate from current practices and the degree of impact planned on the total school, the teacher may consider one or more of these ten guidelines.

1. *Keep the door closed.* Innovators need to examine their motives and decide what their purposes are. Those who elect to gain personal attention, dramatize differences between themselves and others, and criticize and attack the system can be sure they will program for themselves open and hostile opposition. They are their own best enemies. These persons are not innovators by the definition

just given. Rather, they are using their students and the school for other ends. They may be personally frustrated. By not distinguishing clearly between their problems and the problems of the institution, they use the school to work out personal problems. The successful teacher, on the other hand, innovates quietly and without fanfare.

2. *Use a special vocabulary*. If you are aware that school people have a deep fear of change and are jealous of any teacher not conforming to conventionally defined roles and behaviors, you will automatically avoid certain words and phrases. Avoid "change," "fun," "friendly," "excitement," "new," "enjoyment," "kids," "sensitivity," "students' rights," "students' choice," "future." Publicly stress instead "mastering basics," "students' responsibility," "hard work," "respect," "traditional values," "proven," "discipline," and "results."

3. *Identify allies among your colleagues*. As you initiate change, the word will get around about what you are doing. To avoid distorted reports of your program, you have to do your own publicity. Start with at least one other person, but make sure you choose someone who has the respect of many on the faculty. Rather than discussing your program at length, begin by responding to questions only. As others become curious you may be able to provide more details. You will be more successful giving solicited information than trying to impose your ideas on others.

4. *Enlist the students in your game plan*. Tell them what you are doing and suggest ways they can help. If one element of your new program is informality, signified by students using your first name, tell them that applies only in your classroom. Around other teachers ask them to use your title and last name. Make a rule and gain students' agreement that they will not ask other teachers why *they* do not do what you are doing. Comparisons like this will make other teachers uncomfortable and bring down their wrath upon you and your program.

5. *Learn from others*. Ask sincere questions of other teachers, especially those you see as most threatened by what you are doing. If you ask colleagues to share with you their ideas and experiences, you convey your willingness to learn from them. You also indicate that you do not think you and your program are necessarily superior to them and their approaches. Yours may be different, but not superior. If there are other teachers engaged in the new practice, encourage all of them to communicate often with the regular staff and to do much reflective listening to the group not involved in change strategies. By listening with openness, you spread a nonjudgmental attitude and gain the respect of outsiders, rather than their pressure and opposition.

6. *Carry a book around*. Many teachers do not have nor take the time to keep up on new methods and innovations. Often potential blockers will give you more latitude to operate if you appear to know what you are doing, and especially if you can provide a rationale and program description from one or more authors.

When others see you carrying a book around they will be hesitant to write you and your ideas off without knowing the details. Besides being a defense, a book is a conversation starter. You can add to a climate of discussion and thinking by taking the book into the faculty lounge or the lunchroom. Keep the colorful outside jacket on the book, and, as you finish reading the book, place it on your desk in your room and start carrying another one. Put books on your desk only as you finish them. Over the weeks several books will be appearing on your desk. Teachers have high regard for someone who is well-read. You must be sensitive, however, to others' tendency toward inferiority feelings when confronted with informed efforts at change.

7. *Get visibility*. This is a crucial step in your change efforts. By having your program recognized outside the school, you gain protection and leverage. The simplest device is local newspaper publicity. It may help to get your building principal to agree to a brief interview in which he or she pub-

licly acknowledges your program and lends personal support. Another source of visibility is a presentation to the local school board.

Name your program as early as you feel you can. This procedure further legitimizes your efforts, gives you easier visibility, and adds momentum. Make sure the name of your program conveys its purpose and make that name a household word. Sample names are: Project Exploration, Students Being Responsible, Life-Involvement Curriculum, Decision-Making Plan, Community Involvement, New 3R's (Reason, Regard and Responsibility). Use titles which will not alienate the general public.

8. *Get outside support.* Many innovators begin with no outside funding. If you have begun with no extra funds, seek money and other support from any sources you can. For example, if your project involves photography, prepare a list of camera equipment and film needs to submit to the school district. The tendency is to cut back on your budget, so think big. If you can, provide options such as Plan A $200, Plan B $100, Plan C $75.

Make personal calls on all the money sources in your school, district, county office, teachers' association, and, if possible, state department of education. Write your proposal concisely, stating your program goals, methods, time sequence, and budget. Obtain the signature of your department chairman and/or principal if your proposal is to be sent to the district office. For proposals going to agencies outside your district, get a forwarding letter and signature from your superintendent.

Do not overlook teacher education departments of nearby state colleges or universities, public and private. Take on a student teacher or teaching assistant from a psychology, sociology, social work, or other appropriate program. Small local foundations are good potential sources for small grants.

9. *Start regular discussions with other teachers.* Meet on a regular basis (e.g., once a week for lunch), or hold mini-seminars on change in the school. Invite the administration to your sessions periodically and prepare questions to ask them. From time to time invite others to your small sessions, such as university faculty members interested in practical improvements in schools, community artists, selected parents, and professional persons. The idea is to stimulate the thinking of all involved. Announce the seminars at your regular faculty meetings through the school bulletin, newspaper, or a morning newscast.

10. *Start a library and set up a class or workshop.* Ask interested teachers to share their books by placing them on a special shelf in the library or faculty room where other teachers can check out new and interesting books related to the general area of innovation. Make everyone a part of this project and eligible to participate. Through a university extension program, teachers' association, or the district itself, set up a class or weekend workshop for credit on the subject of institutional change (2).

For the Risk Taker

SPECIAL NOTE . . . to the real risk-taker who may want to lose his or her job . . . or exchange it for a better one: Speak out on important issues and problems facing the top person in your school or district. Be direct and critical, but not of any person. Carry out a job or task related to what you are criticizing and become an expert in that field. Express your views strongly and make it clear that you can be useful to the person in charge who is actually facing the problems on a day-to-day basis. You can show this usefulness by providing answers to the problems. Also, open up new problems and suggest other answers. A secondary point is to submit proposals and projects whenever money or other support are made available for new ideas.

Final Challenge

One teacher in her 11th year at the junior high school level admitted recently that she had not read one book about teaching during that entire time. She read some things related to her subject field, but not one thing about human relations, communications, institutional norms, the psychological aspects of young people, learning principles, and patterns of creativity. She decided to shift gears, gather some new ideas, and try out some new approaches to teaching. She has become a respected and successful innovator.

How about you? Do you want to shift gears and approach teaching anew? Do you believe more is demanded of the teacher in today's schools than was required a few years ago? Are students harder to handle? Are you bogged down? Would you like to see some changes made? You too can become a change agent. You can once more share the challenges and joys of that first year of teaching. You can enrich your own life as well as the lives of your students. Begin today. Take the first step.

References

1 This classic analysis of the "equilibrium of change" was developed by the late Kurt Lewin, "Frontier in Group Dynamics: Concept, Method, and Reality in Social Science. Social Equilibria and Social Change," *Human Relations* I, no. 1 (June 1947): 5-41.

2 Skill in teacher-administrator relations and university-public school cooperation is well exemplified by the Salt Lake City Schools, M. Donald Thomas, superintendent.

CHAPTER IV

EMERGING STAFF PATTERNS

Teacher's aides, para-professionals, and teaching assistants are terms that must be understood by the modern personnel administrator. The terms imply new hierarchial definitions, new roles and territorial jurisdiction. Anyone interested in differentiated staffing must be confronted with its more pressing issues and questions, Budahl presents a list of disadvantages and possible pitfalls and procedural suggestions that can lead to "teaching ecstacy". The personnel administrator needs to be aware of the compleax items of the emerging staffing patterns. In addition, the administrator must have knowledge of staffing and elementary school organization and know the necessary ingredients for effective staff utilization. The administrator must have some awareness and knowledge of the strengths and weaknesses of staffing patterns in order to provide professional guidance to the board of education.

DIFFERENTIATED STAFFING:

Some Questions and Answers

JAMES M. COOPER

IN the last three years, there have appeared almost 100 articles, books, position papers, and other writings examining the topic of differentiated staffing for the public schools. Some of these papers extol the virtues of differentiated staffing, while others are sharply critical of the concept. Still others agree that it has merit, but, at the same time, see difficulties with its implementation. In a paper as brief as this, it is impossible to give a comprehensive treatment of the topic. An annotated bibliography is therefore included, which will direct the reader to a variety of positions on the topic. I will attempt only to highlight some of the more pressing issues and questions that should concern anyone interested in differentiated staffing.

What exactly is "differentiated staffing"?

Like "team teaching," most people believe they know what the term means, but each person has a different conception, based on his own experiences. While there are many possible variations, the term "differentiated staffing" implies sub-

NATIONAL ELEMENTARY PRINCIPAL, Jan. 1972, pp. 49-54.

dividing the global role of the teacher into different professional and paraprofessional subroles according to specific functions and duties that need to be performed in the schools and according to particular talents and strengths that are evident within the human resources of any given school community. Some differentiated staffing models also include the creation of a hierarchy, with job responsibilities that are commensurate with the range of pay.

What's new about this? Haven't schools been differentiating for years?

Yes and no. Yes, schools have been differentiating for years, ever since distinctions were made between the principal and the teacher and between social studies teachers and English teachers. However, the concept of differentiated staffing includes other factors that go beyond such distinctions.

What are some of these other ideas?

They include the notion of a career ladder for teachers, a vertical differentiation as well as a horizontal one along subject matter lines, increased decision-making responsibilities for teachers, pay scales for teachers that go upward of $20,000, and a wider variety of career patterns.

What problems do differentiated staffing and these other related ideas purport to solve?

Historically, promotion of teachers lead them away from the classroom, usually into administration. There is very little career incentive for the bright young teacher who traditionally must accumulate x number of years' experience and y credits in order to reach the top of the single salary schedule. Lacking the necessary patience, many talented teachers are forced out of teaching into other occupations or into administration. Creating a career ladder, with increased salaries commensurate with increased responsibilities, would serve to attract and keep talented teachers. By recognizing individual differences in teachers, as well as in students, differentiated staffing attempts to better utilize the talents and energies of the staff by allowing them to do the things that they do well, while not forcing them to perform functions ill-suited to their talents. Thus, by creating more and different kinds of teacher roles, such as evaluation specialist, curriculum developer, and diagnostician of learning difficulties, differentiated staffing tries to match functions to be performed with teacher interest, skills, and abilities more than do traditional staffing patterns. By recognizing the professional competence of teachers, differentiated staffing incorporates more teacher responsibility in decision making regarding curriculum and instruction. In several of the models, many decision-making responsibilities that were previously the domain of the administrator are now taken by teachers.

What implications does differentiated staffing have for curriculum, instruction, school structure, and scheduling?

Staff differentiation in its full meaning recognizes the necessity for concurrent changes in scheduling, curriculum, decision-making power, and individualization of instruction. Merely adding or subtracting personnel and calling it "staff differentiation" is tokenism. Without concurrent changes in scheduling, curriculum, and instruction, staff differentiation is nothing new. In order to best use differentiated staffs, the schedule should be flexible enough to allow teachers to meet with students for varying lengths of time for varying instructional purposes. Also, as teacher talent is released, new curriculum offerings can be made to take advantage of teacher interest and ability.

Is differentiated staffing just an idea, or has it been tried out with all of its ramifications?

There are a number of school districts currently implementing differentiated staffing plans of different types, including districts in California, Florida, Arizona, and Missouri. The oldest and perhaps most well-known differentiated staffing plan in operation is the Temple City, California, plan. Its teaching staff is divided into four professional levels: associate teacher, staff teacher, senior teacher, and master teacher. A schema of their staffing hierarchy is represented in Figure 1. The specific functions to be performed at each of these levels are carefully defined, and teachers are selected to perform these functions on the basis of their competencies. The associate teacher is conceived of as a novice to the profession, and his teaching responsibilities are less demanding than those of the staff teacher. The staff teacher carries a full teaching load but is relieved of most nonprofessional tasks such as yard duty, grading papers, hall supervision, and so forth. The staff teacher is an experienced, probably tenured, teacher. The senior teacher, the first level above the staff teacher, is an expert in a subject, discipline, or skill area. The master teacher is a scholar/research specialist, someone with the technical expertise to apply relevant research to classroom practice. All teachers function as classroom teachers, though not for the entire day.

Some people have charged that differentiated staffing is merit pay in disguise. Is there a difference between the two, and if so, what is it?

The basic distinction between differentiated staffing and merit pay is that merit pay attempts to distinguish who the good teachers are, usually based on someone's judgment, and to pay them more for doing a better job. In this instance, both the teacher who receives merit pay and the teacher who does not perform essentially the same duties and have the same responsibilities, but the merit pay teacher is deemed to perform those duties in a better fashion. The merit pay case usually leaves untouched any change in instructional responsibilities and does not alter the decision-making structure of the organization. Although teachers on a differentiated staff receive different salaries, their functions and levels of responsibility are also different. They are not paid differently for perform-

ing the same duties but for performing very different functions.

What are the reactions of the NEA and the AFT to the concepts involved in differentiated staffing?

The main issue for both organizations concerns the concept of a teacher hierarchy, illustrated by the Temple City model, with its associate, staff, senior, and master teacher levels. This type of vertical hierarchy is seen by the AFT and some organizations of the NEA as a wedge that will separate the solidarity of teacher groups. As Robert Bhaerman, Director of Research for the AFT, has said, ". . . for the time being, we are left with a choice: to pay teachers according to the role they fulfill (who can judge priorities here?) or to pay teachers according to their academic and experience background. . . . Teaching is not competitive; it is a cooperative and communal effort and so it should remain. Nothing must be injected to create divisiveness." [1] Although he accepts the notion of teacher differentiation according to functions to be performed, Bhaerman does not believe that these functions can be ordered in terms of importance and a hierarchy of teacher roles created based on these functions. In March 1971, the Executive Council of the

Figure 1

Temple City Differentiated Staffing Plan, 1969-71

			Nontenure
			MASTER TEACHER Doctorate or equivalent
		Nontenure	
		SENIOR TEACHER M.A. or equivalent	
	Tenure		
	STAFF TEACHER B.A. and Calif. Credential		
Tenure			
ASSOCIATE TEACHER B.A. or Intern			
100% teaching responsibilities	100% teaching responsibilities	60% staff teaching responsibilities	40% staff teaching responsibilities
10 months $6,500-$9,000	10 months $7,500-$11,000	10-11 months $14,500-$17,500	12 months $15,646-$25,000
INSTRUCTIONAL AIDE II $6,000-$7,500			
INSTRUCTIONAL AIDE I $4,000-$7,500			
CLERKS $5,000-$7,500			

AFT supported Bhaerman's position and passed a resolution "opposing any vertical staffing patterns which reduce the total number of fully certificated staff responsible for the education of pupils, which results in an arbitrary reduction of financing for education, and which is a movement away from the concept of the single salary schedule. . . ."[2]

The NEA, composed of many different instructional divisions, does not present a unified position on the issue of differentiated staffing. The National Commission on Teacher Education and Professional Standards (NCTEPS) has enthusiastically endorsed the concept, and a number of position papers on the topic have been published through NCTEPS. The Association of Classroom Teachers, on the other hand, in its position paper echoed the AFT's concern about the establishment of a teaching hierarchy, asking ". . . can differentiated staffing be accomplished only by establishing a new hierarchy within the school system? Might there not be horizontal movement for the teacher rather than vertical movement or a plan of rotating assignments that could be equally effective?"[3]

Although national officials of the two teacher organizations have publicly expressed their opposition to the notion of a teaching hierarchy, there appear to be pockets of support for the idea among teachers at the local levels. In Temple City, for example, the differentiated staffing plan was the result of administrators and teachers developing a plan that was agreeable to both groups. The teachers in Temple City have supported the plan enthusiastically. Because opposition to the vertical hierarchy has become widespread, models have been developed that differentiate only on the horizontal (subject and skill areas) dimension and do not attempt to differentiate teachers with respect to responsibilities and pay scales.

Why should some teachers receive more pay for performing different functions when it is impossible to say with certainty that some teacher functions are more important than others? Why can't teachers perform different functions but be equally compensated?

As a matter of fact, some staffing plans do differentiate according to functions but do not reward differently. Advocates of differentiated staffing argue, however, that those roles that require greater train-ing or skill should receive greater compensation. Since the skillful in other occupations are rewarded more because of their talents and because of their increased responsibility, the teaching profession should be no different. Rather than forcing the talented and ambitious out of teaching because the opportunities for career advancement are practically nil, differentiated staffing advocates argue that opportunities for advancement and increased pay should be made available for the talented.

Another way of viewing the issue is that people who possess certain skills are in less supply than people who possess certain other skills. Since both kinds of skills are necessary for the operation of an instructional program, the people whose skills are in less supply—for example, an evaluation expert—command greater compensation than do those people whose skills are not so unique. When viewed in this manner, higher pay is given according to the law of supply and demand, rather than because certain skills are considered intrinsically more worthwhile and more valuable. Viewed either way, differentiated staffing plans seek to reward teachers for increased responsibility and for particular kinds of competencies.

Is differentiated staffing related to the accountability movement in education and to the ideas of competency-based teacher education and competency-based certification?

Differentiated staffing embodies some of the same concepts as the accountability movement and competency-based teacher education. Before a differentiated staffing model can be constructed, an analysis of the teaching functions to be performed must be made. These functions can then be allotted to specific roles. After functions necessary for the achievement of instructional objectives have been identified, further analysis identifies units of performance, which are called tasks. Tasks are elements of a function that, when performed by instructional personnel in logical sequence, will fulfill the related function. Task analysis provides the teaching performance criteria that must be met in order that the function from which they are derived may be achieved successfully. Thus, in a differentiated staffing model, the stating of tasks in specific job descriptions for employment purposes will provide the formal identification of the teaching performance criteria that will establish a valid base for teacher performance evaluation. For each teacher role identified, there will be specific performance criteria that the teacher occupying that role must meet. In this respect, the teacher will be accountable for achieving the performance criteria associated with his job.

In the Temple City model, for example, teaching colleagues designed the job to be performed by the senior teacher, who was then held accountable to the teachers who received his services for effectively performing his job. Tenure is not granted to persons who occupy senior teacher positions; if they do not perform, they are not reemployed as senior teachers. Fenwick English, former Project Director at Temple City, describes the situation: "By tying the Senior Teacher's role directly to the recipients of the effects of that role and by systematically building into the system procedures whereby roles and role incumbents may be changed, debureaucratization occurs and the dominant one-way communication mode, and with it the traditional superior-subordinate concept, is radically altered . . . services become teacher-centered and teacher-designed."

Does differentiated staffing work on both the elementary and secondary school levels?

There was initial resistance to the Temple City model at the elementary school level. While the vertical differentiation was in terms of a hierarchy, or a teaching ladder, the horizontal differentiation at the secondary level was along subject matter lines—senior teachers in mathematics, science, social studies, and so forth. In essence, this meant that almost no elementary school teacher would be chosen as a senior teacher, because the secondary teachers generally had more expertise in subject matter areas. The problem was solved by creating positions for senior teachers in instruction and in technology who would serve all elementary school teachers on a K-6 basis. When this was done, John Rand, Superintendent of Temple City Schools, reported that the primary grade teachers soon found ways in which a senior teacher could be valuable to them. Thus, the elementary level is differentiating on the horizontal axis along areas other than subject matter. The Temple City school system is currently considering another senior teacher position in human relations. Figure 2 gives a schema that illustrates how the senior teacher would operate for both elementary and secondary schools, as well as a description of the broad responsibilities of the elementary senior teacher.

How can more information about differentiated staffing be obtained?

Readers are referred to the following bibliography and to a more comprehensive one—including films, videotapes, and other media presentations on differentiated staffing—which can be obtained from Mr. Jerry Melton, School Personnel Utilization Resource Center, 908 W. Main, Mesa, Arizona 85201.

Figure 2

Refinement of Elementary/Secondary Differentiated Staffing Model

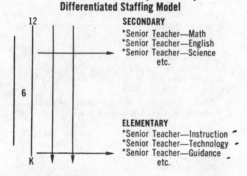

SECONDARY
*Senior Teacher—Math
*Senior Teacher—English
*Senior Teacher—Science
etc.

ELEMENTARY
*Senior Teacher—Instruction
*Senior Teacher—Technology
*Senior Teacher—Guidance
etc.

Responsibilities of Elementary School Senior Teachers

1. **Pupil Diagnosis**
   A. Pupil placement
   B. Pupil behavior analysis
      1) Preventive
      2) Remedial
   C. Parent conferencing

2. **Instructional Analysis**
   A. Program diagnosis/testing
   B. Prescription for learning: individual pupils/groups (to include mode of instruction/appropriate software)
   C. Analysis and utilization of staff

3. **Curriculum Development**
   A. Coordination of curriculum development with master teachers
   B. Development of some curriculum in primary areas

4. **Classroom Teaching**
   A. Regular classroom teaching at least 40% of the time

FOOTNOTES

1. American Federation of Teachers. *Several Educators' Cure for the Common Cold, Among Other Things.* Quest Paper No. 7. Washington, D.C.: Department of Research, the Federation, n.d. p. 6.

2. American Federation of Teachers. "American Federation of Teachers' Statement on Vertical Staffing." Memo from the Federation to the Bureau of Educational Personnel Development, U.S. Office of Education. Washington, D.C.: the Federation, March 1971. (Mimeographed)

3. National Association of Classroom Teachers.

Classroom Teachers Speak on Differentiated Teaching Assignments. Report of the Classroom Teachers National Study Conference on Differentiated Teaching Assignments for Classroom Teachers. Washington, D.C.: the Association, National Education Association, 1969.

A BASIC DIFFERENTIATED STAFFING LIBRARY

Allen, Dwight A. *A Differentiated Staff: Putting Teacher Talent To Work.* Occasional Papers No. 1. Washington, D.C.: National Education Association, National Commission on Teacher Education and Professional Standards (hereafter NEA, NCTEPS), 1967. 7 pp. (Out of print)

Views teachers as interchangeable parts and current staffing patterns as inefficient. Proposes a four-level model and lists advantages of this kind of differentiated staff.

Barbee, Don. *Differentiated Staffing: Expectations and Pitfalls.* Write-In Papers on Flexible Staffing Patterns No. 1. Washington, D.C.: NEA, NCTEPS, March 1969. 7 pp.

Highlights various dangers of differentiated staffing—economy as a goal, using assistants as teachers, creating status and personality conflicts, overspecializing, and increased bureaucracy.

Bhaerman, Robert D. *A Study Outline on Differentiated Staffing.* Quest Report No. 2. Washington, D.C.: Department of Research, American Federation of Teachers, n.d. 22 pp.

Weighs advantages and disadvantages of differentiated staffing. Gives AFT position on differentiated staffing and merit pay. Comments on current differentiated staffing literature. Comprehensive bibliography.

Cooper, James M., editor. *Differentiated Staffing.* Philadelphia: W. B. Saunders Publishing Co., 1972.

A book of readings on differentiated staffing, with chapters giving case studies and exploring differentiated staffing's implications for administration, paraprofessionals, teacher education, and inservice education.

Davies, Don. "Education Professions Development: Investment in the Future." *American Education* 5: 9-10; February 1969.

Former Associate Commissioner of Education, Bureau of Educational Personnel Development, describes the Education Professions Development Act and its objectives to individualize instruction and "open up" the teaching profession.

Edelfelt, Roy A. *Redesigning the Education Profession.* Washington, D.C.: NEA, NCTEPS, January 1969. 17 pp.

Executive Secretary of NCTEPS analyzes the teacher's role, teaching as a career, teacher supply and demand, the promise of a new differentiated staff organization, and the governance of the education profession.

English, Fenwick W. "A Handbook of the Temple City Differentiated Staffing Project, 1965-1970." Temple City, Calif.: Temple City School District, June 1970. (Mimeographed)

An up-to-date revision of the Temple City project, procedures, and policies. Excellent source of information.

English, Fenwick W. "Teacher May I? Take Three Giant Steps! The Differentiated Staff." *Phi Delta Kappan* 51: 211-14; December 1969.

Warns that changing roles are not necessarily synonymous with changing attitudes about learning and analyzes some of the real dangers of differentiated staffing without adequate preparation.

Frinks, Marshall L. *A Readiness for Differentiated Staffing: Questions Relevant to Development and Training Activities.* Information Report No. 2.

Tallahassee: Florida Department of Education, October 1969. 8 pp.

Presents questions any educator must ask before contemplating a change in staffing pattern.

Hedges, William D. "Differentiated Teaching Responsibilities in the Elementary School." *National Elementary Principal* 47: 48-54; September 1967.

Constructs a model for a differentiated elementary school staff. Also a position paper by the Department of Elementary School Principals, NEA.

Joyce, Bruce R. *Man, Media and Machines.* Washington, D.C.: NEA, NCTEPS, 1967. 26 pp.

Pictures a direct instruction team and its support centers. Predicts the school of tomorrow and how students and teachers will function in it—a program designed to complement the nature of learning.

McKenna, Bernard. *School Staffing Patterns and Pupil Interpersonal Behavior: Implications for Teacher Education.* Washington, D.C.: NEA, NCTEPS, 1967. 23 pp.

Builds a staff organization on the basis of human relations and learning tasks. Differentiates teaching roles accordingly.

NEA, NCTEPS. *A Position Statement on the Concept of Differentiated Staffing.* Washington, D.C.: the Commission, May 11, 1969. 8 pp.

NCTEPS endorses differentiated staffing as worthy of trial. Developmental steps are suggested. Definitions consistent with NEA goals are stated.

NEA, NCTEPS. *Remaking the World of the Career Teacher.* Report of the 1965-1966 Regional NEA-TEPS Conferences. Washington, D.C.: the Commission, 1966. 228 pp.

Composite of speeches and papers focusing on the title subject. An attempt to define excellence in teaching and to redefine the teaching role.

NEA, NCTEPS. *The Teacher and His Staff: Differentiated Teaching Roles.* Report of the 1968 Regional NEA-TEPS Conferences. Washington, D.C.: the Commission, 1969. 143 pp.

Ten papers deal with the need for teacher specialization, relevant curriculum, principalship, team teaching, teacher education, planned-change strategy, and critiques of current education assumptions.

Rand, John M., and English, Fenwick W. "Towards a Differentiated Teaching Staff." *Phi Delta Kappan* 49: 264-68; January 1968.

Fundamental and global rationale for differentiated staffing. Role description; resistance to change.

Ross, Marlene. *Preparing School Personnel for Differentiated Staffing Patterns: A Guide to Selected Documents in the ERIC Collection, 1966-1968.* Washington, D.C.: Educational Resources Information Center, 1969. 74 pp.

An ERIC publication listing 114 documents on differentiated staffing. Teacher-administrator relationships, media, roles, team teaching, curriculum organization, and innovation are included.

Ryan, Kevin A. *A Plan for a New Type of Professional Training for a New Type of Teaching Staff.* Occasional Papers No. 2. Washington, D.C.: NEA, NCTEPS, 1968. 12 pp.

Education courses and student teaching are viewed skeptically. Sequence performance criteria and simulated teaching experiences are suggested training for candidates for a differentiated staff.

Stiles, Lindley J. "Certification and Preparation of Education Personnel in Massachusetts." *Phi Delta Kappan* 50: 477-80; April 1969.

Summary of an advisory report on certification for Massachusetts; advocates distinctive performance levels and teacher self-regulation.

Necessary Ingredients
for Good Team Teaching

Clyde H. Colman
Leon Budahl

ALTHOUGH team teaching has grown dramatically since the late fifties, it poses no real threat to the one-teacher classroom.

Limitations of Teaming

Proponents of team teaching are quick to point out its strengths, but its opponents are just as quick to identify its limitations. Some of these limitations are listed below.

1. Many teachers are not suited by training or disposition to engage in the cooperative planning and varied use of procedures, resources, and personnel that are essential to team teaching. In fact, it is often maintained that if a teacher is thoroughly competent in teaching his particular subject, team teaching is not necessary.

2. Team teaching calls for the use of special physical facilities that must be provided at considerable expense if not already available. Many older schools simply do not have the necessary large rooms for some phases of teaming.

3. Special planning periods must be scheduled at a time when all team members can meet. In order to make such meetings

NASSP BULLETIN, Jan. 1973, pp. 41-46.

possible, the administrator sometimes must ask for concessions for team members or impose restrictions on non-team members.

4. The per-student cost of team teaching is sometimes higher than the per-student cost of conventional teaching, because many teams are comprised of nonprofessional aides, paraprofessionals, and clerical assistants in addition to full-time certified teachers.

5. The necessary impersonality of large-group instruction hampers the emotional, social, and academic progress of certain students who need consistent, individual contact with their teachers. Team teachers seldom become well-enough acquainted with individual students in a large group to be able to meet their needs effectively.

6. Planning essential to productive team teaching often becomes unduly complicated, and the end result may not justify the expenditure of professional time and energy. If individualized instruction and instruction in both the small and large groups is not planned with great care, team teaching may be less effective than traditional classroom instruction.

Basic Principles of Teaming

Reports of team teaching projects reveal common principles basic to success. A number of these principles are listed below.

1. The chief purpose of team teaching is to improve the quality of instruction and learning by using the school staff as efficiently as possible.

2. The effectiveness of team teaching largely depends upon individual team members, various strengths and their ability to work together as a group. In team teaching, teachers should be able to capitalize on their particular strengths and minimize their weaknesses.

3. Team teaching requires cooperative planning and capitalizes on group thinking.

4. Certain kinds of subject matter lend themselves to different methods of teaching—independent study, small groups, or large groups.

5. In order to serve the needs of different instructional situations, teaching teams can be organized to teach the same subject to combined groups, to cross subject-matter boundaries, to take advantage of unique facilities and individuals within a com-

munity, or to individualize instruction as dictated by student needs.

Human Relations Problems Arise

Effective team teaching doesn't happen by chance; it is the result of careful planning. The various segments of instruction taught by different participants have to be correlated. What happens when team teaching is not thoroughly planned is illustrated in the following examples.

Four teachers were involved in a program of history, English, art, and music. One paraprofessional was utilized to supervise independent study and to handle official school paperwork. The class of 120 highly capable students was held within a two-hour block of time.

For the first several weeks of the school year, the basic concepts of good team teaching held fast. The four-member team and the one paraprofessional felt united in their common pursuit. It was an almost classical view of unrestrained communication and sincere sharing with no evidence of selfishness. One element, however, turned the promising year into a teacher's nightmare: human relations.

Two factors can destroy a teaching team: incompetency (which possibly can be eliminated with inservice education) and lack of compatibility. When a conflict arises within a teaching team, it generally has a slow, smouldering quality, not immediately detectable by those who could possibly have some ameliorative effect. Perhaps if the conflict were to blaze up, it could be recognized and dealt with quickly and efficiently. But, in the incident cited here, the fire did not begin to blaze until all of the team members were trapped within their own structure. The conflict, when finally identified, was beyond control and the team had to operate throughout the last part of the year under great strain.

Two incidents during the second quarter of the year led to the breakdown of human relations. Both would seem relatively minor to the outsider, but they led to a pressurized situation.

The principal, very proud of his school's humanities program, had given a talk during the previous semester to prospective teachers at a nearby university. The chairman of the education department there had asked him if he could place a student teacher in the principal's school to work with the humanities team during

131

the second half of the fall semester. Permission was given, and this relatively innocent act led to the first problem encountered by the team.

The student teacher seemed competent and affable. After a week of observation, she began her student teaching assignment with a lecture in Greek history. The team's history teacher was extremely upset with the presentation, although no other team member realized this at the time. In retrospect, it could be determined with a great degree of accuracy that the cause of this conflict was the fierce pride of the team's history teacher. Simply stated, she felt that the student teacher's presentation had cheated the students of the benefit of her vast knowledge. Indeed, her knowledge was quite awesome, as she was definitely considered by the administration a master teacher.

A personality conflict, unrecognized by the other team members, arose immediately between the history teacher and the student teacher. The student teacher, very frightened of her supervising teacher, avoided her; and the supervisor interpreted the avoidance as rebellion to authority. Step by step, a complete misunderstanding developed between the two individuals.

During the year a second such drama arose with a completely different cast of characters.

In February, the principal asked for volunteers to participate in the twelfth-grade English team experiment to begin the following year. Three of the 10 twelfth-grade English teachers volunteered, each having had three or more years of successful experience and each eager to try out the new procedure.

Mr. Z, the senior member of the team, was appointed chairman. Because the teachers assumed it was not necessary to rework units they had taught successfully before, they decided that planning could be deferred until one week before school started, when they would devote full time to the task. When school opened, the team members were still attempting to think through the methodological implications of team teaching. The principal set aside time for a common planning session in which the teachers could meet together three times a week. Large-group instruction for 85 students (three sections) was scheduled for twice each week.

The three team teachers soon found themselves planning and teaching on a day-to-day basis, hoping that somehow they would be able to reap some of the benefits of team teaching. In their

132

insecurity they reverted to the traditional procedures in which they had confidence. Unit planning geared to team teaching and utilizing the special abilities of team members was largely overlooked. Mr. Z, a dominant personality, assigned himself the major responsibility for teaching the large combined group, and the other team members yielded submissively. Poor planning as evidence here can be as destructive as poor human relations.

Procedural Suggestions

If the teachers planning a team teaching approach can agree on their philosophies of the mutual undertaking, they are in a good position to proceed with their ideas.

The next step would be to present their plans to the administration with a written course of study and a proposed budget. If the administration gives any indication of lack of support, the teachers should perhaps revamp the plans or try to reorganize their course of study to suit administrative policy. If the plan is approved by the administrators, the team, with administration, should determine whether adequate facilities are available for large group meetings, seminars, small group meetings, and independent study. If the above criteria are not met, the experiment does not have a fair chance of success.

Although the newcomer to team teaching is apt to need particular guidance, both the inexperienced and the experienced teacher may receive helpful directions from the following suggestions.

RECOMMENDATIONS

1. Prepare thoroughly before engaging in team teaching; be sure that the other team members also can plan carefully.

2. Select team members who possess specific qualities that contribute to team effort as well as to general instructional competence. Team teaching can be only as effective as the quality of team members permits it to be.

3. Become informed on the current projects involving team teaching that are being tried throughout the nation.

4. During the planning phase of each unit, identify the precise role each member of the teaching team is to play.

5. Make sure that the psychological principles of learning are not violated during large-group lectures.

6. Make sure that the necessary personal contact between team teacher and individual student is maintained in spite of large-group instruction.

7. Work for consistent improvement in team teaching even after one or two experimental years have been completed.

8. Be sure that the design for team teaching makes it possible to arrive at verifiable conclusions about its success or lack of success. Work out procedures for evaluating the efficiency of all aspects of team teaching.

CAUTIONS

1. Do not assume that educational achievements are unimportant because they cannot be tested by paper-and-pencil test. Student interest, teacher-student relationships, and appreciation for the subject—all of which may be positively affected by team teaching—are important educational gains that do not lend themselves readily to objective measurement.

2. Do not assume that all instructional experts are proponents of team teaching. Remember that the current evaluation of team teaching frequently is based on personal opinion.

3. Do not launch into an extensive program of team teaching unless the first experimental efforts prove to be unusually rewarding.

Conclusion

Team teaching offers the educator unique and challenging opportunities that would otherwise be denied him in the self-contained classroom. Becoming a useful and productive member of a team could be likened to the opening of a door and allowing fresh air to enter the room, fresh air to be breathed and enjoyed by both teachers and students.

With highly competent teachers, the blessings of the school administration, adequate facilities, above-average budget, eager students, and good planning, a program of team teaching can be productive and educationally stimulating. In rare instances, it can even be an exercise in teaching ecstasy for all who are involved.

STAFF UTILIZATION RECONSIDERED

Hollis H. Moore

FOR the last three years, the U.S. Office of Education through funding from the Education Professions Development Act (EPDA) has been supporting pilot differentiated staffing efforts to explore, develop, and implement more effective school personnel utilization. Although the number of funded projects has been small, their efforts, both individually and combined, are demonstrating new avenues for staffing public schools. For the 1971-72 school year, there are seventeen of these funded projects, almost all of which involve elementary schools.

This article attempts to: 1) review some of the deficiencies of conventional elementary school organization and staffing, 2) describe some specific attempts being made by one of several elementary schools involved in the Marin EPDA Staff Differentiation Project,[1] and 3) summarize some necessary ingredients for effective staff development and utilization for improving elementary education.

It must be emphasized that school staffing arrangements cannot be viewed in isolation from many other influential variables, including instructional objectives and programs, the use of time and space, the available financial and material resources of a school, and other obvious factors influencing the degree of change that can be successfully implemented. A combination of major structural changes is necessary in the organization of public schools. However, it must be stressed that there is no one model or one approach that is appropriate for all school situations.

Conventional elementary schools have been organized with the self-contained classroom as the basic instructional unit. As G. Sidney Lester, a social studies consultant in California, has concisely pointed out, "The evidence clearly indicates that the self-contained teacher working alone in a self-contained classroom in a self-contained school is an out-dated approach for keeping pace with the obvious changes within our society and the expanding challenges facing educators."[2]

Some even refer to the "self-contaminated" classroom. Donald Davies, acting Deputy Commissioner for Development, U.S. Office of Education, has stated: "It has long been apparent that no single individual has the energy, competence, or time to deal with all of the responsibilities assigned to one teacher in one classroom. . . . Differentiated and flexible ways to organize and use time and talent are essential to a more efficient learning operation."[3]

A critical analysis of conventional elementary school organization points to several deficiencies, which include:

An unrealistic, omnicapable teacher model. Every teacher is expected to be all things to all students, working in an isolated self-contained classroom for, in most cases, every hour of the instructional day. It is unrealistic to expect the teacher alone to competently cover fifteen to twenty different subject areas on an individualized basis!

No scheduled time for team planning and professional growth. There is little, if any, time for working constructively with colleagues, for needed curriculum development, for continuing inservice training, for truly individualizing an instructional program, for participating effectively in school decision making, for better articulation and coordination of instructional objectives and program components, for conferencing with students and parents, and for individual and team

NATIONAL ELEMENTARY PRINCIPAL, Jan. 1972, pp. 63-70.

planning to utilize effectively varying strengths and interests of the teaching staff. The isolation of self-contained teachers prevents constructive communication and feedback in terms of enhancing their own teaching skills and relationships with students and other members of the teaching staff.

Inefficient use of manpower. Staffing schools with only certified teachers results in an inefficient utilization of manpower because teachers spend a large proportion of their time—from 20 to 50 percent—doing necessary but nonprofessional, routine, and clerical tasks that could be done as effectively by less highly trained and lower paid aides or even volunteers.

Limited opportunities for students. The confining use of space and time severely limits the variety of experiences preferable for elementary aged children growing up in a dynamic, pluralistic, and continually changing society.

Inefficient use of educational resources. Duplication of many instructional resources is required, especially in terms of reference books, individualization materials, manipulative games and simulation materials, audiovisual materials and equipment, and so on, which creates an inefficient use of instructional resources. By exploring different staffing, scheduling, instructional modes, and space arrangements, resources can be better concentrated in learning or interest centers and instructional grouping can be more functional. These arrangements can provide for more in-depth and varied resources and experiences in each subject area.

Little professional accountability. The building principal is required to serve as the "evaluator" of the teaching staff, an almost impossible job due to his large span of control. Without collegial interaction and assessment, meaningful and constructive professional evaluation systems tend to falter and not be implemented in a thorough way.

Ongoing self-renewal is stifled. Because of these interrelated factors, significant innovative breakthroughs are usually doomed to failure. Without an oppor-

tunity for staff members to work cooperatively together on a regular basis, with planning and development time built into the normal work week, there is little chance that innovation will have a lasting impact on elementary school programs. All too often, change strategies have relied primarily on isolated, individual, self-contained classroom teachers who usually have inadequate follow-through support for successful implementation.

An Attempt to Improve School Staff Utilization

One specific example of some new developments in staff utilization can be found in the Wolfe Grade Elementary School in the Kentfield School District, Marin County, California. Deliberate efforts were made to explore alternatives prior to major program implementation. The first year was devoted to studying staffing possibilities that could offer potential solutions to many of the deficiencies in conventional elementary school organization. For the fall of 1971, the staff decided on implementing a new pattern of staff utilization, which they would further develop and refine during the 1971-72 school year.

The major components included in the first operational phase are:

1. The instructional staff has been divided into four personnel units serving as instructional teams.

2. The school is developing an administrative team working together on a School Council.

3. Two working committees have been established focusing on:

a. Training and staffing

b. Social studies curriculum and instruction

4. An Expanded Learning Program in the afternoon portion of the school day is being organized to provide:

a. More individualized reinforcement, special assistance, and personalized attention with an improved adult-student ratio (already over 100 volunteers are working at the school in various capacities)

b. A variety of enrichment opportunities

c. Concentration of state mandated and district provided curriculum in such areas as physical education, music, art, and Spanish to avoid interruption in the basic academic areas

d. Regular time within the normal school week for members of the staff to work together on the School Council, the two commitees, and on their own team planning efforts

5. A large number of student teachers are being trained as contributing members of the staff.

It is interesting to note that the four personnel units at Wolfe Grade School have moved in quite different directions in their development and program implementation. The number of teachers on each team varies from six to two. The teams were established by consensus based on results from a staff attitude and interest survey and an assessment of teacher strengths with regard to complementing one another in the instructional program. The staff also attempted to assess student learning styles and needs. A beginning effort was made to match teaching styles with student learning styles to provide for more compatible and effective learning relationships within each personnel unit.

The teams have considerably different features, as described briefly:

Personnel unit 1 (grades K-3), early childhood. The new program in early childhood provides the opportunity for students to work with a variety of teachers in different settings to better meet their individual learning needs. At the same time, there is continuity provided for in the program with a "homeroom" for each child to get to know one teacher especially well and to provide for personalized contact with both children and parents. The major purposes include more individualized instructional programs for students so that they can progress at appropriate rates and more effective utilization of the special strengths, interests, and competencies of team members.

The classroom space has been divided into different functional areas. The art and music programs are centered in one room, a math-science laboratory and construction area in another, a reading and listening center for drill and reinforcement exercises in another, and two small group seminar areas in a divided classroom. Doorways were provided between the rooms for an easy flow of students and staff to accommodate the needs of the flexible instructional program. Volunteer aides have been recruited to supervise the reading and listening centers, to employ drill materials, and to assist in various other instructional activities.

The kindergarten students will be absorbed into the academic program at the chance that innovation will have a lasting impact on elementary school programs. All too often, change strategies have relied primarily on isolated, individual, self-contained classroom teachers who usually have inadequate follow-through support for successful implementation.

An Attempt to Improve School Staff Utilization

One specific example of some new developments in staff utilization can be found in the Wolfe Grade Elementary School in the Kentfield School District, Marin County, California. Deliberate efforts were made to explore alternatives prior to major program implementation. The first year was devoted to studying staffing possibilities that could offer potential solutions to many of the deficiencies in conventional elementary school organization. For the fall of 1971, the staff decided on implementing a new pattern of staff utilization, which they would further develop and refine during the 1971-72 school year.

The major components included in the first operational phase are:

1. The instructional staff has been divided into four personnel units serving as instructional teams.

2. The school is developing an administrative team working together on a School Council.

3. Two working committees have been established focusing on:

a. Training and staffing

b. Social studies curriculum and instruction

4. An Expanded Learning Program in the afternoon portion of the school day is being organized to provide:

a. More individualized reinforcement, special assistance, and personalized attention with an improved adult-student ratio (already over 100 volunteers are working at the school in various capacities)

b. A variety of enrichment opportunities

c. Concentration of state mandated and district provided curriculum in such areas as physical education, music, art, and Spanish to avoid interruption in the basic academic areas

d. Regular time within the normal school week for members of the staff to work together on the School Council, the two commitees, and on their own team planning efforts

5. A large number of student teachers are being trained as contributing members of the staff.

It is interesting to note that the four personnel units at Wolfe Grade School have moved in quite different directions in their development and program implementation. The number of teachers on each team varies from six to two. The teams were established by consensus based on results from a staff attitude and interest survey and an assessment of teacher strengths with regard to complementing one another in the instructional program. The staff also attempted to assess student learning styles and needs. A beginning effort was made to match teaching styles with student learning styles to provide for more compatible and effective learning relationships within each personnel unit.

The teams have considerably different features, as described briefly:

Personnel unit 1 (grades K-3), early childhood. The new program in early childhood provides the opportunity for students to work with a variety of teachers in different settings to better meet their individual learning needs. At the same time, there is continuity provided for in the program with a "homeroom" for each child to get to know one teacher especially well and to provide for personalized contact with both children and parents. The major purposes include more individualized instructional programs for students so that they can progress at appropriate rates and more effective utilization of the special strengths, interests, and competencies of team members.

The classroom space has been divided into different functional areas. The art and music programs are centered in one room, a math-science laboratory and construction area in another, a reading and listening center for drill and reinforcement exercises in another, and two small group seminar areas in a divided classroom. Doorways were provided between the rooms for an easy flow of students and staff to accommodate the needs of the flexible instructional program. Volunteer aides have been recruited to supervise the reading and listening centers, to employ drill materials, and to assist in various other instructional activities.

The kindergarten students will be absorbed into the academic program at the appropriate time for reading readiness. The students work in small groups more frequently to meet their individual needs better. The program stresses more careful diagnosis, prescription, and progress assessment so that grouping can be properly adjusted as necessary. Reading and language arts goals and objectives have been developed, as well as a physical education program checklist. Similar materials are in the process of being developed for the math and science areas. These efforts are designed to help assess and monitor student progress more effectively.

Personnel unit 2 (grades 1-4). This personnel unit consists of five teachers responsible for the instructional program for students aged 6 to 9 years, working together in a hexagonal open space building. The team has grouped learning activities according to children's needs in a way that would be comfortable for both children and teachers. The first month of school was spent diagnosing needs and preparing students for flexible grouping and independent learning.

The team is engaged in developing a revised social studies program. A major objective of this effort is to design ways of teaching children the value of the contributions that children of different ages can make to one another's learning and to accustom the students to cross grade level groupings. It will also provide children the opportunity to work with different teachers on the team.

Independent learning centers in math, science, language arts, and art have been placed near the back of each class section. The walls are open so that students can move easily around the perimeter of the hexagon building. Children have an opportunity to visit these centers during the week either individually or in small groups. The center may or may not be adjacent to their class meeting place. The children are being taught to use the materials in the centers independently and to become accustomed to moving about in the building for learning purposes without disturbing teaching and learning going on in nearby areas.

One room of the building has been provided with work stations for quiet study. The teaching team members have desks here for team planning and individual work. The wall has been opened from this room to the small center area of the building and a comfortable reading area has been provided there.

Personnel unit 3 (grades 4-5). This two-teacher team was formed because there were a number of fourth- and fifth-grade children achieving below grade level. It was decided to cluster them in two adjoining rooms teamed together. Several student tutors were placed in both classes to help foster a "buddy" system for learning. From this plan evolved both an initial grouping of the children for all basic subject areas and the physical layout for the two classrooms.

One room is set up to accommodate both classes in large group discussions, presentations, and other activities. The other room has many varied activity centers, which include a reading corner, listening center, math center, and science center. A special interests section where children are encouraged to investigate many different techniques in art was also provided. Here they can also pursue hobbies such as model building, puzzles, sewing, stitchery, and baking during their elective time. This feature is designed to help motivate children to share their interests with others and thereby expand the buddy system not only in an educational way but also in a social and more personal way.

Personnel unit 4 (grades 5-6). This instruction team of four teachers is attempting to utilize teacher strengths and interests better by dividing up subject matter responsibilities in the instructional program. Two teachers are working together in each of four areas: individualized language arts, math, social science, and science. Efforts are being made to develop new lab materials and diversified learning activities. The teachers share together with the instructional planning in their subject concentrations. The total team meets at least once a week to plan, evaluate, and revise their program as needed to meet student instructional needs more effectively.

In addition, the school has a pilot program for 16 student teachers, both graduate and undergraduate, from Dominican College, San Rafael, California. They spend approximately 10 hours a week observing and working at the school in the first semester. As part of this program, two college faculty members work regularly at the school with both student teachers and staff members.

In the second semester these students will be spending almost full time at the school helping to teach. To guide them through this program, 60 performance objectives have been developed by the college staff, teachers, and college students. These objectives, complete with identifiable behaviors, specific conditions for their achievement, and described success criteria, serve as the basic requirements for the students as they move individually through their training experiences.

Probably the three most unique qualities of this student teaching program are:

1. Placing a major portion of the program in the real world of the school
2. Providing some success criteria in terms of what happens to the pupils with whom the student teacher is working
3. Providing appropriate options for the student teachers individually as they set out and complete the program.

The total staffing program is also attempting to develop an accountable administrative team enabling staff members to participate actively in decision making. This effort is being based on several assumptions and guiding principles, one of which is that those people who are directly responsible for implementing a decision should influence the decision to the greatest degree. This generally results in the largest commitment to implement the resulting decision and the greatest acceptance of the responsibility that that decision implies. The Wolfe Grade staff is attempting to clarify, through its School Council, the decision-making process and the appropriate procedures for effective management of the school's operations and instructional program.

The combination of these adult resources greatly improves the adult to student ratio at the school, providing more personalized attention for students, more effective varieties of learning experiences, and more productive use of the professional teaching capacities of the certified staff. The restructuring of school time and use of space offers many new instructional opportunities. The differentiation of roles and tasks, teamed together in effective ways, offers the potential for ongoing program improvement.

General Requirements
For More Effective Staff Utilization

The combined experience of the Marin Staff Differentiation Project, involving Wolfe Grade and several other elementary schools, would suggest the following factors as being especially important for the development of more effective staff utilization:

The role of the principal needs to change. The principal is in the key position to facilitate growth within a staff or to thwart such growth. The role of the principal needs to be reexamined as much, if not more, than any other single role within the elementary school to allow for maximum staff involvement and professional development. Traditionally, principals have tended to work separately with individual teachers. Total staff meetings usually have been used to cover only administrative detail or trivia. The principal has traditionally held the formal decision-making authority. A paternalistic style of school administration has been the rule rather than the exception.

The role of the teacher needs to be redefined. Due to the knowledge explosion and growing expectations of professional teachers, the teacher role also must be critically reexamined and redefined. Differentiated responsibilities are necessary to make the school a more effective instructional organization, and the specific skills utilized by teachers need to be reordered in terms of their priority. Teachers need to view themselves more as learning catalysts than as primary disseminators of information. In today's society, there are so many other sources and means of information dissemination that the teacher's primary task should become instead the effective management of learning processes, information resources, and growth experiences.

In redefining the role of the professional teacher, greater emphasis must be placed on the diagnosis and prescription phases of individualizing instruction. Teachers must become more skilled in assessing student learning needs and prescribing appropriate materials and activities to foster growth. Ongoing assessment techniques to evaluate the results of instructional programs need to be developed. Schools need to place greater emphasis on continuing professional growth, especially for instructional teams and total school staffs.

Teachers need additional expertise. Teachers need time and opportunities to develop the necessary expertise to effectively improve the school's instructional program. Most elementary school teachers do not have the planning, organizational, decision-making, and interpersonal communication skills to work effectively with colleagues on a professional level.

Diversified staffing must become comfortable. Everyone needs to become accustomed to having more individuals working within the school due to the introduction of paid aides, parent volunteers, resource volunteers, student teachers, intern teachers, and peer tutors. The teaching staff must become less sensitive to other individuals observing them in their instructional activities. New staffing patterns, whether in separate classrooms or in open space schools, provide greatly increased adult-to-adult interaction.

It is also very important to provide orientation and training not only to the variety of support personnel but also to the teaching staff in terms of how to utilize these individuals effectively and how to relate to them in a positive and professional way.

Variability in team teaching must be nurtured. In developing more effective work groups, the establishment of teaching teams offers considerable potential. The formation and the functioning of teaching teams in the Marin Project suggest the following points:

1. It is necessary to expect that teaching teams will vary in direction and will develop at different rates of speed. It is ineffective and even detrimental to push all teaching teams in the same direction. There are too many variables influencing the formation of effective teaching teams to make such an expectation or demand realistic.

2. Some teams need to select a single leader to organize and coordinate the team's activities. Other teams do not respond enthusiastically to the notion of designating a leader, but instead wish to divide team responsibilities in a way that involves more team members in varied leadership roles. In either case, it is highly desirable to consider carefully necessary leadership functions and to clarify how these functions are going to be served within the team.

3. Developing team relationships can be a frustrating and slow moving process. It is necessary to reinforce and support the commitment and effort made by instructional teams attempting to function effectively.

4. Teams need to learn from their own experiences in order to decide which forms of team interaction and organization work best for them. It is important to encourage reflection and modification of team programs so that team members do not feel rigidly locked into a particular approach. Flexibility is necessary for team development of a better understanding of the process of working on a professional level with other adults and for joint improvement of the instructional program for their students.

Reallocation of educational resources is required. In developing more effective school staffing patterns and instructional programs, educational resources must be reallocated. Higher teacher salaries and smaller class sizes will not solve education's problems. A new mix of resources allowing for an efficient combination of personnel and instructional materials must be developed. Through such reallocation of resources, instructional teams can become more effective, be more productive, and provide increased learning opportunities for children on a more personalized and individualized basis. In other words, differentiated staffing can provide a better return on the public's investment.

It is encouraging that elementary schools are attempting to find better ways of utilizing personnel and other resources to improve learning. Many alternatives are being explored, tried, and assessed. The prospects look good for breaking away from some of the deficiencies of the self-contained classroom model of elementary education.

FOOTNOTES

1. Further information concerning the Marin EPDA Staff Differentiation Project and differentiated staffing concepts may be obtained from: Hollis H. Moore, Director, Marin County Superintendent of Schools Office, 201 Tamal Vista Boulevard, Corte Madera, California 94925.

Annotated bibliographies on *Team Teaching, Differentiated Staffing—An Addendum, School Volunteers, Teacher Aides,* and *Individualizing Instruction* have been prepared by the Project.

Information regarding the other sixteen funded EPDA Differentiated Staffing Projects may be obtained from: Raymond G. Melton, Director, National Cluster Coordination Center, 809 West Main Street, Mesa, Arizona 85202.

2. Lester, G. Sidney. "Marin Perspectives on Differentiated Staffing." *Marin County Schools Reporter* May 1970. p. 9.

3. Davies, Donald. "Education Professions Development—Investment in the Future." *American Education* 2: 9-10; February 1969. p. 10.

Differentiated Staffing—
Its Rewards and Pitfalls

THE REV. J. W. KEEFE

SPECIALIZATION has become one of the most significant words of the Space Age. Most of the extraordinary achievements in our era have resulted from a systematic utilization of talented people. There is scarcely a gain worth mentioning in science, medicine, business, or management, and indeed in professional education, that does not reflect an enlightened application of staff utilization theory.

This has not always been so. The time is not very remote when most great discoveries and ideas were developed by creative minds working alone, often in cloistered places and frequently with little public recognition. Theirs was a solitary specialization. Our age has seen the dawning of a team approach to specialization, in which men and women of differing talents and training combine their skills to provide an increasingly more efficient attack on the limits of knowledge.

This concept of specialization within a team has led to the development of many of today's most promising educational in-

NASSP BULLETIN, May 1971, pp. 112-118.

novations, among them team teaching and differentiated staffing. Since the role of the teacher is central to the progress of modern education, much contemporary research has focused on the problem of providing a more efficient format for teaching than that experienced by the jack-of-all-trades teacher of former times.

The present concept of the teaching role dates back to the nineteenth century, when the teacher typically had a limited education and was expected to function in all or several fields of knowledge. All teachers were expected to be fundamentally alike. They were interchangeable. They were all expected to have the same basic skills and the same inherent limitations. Promotions then and now generally took teachers away from students. If a teacher shows unusual promise, he may become a department chairman or a counselor or an administrator. In all of these cases he meets fewer students; as he advances, he moves further away from the thing that he does best. Perhaps this is a good example of the "Peter Principle" in operation. This, unfortunately, should not be the case, but will continue to be so until the concepts of staff utilization, staff differentiation, and true specialization are generally applied in our schools.

The Trump versus *the Allen Plan*

In a recent article of particular excellence, James Olivero quotes an insightful definition of differentiated staffing as proposed by Don Barbee.[1] "Differentiated staffing is a concept of organization that seeks to make better use of educational personnel. Teachers and other educators assume different responsibilities based on carefully prepared definitions of the many teaching functions. The differential assignment of educational personnel goes beyond traditional staff allocations based on common subject matter distinctions and grade level arrangements and seeks new ways of analyzing essential teaching tasks and creative means of implementing new educational roles." As early as 1959, J. Lloyd Trump recommended that secondary schools reorganize their teaching staffs along differentiated lines to include professional teachers, instructional assistants, clerks, various kinds of aides, community consultants, and staff specialists. Departing somewhat from the Trump approach, Dwight

---

[1] James L. Olivero. "The Meaning and Application of Differentiated Staffing in Teaching." *Phi Delta Kappan*, Vol. LII, September, 1970; pp. 36-40.

Allen of Stanford University proposed a model of differentiated staffing in 1964 that projected four levels of professional teachers and three levels of nonprofessionals. These two models by Trump and Allen have served as the basis for all significant differentiated staffing proposals in the decade of the sixties.

The Trump plan supports the concept that there must be differentiation in school administration, in the teaching staff, and among the paraprofessional assistants. It presumes several levels of function and competence, but the organization on each level is more horizontal than vertical. The administrative staff includes a principal, who is defined as an instructional leader; an assistant principal, or several if the school is large, who has as his primary responsibility curriculum and instructional leadership; a building administrator, who is responsible for the school plant, the cafeteria, the transportation system, and various administrative details; an external relations director, whose responsibility is to develop a statement of the school's financial needs for the central office, governmental agencies, and other groups; a personnel administrator, who has responsibility for supervising attendance, discipline, guidance, and liaison with community and public agencies; and an activities director, who is responsible for faculty social events and student extracurricular activities.

The Trump design envisions a departmental or interdisciplinary teaching team which builds on the varying talents and individual differences that exist among teachers. The plan suggests a team teaching approach, with differentiated functions allocated among teachers in somewhat the way the school hopes to provide for individual differences among pupils. This concept, however, does not imply a hierarchy of teachers; it proposes a team of peers working together, utilizing their different talents for the common good of the students. It means that the school deliberately employs a staff with divergent training, competencies, and interests, thus capitalizing on the differences among teachers rather than attempting to push them into traditional molds. These professional teachers, in turn, work with three kinds of paraprofessional assistants: instructional assistants with the equivalent of two years of college or similar training, who supervise independent study areas, help prepare materials and evaluate student progress; clerical assistants, who are hired on the basis of their skills in typing, duplicating, record keeping, and

145

the like; and general aides, no specific training required, who handle general kinds of supervision and assist in miscellaneous ways.

The Trump plan sees the teacher in the role of "facilitator of learning" and teacher-adviser. It is basically a nonhierarchical design. The Allen plan, on the contrary, is basically hierarchical in its approach. This design has been systematically developed in the Temple City Unified School District in California. Professional teachers are organized on four levels: associate teachers, who are interns or "novices," given a formal schedule but few responsibilities; staff teachers, who have a regular teaching load and are aided by paraprofessionals; senior teachers, defined as "learning engineers," who are expert in particular subjects or skill areas; and the master teacher, who is the resident scholar and research expert. Teachers higher in this hierarchy have fewer teaching responsibilities and more professional advisory functions. Staff teachers are assisted by three levels of paraprofessionals: academic assistants, who serve as instructional aides; educational technicians, who bring multi-media skills and talents to the teaching team; and clerks, who function in the same capacity as in the Trump plan. The major areas of responsibility delineated in the Allen plan are instructional management, curriculum construction, and the application of research to the improvement of instruction.

Which of these two designs proves to be the more successful will be determined in the laboratory of time and experience. Undoubtedly, the most significant fact about both approaches is that they are widely criticized by those who feel that the status of the professional teacher is jeopardized by the introduction of paraprofessional personnel. The Allen plan is criticized as a subtle merit pay proposal, although under most merit pay plans teachers have the same responsibility but get different compensation. The Allen-Temple City plan defines *differentiated* functions for teachers, and the salary scale is based on these divergent responsibilities. The Trump plan attempts to avoid the merit pay pitfall by emphasizing a peer relationship among teachers who exercise a differentiated responsibility.

Every experimental design has its measure of success and failure. Since there has been so little systematic implementation of differentiated staffing, however, at this stage of development it is much more valid to speak of pitfalls and rewards. There are certainly several significant rewards flowing from such a staffing concept:

1. A differentiated staff encourages innovation. Teachers are not isolated in their attempts to introduce new content and new methods. When responsibilities are differentiated, the management of change is more systematic and therefore less traumatic.

2. Curriculum organization and improvement are facilitated. Team planning establishes the context for the diverse educational interests and insights of the staff and provides fertile ground for the mutual consideration of student performance objectives, continuous progress sequencing, and team evaluation.

3. The professionalization of teaching is solidly advanced. Staff differentiation provides abundant opportunities for leadership and followership. There is opportunity for peer-group recognition and individual study opportunities in depth. Teacher planning time is available during the school day through schedule modification, and there are many in-service education possibilities. There is also opportunity for teacher specialization as well as expansion of broad knowledge in related fields. In addition, the supervisory roles of teachers and administrators are enhanced and teachers and students both have opportunity for variety during the entire school day.

4. Individualization of instruction is promoted because staff differentiation makes possible a nongraded structure in the school, with continuous progress and individual diagnosis, prescription, and evaluation of student needs and goals.

There are, of course, a number of pitfalls. The major disadvantages tend to arise from the attitudes of staff members.

1. Differentiated staffing patterns require changes in role behavior on the part of administrators and teachers. These role changes presume and require adequate if not excellent communication between levels and an understanding of the differentiated role and a strong desire on the part of all involved to implement it. Obstacles arising in this area include a failure to communicate clearly, freely, and openly and the danger that a lack of attention will be paid to details and follow-up activities. There is the possibility that teachers may not utilize their time well. There is also the danger of a prima donna emerging whose main concern is to advance his or her ideas and to monopolize meeting time. There is, of course, the possibility that some teachers may not be open enough to survive evaluation arising from close professional contact.

2. We must be concerned that differentiated staffing does not become an end rather than a means to an end. Proper staff utilization means that teacher specialists can be made available to students with varying interests and aptitudes. The aim of this process is the greater individualization of instruction and the more efficient motivation of student learning. The structure is not as important as the way the structure functions.

147

3. A final pitfall is the risk that differentiated staffing may foster the evolution of a more rigid hierarchy than the one that now exists in schools with self-contained classrooms. A system is only as valuable as its flexibility and level of performance. We will have to focus strongly on the fact that the primary purpose of the differentiated staff is to provide specialization within a flexible framework.

Differentiated staffing structures are not yet a reality in many of our schools. There are, of course, notable examples in the Temple City project, in the various Trump schools of the Staff Utilization Project, and the current Model Schools Project. There are also schools utilizing systematic team techniques to implement individually prescribed instruction and computer assisted instruction. The returns are far from complete and the outcome is by no means determined. Many of the problems of staff utilization have resulted from an unhappy mix of teachers and administrators who could not work well together. Those schools that have experienced even a modicum of success have worked systematically to develop good horizontal and vertical communication among staff members and to enhance leadership by employing modern management techniques.

Conclusion

Experience forces me to conclude that schools will not be successful in implementing differentiated staffing unless they take seriously McGregor's distinction between adversary and participative modes of leadership. The rapid changes in our modern world, the greater sophistication of both adults and young people, and the long and developing tradition of a democratic style of life have tended to make obsolete the authoritarian style of leadership in many areas of American life. A successful differentiated staff may well depend upon a principal and an administrative staff that can use participatory modes of management in the identification and achievement of goals. When an *administrative staff* can work together as a team of professionals to achieve a sense of mutual confidence from goals and tasks determined by consensus, then *teaching teams* also may be able to see the value of a truly democratic form of team planning. Innovations are successful only when they are understood and implemented on the grass-roots level. Students will not begin to reap the rewards of appropriate staff utilization until teachers acting in educational teams are able to define goals, diagnose the needs of each individual student, prescribe appropriate curriculum materials, and evaluate student progress in the light of these mutually defined objectives. Perhaps differentiated staffing will be totally unworkable in an authoritarian environment; it will certainly be less successful. It will thrive only when our administrative and staffing structures have achieved a competent systems approach based on contemporary management design and a clear definition of mutual goals.

CHAPTER V

The Status and Development of Paraprofessionals

In the previous chapter various staffing patterns were
reviewed. In these staffing strategies there are described
various "positions" of a non-professional nature. These
non-professionals can emerge as a hierarchy of positions
with at least two major divisions: the paraprofessional
specialist with two to four years of advanced preparations
and sub-professional personnel with limited training.[1]
Whatever the case, there will be a significant number of
people who serve in a supportive role in the teaching-
learning situation.

Because of the newness of the para-professional, there
will be a great deal of ambiguity of expectations of paraprofessionals among teachers and administrators. Confusion
will reign regarding what teacher aides are doing and what
they will be expected to do. There is hope that teachers
will be free of the many non-instructional activities so
that they can perform the teaching tasks or better enable
them to design learning strategies which will assist the
individual student.

The success of any paraprofessional program will depend upon the inservice training of the paraprofessional.

1
Bozeli, Frank P. "Organization and Training of Paraprofessionals", The Clearing House, December 1969, pp. 206-
209.

TEACHER-ADMINISTRATOR EXPECTATIONS IN DEFINING ROLES FOR PARAPROFESSIONALS

Robert Lynn Canady

John T. Seyfarth

It has been said that "the sixties will probably be noted in educational history as the period of greatest growth in the use of paraprofessionals in the public schools of this nation."[1] A number of forces operating during the past decade facilitated the movement to add a new position to the staffs of the nation's schools. Among those forces were the increased participation of the federal government in educational activities, increased attention to the need for programs designed to help disadvantaged students, and greater demands for educational services.

The use of paraprofessionals was a logical extension of the idea of a differentiated staff, which had been supported by a number of leading educators as a means of attracting and holding more capable teachers and making better use of their abilities. The position of paraprofessional was viewed by some as the first rung on a career ladder which would make teaching a more attractive career as well as making it more accessible to minority and lower-class groups.

Despite the growing use of paraprofessionals in the classrooms and the general enthusiasm with which they have been received, however, "a clear conceptualization of the role of the teacher aide has not yet emerged."[2] Nor does there exist among professionals a consensus regarding the proper means of recruiting and training paraprofessionals, the qualifications to require, or what pay scale to offer.

Further, there still is no theoretical basis for determining the kinds of tasks paraprofessionals should or should not perform,[3] as pointed out by Tanner and Tanner in the May, 1969, issue of *Educational Leadership*. Although empirical research is needed to develop a sound theoretical base for the utilization of paraprofessionals, the expectations professionals hold for paraprofessionals will strongly influence their utilization. Hence, sociological role theory offers a departure point from which to examine the developing paraprofessional services in the schools.

Role theory holds that a person's behavior in an organization is influenced by by the expectations others in and out of the organization hold for the position he occupies. Foskett and Wolcott summarize the view with respect to education:

There is a complex or structure of norms, involving behavior of teachers, principals, pupils, parents, citizens, and others in regard to the formal educational process. The nature of this structure, the kinds of expectations the members of these groups have for themselves and for each other, and the extent of agreement among the members of each group and between groups, will have an effect on the relations of individuals and the effectiveness of the total educational program.[4]

Public school teachers and administrators have participated in the educational process for more than a century, and their images and role expectations have become institutionalized. There is a high degree of consensus among persons both in and out of education regarding the expected behavior of these two groups. This fact

EDUCATION, Feb./Mar. 1972, pp. 99-102.

may account in part for the difficulty one encounters when attempting to change educational practices, especially when those changes require redefinition of roles. In contrast, there is relatively low consensus among educators and others regarding the new position of paraprofessional. This ambiguity of role provides an opportunity for professionals and others to participate in shaping and defining the new position. Labor unions, federal agencies, and community groups are likely to participate in this process.

Foskett and Wolcott found that "in the absence of a clearly defined role there is always a tendency to play it safe and not do too much to risk the ire of others by doing something that is not generally accepted as proper."[5] The import of this finding is that the lack of consensus regarding the paraprofessional's role is likely to lessen this contribution. Moreover, this lack of agreement is likely to result in the paraprofessional's duties and qualifications being patterned after the qualifications of principals and teachers, although such a practice may not be the most profitable use of paraprofessional talent.

Research conducted by the principal investigator in the State of Tennessee during 1968 and 1969[6] confirmed the fact that formal educational requirements for paraprofessionals[7] are similar to those required for teachers. Of 126 superintendents responding to inquiries about the use of paraprofessionals in their schools, the majority cited some type of educational requirement as a criterion for employment as a paraprofessional. The results are tabulated in Table I.

The most frequently cited requirement was that a prospective paraprofessional must have attended high school. About two-thirds of the superintendents reported requiring at least graduation from high school. A large majority reported that the ability to assist with instruction was either required or desirable, and about one-third wanted paraprofessionals who could teach a class. About 80 percent of the respondents felt that paraprofessionals should possess clerical skills (required or desirable), and about three-fourths would like persons who had had successful experience working with children.

TABLE I

Employment Qualifications for Paraprofessionals
Reported by Tennessee Superintendents

Qualifications	Per Cent*		
	Required	Desirable	Unnecessary
Education:			
Secondary school attendance	75	14	0
Secondary school graduation	65	22	1
Post secondary study	3	71	12
College degree	1	27	52
Other Characteristics:			
Clerical skills	21	62	2
Successful experience with children	13	63	5
Parent of school age child	2	35	44
Ability to assist with instruction	16	59	10
Ability to teach a class	2	33	48

*"No response" category deleted

When the responses of superintendents were compared with those of teachers and principals in the state, differences were noted. Tasks which the teachers rated as most important for paraprofessionals to perform, in order of preference, were: (1) provide clerical assistance, including duplication of materials, (2) prepare audio and visual materials for instruction as determined by the teacher, (3) file and catalogue materials, (4) help with supervision of children during lunch periods and bus loading, and (5) assist teachers in utilizing materials in large group lessons and demonstrations. Four of the same tasks were also identified by principals as most appropriate ones for paraprofessionals; but "serve as library materials assistant" was substituted for item (4), help with supervision of children during lunch periods and bus loading.

Although both administrators and teachers responded favorably to all of the 24 suggested duties,[8] they consistently ranked instructional tasks lower than noninstructional tasks. If it is true, as was assumed, that paraprofessionals will primarily perform duties expected by professionals, then it seems likely that paraprofessionals will not perform significant amounts of instructionally related duties in the schools. This conclusion contrasts with the relatively high emphasis which superintendents placed on education and instructional ability in hiring paraprofessionals.

The data from the study[9] also suggest that a dichotomization of tasks into professional and nonprofessional, as suggested by Tanner and Tanner,[10] may not be a fine enough distinction to identify those duties which professionals consider desirable for paraprofessionals to perform. Although two professional groups—teachers and principals—were in general agreement that instructional tasks were less preferred,[11] they differed considerably within the categories of tasks which could be classified as non-instructional. Further,

these findings showed that teachers with differing years of professional experience responded differently to the tasks they expected of paraprofessionals.[12] Teachers with five years or less experience were significantly less positive than more experienced teachers to the paraprofessional role category of educational materials assistant.[13]

The study also indicated that teachers who had experienced a working relationship with paraprofessionals felt significantly less positive toward paraprofessionals than teachers who had never worked with them, although teachers with experience with paraprofessionals were in favor of the trend toward employing more paraprofessionals.[14] Teachers who had experience working with paraprofessionals apparently viewed contributions of paraprofessionals more realistically and recognized the need for more teacher training and assistance in adequate utilization of paraprofessionals in the classroom.

Colleges of education have done very little to prepare teachers to work with paraprofessionals, although the paraprofessional position is becoming a standard assignment in many school districts. One recent report noted that "young teachers, in particular, appear to have difficulty in working with aides, and since aides are a permanent and growing part of American education, it is essential that training for their use be provided."[15] A national survey found that teachers feel their greatest need for inservice training is learning how to work with paraprofessionals effectively.[16]

Training of paraprofessionals is another need which the colleges, and particularly community colleges, are only now beginning to serve. The National Commission on Teacher Education and Professional Standards has appealed for differentiated training for paraprofessionals based on realistic assessment of the duties they will perform in classrooms. The Commission's statement follows:

Since all auxiliary personnel will not have the same skills or serve the same function, their qualifications and salaries should vary. The lunchroom aide, for example, does not need the degree and kind of skills a lay reader needs. A clerical aide might need only a high school education with emphasis on clerical skills, but a graphic artist hired to prepare instructional materials might need two or more years of college. Teachers and others must develop job classifications, and a specific job will dictate the aptitudes needed, the qualifications to be met, and the pay to be received.[17]

In considering the role theory approach to defining roles for paraprofessionals, a question which must be answered is whether professionals' expectations of paraprofessionals should be accepted and paraprofessionals trained to meet those expectations, or whether teachers should be trained to expect from paraprofessionals those tasks which research indicates to be most effective and useful in the school setting. This, of course, is a question which cannot be answered by research alone; it is a policy question and ultimately involves value judgments. However, continued research is needed to collect data on which such a vital decision can be based.

Footnotes

[1]Donald W. Dunnan, "A Point of View," *The School Administrator* (Washington, D.C.: American Association of School Administrators, April, 1969), p. 11.

[2]*Research Bulletin* (Gainesville, Florida: Florida Educational Research and Development Council, College of Education, University of Florida, March, 1966), p. 15.

[3]Laurel N. Tanner and Daniel Tanner, "The Teacher Aide: A National Study of Confusion," *Educational Leadership*, XXVI (May, 1969), p. 765.

[4]John M. Foskett and Harry F. Wolcott, *Self Images and Community Images of the Elementary School Principal: Findings and Implications of a Sociological Inquiry* (Eugene, Oregon: Center for the Advanced Study of Educational Administration, University of Oregon, May, 1966). (Mimeographed.)

[5]*Ibid.*, p. 36.

[6]Robert Lynn Canady, "Role Descriptors for Paraprofessionals in the Tennessee Public Schools: An Investigation of Perceptions at Various Professional Levvels" (unpublished doctoral dissertation, The University of Tennessee, Knoxville, 1970).

[7]Qualifications taken from a study *Teacher Aides in the Classroom*, a cooperative regional project of the six New England states funded under Title V, Section 505, of the Elementary and Secondary Education Act of 1965 (Providence, Rhode Island: The New England Educational Assessment Project, November, 1967).

[8]Duties were largely determined by a New England study conducted in 1967. *Ibid.*

[9]Canady, *op. cit.*, pp. 109-113.

[10]Tanner and Tanner, *op. cit.*, p. 769.

[11]Canady, *op. cit.*, pp. 79-80.

[12]*Ibid.*, pp. 88-89.

[13]*Ibid.*, pp. 89-90.

[14]*Ibid.*, pp. 84-86.

[15]*Education Daily*, January 7, 1970, p. 5.

[16]"Teachers' Needs for Inservice Training," *NEA Research Bulletin*, XLVI (October, 1968), p. 80.

[17]National Education Association, *Auxiliary School Personnel* (Washington, D.C.: National Education Association, National Commission on Teacher Education and Professional Standards, 1967), pp. 10-11.

Paraprofessionals in Schools

BEATRICE M. GUDRIDGE

$\mathcal{P}$ARAPROFESSIONALS—the umbrella term covering cafeteria aides and reading tutors, instructional aides, community workers, and many other educational workers —have become the fastest growing body of employes in U.S. schools.

Like the loyal army of school volunteers who manned (and still are manning) so many vital school posts over the years, paraprofessionals are noneducators whose work in and around the school frees the teacher to perform the professional functions for which he was trained. One state—Florida—defines the paraprofessional as "any person assigned by a school board to assist a member of the instructional staff in carrying out his instructional or professional duties and responsibilities." Unlike the volunteer, however, the paraprofessional is paid, receives certain employe fringe benefits, and gets careful in-service training in an increasing number of school systems.

Currently 200,000 to 300,000 paraprofessionals work in and around public schools, and by 1977, says the National Congress of Parents and Teachers, their numbers may swell to 1.5 million. A 1969 study by the Research Division of the NEA showed that one classroom teacher in four had the support of a teacher aide. Economist Leon H. Keyserling, in his projections on education manpower needs for this decade, predicted that the ratio will eventually become one aide to every two teachers. The U.S. Office of Education (USOE), through its $24.3 million Career Opportunities Program (COP), is helping 8,000 low-income participants, many of them Vietnam war veterans, to work as school aides and at the same time aim toward a full-time career in education. The California Teachers Association has reported that one-third of all school districts in that state are using some type of classroom aide, and in New York City alone there were 15,000 education paraprofessionals on the job in 1971.

The significance of the paraprofessional movement has not been lost on the two big teacher organizations, the NEA and the American Federation of Teachers

• • • • • • • • • • • • •

Condensed from PARAPROFESSIONALS IN SCHOOLS: HOW NEW CAREERISTS BOLSTER EDUCATION, A Special Report prepared by the staff of Education U.S.A. 1972 National School Public Relations Association, Washington D.C. 1-2, 6, 48, 54.

(AFT). Eighteen years ago when Bay City, Michigan, launched the nation's first major experiment in the use of teacher aides, organized teacher groups recoiled in horror. They were convinced it was a scheme to cut school costs and balloon class sizes. This still worries AFT and NEA, but on the principle that "if you can't lick them, let them join," both organizations are now actively courting paraprofessionals.

AFT welcomes paraprofessionals into its teacher locals as full members, and since 1968, almost every set of teacher-initiated contract demands drawn up by local unions has included provisions for the hiring of teacher aides. In New York City, the United Federation of Teachers, an AFT affiliate, has won a landmark contract for 10,000 of that city's paraprofessionals.

The NEA, through its Association of Classroom Teachers, has been interested in the paraprofessional movement since 1967 and is now flexing for a full-scale organizing drive with the blessings of the 1971 NEA Representative Assembly. Eventually, NEA expects to organize a separate membership category within its constellation for school auxiliary personnel. NEA leaders believe, however, that the organizing push should start at the local and/or state level. To promote this development, NEA is offering promotional savvy and some financial help to its affiliates.

Who are the paraprofessionals and what do they do? What impact is their work having on pupil achievement, teacher morale, principal efficiency, and parent satisfaction?

The school paraprofessional can be a teen-ager or a white-haired grandmother, an elementary school dropout or a Ph.D. holder, a suburban housewife or a retired businessman. Women, however, greatly outnumber men in these posts, and although paraprofessionals work at all levels from preschool through high school, most are found in the early grades.

Paraprofessionals wear a multitude of labels—instructional aide, teacher aide, education aide, school aide, community aide, media aide, clerical aide, teacher assistant, educational associate, family assistant, family worker, parent/community aide, social worker aide, and community liaison worker. Some school districts describe more than 170 functions performed by aides.

Impact

Once having used aides, school district spokesmen say they would be "very reluctant" to give them up. Indeed, federal funds have been supplemented by many systems to ensure stability and increase the scope of the aide program. In an NEA study, 9 out of 10 teachers said aides were helpful. More than one-half of the teachers declared they were of great assistance. Administrators view aides favorably because they make it possible to use instructional resources wisely. Parents and pupils react positively, and the aides themselves are so sold on their work that many plan to make education a lifetime career.

Studies show that aides are fulfilling the major purposes expected of them: increasing the learning achievement of students and freeing teachers to use diagnostic, planning, and decision-making skills. And some surveys indicate that although installing an aide program takes additional funds, the per-pupil instructional costs can be lowered by using paraprofessionals.

A study of aides in grades 1-4 of the Portland, Oregon, schools, for example, found that their use led to more constructive utilization of time for pupils from the aide and the teacher; teacher aide teams delivered instruction at a lower per-hour cost than teachers alone; and pupil learning showed a favorable effect. The Portland study, conducted by Eaton Conant of the University of Oregon, showed that during a five-hour day, teachers alone in classrooms spent 92 minutes on instructional activities. With the introduction of an aide, teacher time in instruction rose to 109 minutes, with the aide providing an additional 129 minutes of instructional activity. Average total cost for an hour of instruction of a teacher aide, Conant said, was $8.80, compared with over $16 for a teacher alone. These differences came about, he said, thanks to the additional instruction provided by both teacher and aide, and the lower salary for the aide.

Because the aide concept is still new, hitches sometimes develop in assignment of aides. "I think teachers should sit down and find out right from the start what the aides' skills are and not just assign us to clerical work," one aide said.

Sometimes the aide program fails when well educated helpers become dissatisfied with the limitations of their aide work. College graduates who have taught several years before marriage feel they are wasting their time because they cannot teach. Their disappointment may be due to lack of proper orientation and in-service training in which they might have been reminded that educational theory and practice change, and previous teaching experience might now be inadequate. On the other hand, an in-service training program for teachers might have suggested ways they could make use of a former teacher's experience.

A final major factor inhibiting a more rapid spread of the paraprofessional movement is the shortage of funds. James F. Garvey, assistant superintendent of La Canada, California, Unified School District says, "The most important question is whether advantages from auxiliary personnel services are worth the additional cost."

All in all, the pluses of the paraprofessional movement appear to far outweigh the minuses—but the gains will not come automatically. The movement will succeed only if educators and citizens are willing to do the planning and provide the funds to accomplish the goals that aides may make possible. □

TEACHING AIDES:

How well do they perform in the secondary schools?

By BRIAN S. GIERSCH

Introduction

For the past two years Prince George's County Public Schools, Maryland, has conducted an instructional aide program at the secondary level as part of our federally funded Emergency School Assistance Project. While aide programs are not unique, the deployment of instructional aides at the secondary level is rather uncommon. With the increased availability of federal funds, especially to disadvantaged schools, the lessons of our experience may be of value to others interested in the establishment of a similar program. What appears below, then, is an outline of our program, a review of its evaluation, and recommendations for the improvement of this or similar programs.

THE CLEARING HOUSE, Jan. 1973,

pp. 267-272.

Program Summary

Authorized by the U.S. Office of Education, under the Emergency School Assistance Program, the Prince George's County Public School System received in federal grants $532,709 for the 1970–71 school year, the intent of which was to provide financial assistance in implementing desegregation plans. The activities funded by this grant included, among others, instructional aides for nine of the secondary schools affected by the shifting of attendance boundaries. An extension of this program, but on a more limited basis, was granted for the 1971–72 school year. The ESAP Instructional Aide Program, as implemented this past year, provided 36 full-time instructional aides and one aide coordinator for nine of the junior high schools originally affected by the 1970–71 desegregation plan. At this level, reinforcement and remediation of basic skills in language arts and math was expected to have a significant effect on future academic performance, which, in turn, would affect the child's self-concept and his peer relationships.

Aide Staff

The majority of the aide staff, as it was finally composed, consisted of persons with previous aide experience and/or some degree of college training. Our completed staff had a racial breakdown of 25 black and 11 white aides, with each school being assigned four ESAP aides. A significant result of the care taken in selecting our aides was the extremely low turnover rate experienced during this past school year (5 per cent), as compared with our 1970–71 experience (17 per cent).

Orientation and In-Service

As soon as our aide staff was complete, a two-day orientation program was conducted by the aide coordinator for all 36 aides. A similar one-day program was held for approximately 70 of the teachers working with our aides. Both programs provided discussions of the duties of aides, the teacher-aide team concept, the need for planning, the role of the aide coordinator, the purpose of the program, and suggested techniques for utilizing aides.

October and November saw the aide coordinator, in addition to providing the two orientation programs, conduct orientation and planning meetings within each of the schools for those members of the administrative and teaching staff closely associated with the program. The majority of these meetings were conducted following a full day of observation in each school and centered on specific techniques for utilizing aides effectively, demonstrating materials, or clarifying specific concerns raised by teachers or aides.

One recurring concern regarded the lack of inexpensive materials available for individualized instruction. To rectify the situation, the aide coordinator gathered ideas from a variety of sources and reproduced them in the form of learning stations or instructional games. These materials then became the focus of a continuous program of workshops for teachers and aides that ran from December until May. During this period, 11 workshops were held for individual schools. Substitutes were hired, using ESAP funds, so that teachers, as well as the aides, could take part in these programs. In addition, one major program was developed for 70 participating teachers which centered on vocabulary and organizational skills, with emphasis on techniques which the teacher and aide, as a team, could employ to reinforce these skills. The winter and spring were also devoted to periodic meetings with the various personnel involved in the program either individually or in groups, to discuss and resolve problems identified through observation or raised by the staffs within the respective schools.

Activities of the Aides

With few exceptions, each aide was assigned to work with two or three teachers whose classes contained large percentages of students having demonstrated relatively low levels of academic achievement and requiring additional assistance in the reinforcement and remediation of their basic language arts and math skills. As a result, in those schools with this type of scheduling, approximately 24 different classes were receiving the assistance of an instructional aide each day. The majority of these were English, Core and Math classes. In most instances, the aides worked with small groups of students or individual students within these classes in an attempt to provide remediation and reinforcement, as directed by the classroom teacher.

In addition to their regular instructional role, the aides were also involved in extracurricular activities such as student clubs, field trips, thespian activities, and musical organizations. The presence of the ESAP aides, then, affected all areas of student endeavor, both academic and cocurricular.

Program Evaluation

To facilitate a meaningful evaluation of the ESAP Instructional Aide Program, a survey form was developed and distributed to all aides and teachers associated with the program. While this is, admittedly, a subjective means of evaluation, it must suffice as no provision was made in the program proposal or in the approved budget for an objective means of evaluation. The results of this evaluation are presented here under two categories: benefits; and weaknesses.

Benefits of the Program

On the outset of the current program year, four assumptions provided the basis for the existence and continuation of the ESAP Instructional Aide Program. These assumptions appear below as they were rephrased for the survey mentioned above, accompanied by the percentage of teachers and aides responding in a positive manner to each statement.

Survey Statement	Teachers	Aides
Students have benefitted academically from the assistance of aides.	96%	93%
Student's self-concept has improved as a result of the assistance of aides.	85%	93%
Human relations (among students) has improved as a result of the assistance of aides.	86%	92%
Aides have contributed to improved classroom instruction.	95%	N/A*

* While the aides did respond positively (62 per cent), only the professional educator can best make this judgment.

In terms, then, of the subjective responses outlined above, the program has been a success as judged by the persons most closely associated with its daily operations.

To make provision for evaluation by the administrators of the participating schools, each principal was requested to provide, in essay form, a statement regarding the effectiveness of the program within their respective schools. The following statements have been excerpted from the nine letters received as they provide further insight regarding the overall benefits of the aide program:

An aide program . . . [enables] more individual and small group attention to junior high students, who desperately need identity and inclusion, and not oblivion in the transition from elementary to secondary [schools].
. . . the Instructional Aide Program made it possible to more effectively implement the Right to Read Program through individualized grouping according to the instructional needs of the students. . . . Not only did the aides help in instructional follow-up and materials preparation, but in some instances they created materials tailored to the individual interests of groups.
Student achievement has improved in those cases where students have been able to work in small groups or on an individual basis with the teacher or aide. As students have begun to experience success instead of failure, they have developed a more positive self-concept, and consequently, their behavior has been modified in a constructive direction.

Characteristics of the Aides. The current literature regarding aides and the benefits derived therefrom indicated almost unanimously that one of the major strengths of paraprofessionals employed in an instructional role is their ability to relate well with students in need of instructional assistance. It is significant that more than one-third *of all responses* to an open-ended question asking about the strengths of aides related to the successful manner in which aides, as non-authority figures, could communicate, support, and encourage their students, especially the "slow learners."

Effect on Instruction. One of the most obvious effects that instructional aides should be expected to have on instruction would be in the area of individualization. In response to this very concern, 93 per cent of the teachers indicated that their aides had enabled them, as teachers, to provide more individualized instruction. Further support for this contention was obvious when 43 per cent *of all comments* made in an open-ended question relating to the strengths of the program indicated that the presence of aides did foster more individualized instruction for students. As a sign that the instructional program had been improved as a result of the aide program, 88 per cent of the teachers reported that aides had enabled them to offer more variety in their instructional activities.

Weaknesses of the Program

The discussion provided above has alluded to a number of problems which became evident during the course of the 1971–72 Instructional Aide Program and, to some extent, prevented optimum performance from the program. The most significant of these weaknesses will be outlined below and the final section of this article, "Recommendations," will deal with the corrective measures which should be adopted to improve the quality of any secondary instructional aide program.

Planning Time. In establishing guidelines for the scheduling of aides, the aide coordinator suggested that each aide be provided daily planning time with each of the teachers to whom she would be assigned. While sufficient planning time was incorporated into the schedule of each aide, the utilization of this time left much to be desired. Surprisingly, the teachers were openly cognizant of the problem, as is reflected by the data provided below:

Survey Statement	Teachers	Aides
Teachers utilize scheduled planning time to meet and plan regularly with aides.	58%	78%

Orientation and In-Service. These two areas of staff development received, unfortunately, the lowest percentage of positive reaction, as compared with all other items on the survey and, as a result, much attention should be focused on the development of more meaningful and numerous in-service experiences for any future aide program. Rather than provide an extensive discussion of the matter here, survey statements will be provided with recommendations offered later.

Survey Statement	Teachers	Aides
Adequate in-service was provided for the aides.	46%*	67%
Adequate in-service regarding the use of aides was provided for teachers.	52%	36%*
The duties and responsibilities of aides were clearly defined.	70%**	74%**

* These should be considered as the more significant features.

** While these figures are well above 50 per cent, much higher figures would be desirable.

In-School Leadership. As was experienced during the 1970–71 school year, a continuing problem was that of the leadership available to the aides within a number of the participating schools. Occasionally, it was leadership that cared little for the successful implementation of the program, in spite of its benefits, and, as a result, tended to stymie the efforts of the aides, teachers, and aide coordinator. In other cases, it was leadership imposed upon the aides which channeled their efforts in unproductive directions.

Program Evaluation. No provision was made in the budget of the aide program for an objective means of evaluation, which would effectively determine to what extent the aides actually have affected the academic achievement, self-concept, and human relations of the children with whom they have contact. Until such time as objective testing is utilized for evaluation purposes, the subjective data sought instead will always be viewed with some degree of skepticism.

Recommendations

Assignment of Aides

Regarding specific classroom assignments of aides, the number of teachers to which any one aide is assigned should be limited to a maximum of three. Eighty-nine per cent of all teachers and 94 per cent of all aides responded positively to a survey statement suggesting that assignments be limited to two or three teachers per aide. Many of the responses to an open-ended question regarding recommendations indicated that three teachers per aide may be undesirable and that aides be limited to working with no more than two teachers.

Orientation Programs

Administrative Orientation. Considerable dissent was voiced through the evaluation survey regarding the excessive use of aides in the administrative offices of certain schools and as emergency substitutes. While the program guidelines specifically regarded these activities as undesirable, various administrators ignored them and misused the ESAP instructional aides. One solution to this matter might be a pre-program orientation meeting for all principals of those schools scheduled to be staffed with aides. Such a meeting would provide a forum for the aide coordinator to discuss in detail the job description of instructional aides, as well as allow the principals to voice their concerns and discuss their particular problems regarding this matter.

Teacher Orientation. One of the most serious deterrents to a successful program has been the lack of orientation for teachers prior to the introduction of aides to their schools and classrooms. Some provision must be made for a pre-school teacher program which would enable teachers to discuss the aides' duties, tentative scheduling for aides, specific techniques for utilizing aides, and to become aware of the goals of the aide program as it relates to the aides and classroom instruction. Such a program, combined with continuous and more frequent follow-up programs of a group and/or individual nature, should enable teachers to more effectively utilize their instructional aides.

Aide Orientation. While aides, in most cases, were satisfied with the workshops sponsored for their benefit, both teachers and aides expressed a lack of enthusiasm for the aides' in-service and orientation programs. Survey recommendations indicated that topics such as specific content matter, child growth and development, group dynamics, and human relations be incorporated into these programs and that there be more frequent in-service programs of this nature provided for the aides. One very specific recommendation was that each professional day for teachers be utilized for the aides as a day of professional growth by scheduling a program for all instructional aides on a special theme.

Supervision from the Aide Coordinator. In addition to providing all of the forego-ing services, many teachers and aides suggested in the evaluation survey that more classroom observations be made by the aide coordinator, both announced and unannounced. The observations, as well as the concerns of the school-based staff, would provide the agenda for regularly scheduled, one-per-month team meetings, which would include the aide coordinator, principal, teachers, and aides in any one of the program's schools.

Supervision of the Program

At the school level, while principals and vice-principals are, naturally, concerned with the success of an aide program for their students' benefit, the leadership within the respective schools for the aide staff should not be placed here. Because language skills are the focus of the aide program, leadership should come from those who possess the expertise in this field. Specifically, the reading resource teachers should have this responsibility as their schedules are most flexible, they have fewer conflicting commitments than do principals, and their concern parallels that of the aide program. Should job descriptions present a problem (no such conflict has appeared over the past two years), compensatory emoluments might be considered.

Objective Evaluation

One final recommendation remains to be made for the purpose of improving the quality of the instructional aide program; that of objective evaluation. To date, neither year of the ESAP program has provided formal testing procedures to determine the effects of instructional aides at the secondary school level on the basic skills and peer relationships of students. It has been suggested that a test battery (e.g., Iowa Test of Basic Skills) be administered in the fall as a pre-test. After identifying a control and experimental group, selected portions of the same battery could be readministered in the spring as a post-test; the results of which should provide some hard data on the effectiveness of the program on academic achievement. The cost of such a testing procedure should be less than 100 dollars. Attitudinal scales could be utilized in a similar manner to indicate the effect aides have on the group relations of students.

✤

CHAPTER VI

The Evaluation of Teachers and Teacher Performance

The proverbial and hitherto persistent "teacher shortage" that has prevailed for much of the post World War II era appears to have lapsed into history along with the little red schoolhouse. The factors contributing to this are numerous and can be found in the economics, and the politics and sociology of the time. In the face of increased competition for a limited number of teaching positions available, selectivity processes inevitably become operant in the screening of candidates. In addition to this, the evaluation of teachers-on-the-job takes on greater significance both for employer and employee. The possession of minimal or basic skills and attitudes by a successful candidate for a teaching position is only an entree to a place on the staff. As that individual carries on his tasks, he is expected to sharpen and refine those basic qualities which caused him to be selected. His responses to the daily challenges of the classroom and his equally imporatant responses to the inservice improvement program of the school system will provide necessary data and information in evaluating his professional appropriateness for that job, that school and community.

The resurgence of actively expressed public concern for quality education is another source of motivation for the attention which is being given to the evaluation of teachers. One of the key factors in establishing this motivation is a well-planned and carefully implemented teacher evaluation program. Considerations must be given to evaluations with wide focus and factors that shape the effectiveness of the teaching and learning process in schools. In order to produce the quality education which the public is seeking, staff evaluation policies or practices are not adequate. We must go beyond this and use student evaluations/ assessments of teachers to the best advantage, evaluation of administrative performance by the school's teaching staff, and self-appraisal techniques. Individuals who are providing leadership must be implementing changes in teacher evaluation for greater growth and efficiency in our school systems.

EVALUATING TEACHERS — PLAN OR PLOT

By

WILLIAM G. KEANE

The sudden surplus of teachers has created a new set of problems for school boards and administrators as well as for the thousands of young men and women who are competing for the diminishing number of vacant positions. Since teachers are currently earning salaries equal to or better than those paid to many of the taxpayers they serve, a critical eye was bound to be cast on the quality of classroom performance. Add to this situation the public's knowledge that there is a vast contingent of certified and unemployed teachers who are young, enthusiastic, and competent (and less expensive than their more senior colleagues), the motivation for school officials to examine the quality of instruction taking place in each district has increased sharply.

Clear indications of this sudden enthusiasm are not hard to find. This year the Michigan Association of School Administrators (MASA) chose the topic of "Teacher Evaluation" as the subject for all day in-service workshops in each region throughout the state. The Michigan Association of School Personnel Administrators set up a state-wide conference on the same topic. As a further indication that the heat was on everybody, the MASA fall conference was devoted exclusively to the subject of administrative evaluation.

Now that the subject of evaluation has emerged from the periphery of school leadership tasks to become a prime concern and significant undertaking, it is critically important that school officials carefully think through the purposes of any contemplated program before moving mindlessly in the wrong direction or, perhaps worse, in five different and possibly conflicting directions at the same time.

There are many needs that a newly installed teacher evaluation program might meet. The biggest temptation might be simply to do SOMETHING, anything, in response to community pressure. Almost any program would meet this objective provided it is eminently visible and well publicized.

Others might see the primary goal of an evaluation program as the gathering of specific documentation in order to enable dismissal actions to stand all court and Tenure Commission tests for due process. Still others might view evaluation programs as a primary means to put teachers on notice that the Board and administration mean business about accountability.

However, it is unlikely that a thoughtfully conceived and carefully conducted evaluation program can spring from these relatively superficial motives. A sound evaluation effort undoubtedly will produce lots of documentation about teacher performance. It will generate specific information about student learning (which is, after all, accountability in its best sense) and it will give citizens reason to believe that school operations are being carefully monitored. However, these outcomes will be more by-products than goals. Rather, the teacher evaluation program should be viewed and developed as but a part of a total process whereby a school district examines its performance to determine whether the objectives of the organization are being met. Thus all inputs, processes and outputs, and *all* personnel responsible for activity in each of these areas, will be subject to evaluation. The chief outcome sought in such a program is improved instruction and the attitude of each evaluator in the total process is characterized by the desire to establish a helping relationship.

Nevertheless, no matter how positive and constructive the attitude of those who initiate a teacher evaluation program, no matter how well based on sound theory and proven practice it may prove to be, there will be obstacles to overcome. A force field analysis of the district's situation prior to implementation would appear a desirable first step to take. It is likely, for example, that the following barriers to and sources of encouragement for a teacher evaluation program would characterize virtually all situations.

Perhaps the biggest hurdle to be overcome in getting the program started would be the benign inertia of past practice. Until the last few years most districts used a teacher monitoring program that was called on to identify and document only the most flagrant examples of gross incompetence among probationary teachers since the perennial teacher shortage limited the amount of selectivity the district might exercise. Only a most unusual school district would have carried out a systematic evaluation program of tenure teachers in this period.

An impediment of more recent vintage is the not totally unfounded fear on the part of teachers that the accountability bandwagon will deposit its evil cargo right at their doors. Thus, if the program isn't planned with meaningful and complete involvement by teachers, and if the goals of the program aren't genuinely congruent with the best interest of teachers as they view them, teachers associations will vigorously resist every step of the way.

Finally, there are few models of evaluation systems with wide dissemination that have given teachers reason to expect that the one developed by the district will be fair, positive in orientation and genuinely helpful. In other words, there may be effective evaluation systems, but few teachers know of one or know of other teachers who know of one.

MICHIGAN ASSOCIATION OF SCHOOL BOARD JOURNAL, July 1973, pp. 17-19.

Though one should be aware of these potential impediments in starting out to design an appropriate system, there are also sources of encouragement for the task at hand. As Redfern[1] and others have pointed out, teachers associations, particularly at the state level, have been on public record for decades as encouraging the search of valid, constructive evaluation systems. Their position on this subject is too widely publicized to permit retreat at this point.

In addition, public dissatisfaction with education is too widespread and too well documented for teachers not to understand the need for boards of education and administrators to examine all district operations with care. It is just plain good politics as well as good public relations for a local teachers association to cooperate with administration in developing an effective system. However, this advantage can be counted on for a limited time. Unless school officials are genuinely interested in giving teachers meaningful input into the developmental process, political and public relations considerations will give way to more fundamental interests of teachers.

Lastly, teachers recognize that their vigorous struggles for due process rights waged both in the courts and before the Tenure Commission have made the need for a comprehensive well documented teacher evaluation program an absolute necessity in every district. In the January, 1973 issue of the *Michigan School Board Journal* Arthur Rice, Jr., an Associate Executive Secretary for the Michigan Education Association, clearly affirmed this position: "Periodic evaluation of teachers in conformance with locally negotiated procedures is necessary."[2]

Though, as indicated above, no evaluation program can have much hope of real success unless teachers have significant input into designing the system, those in a leadership position need to have some concept of the type of system they would like to propose. Without wishing to oversimplify, one might say that there are only three basic types of evaluation formats: one that is essentially subjective in its data gathering method, one that is largely objective and one that seeks to use both subjective and objective data. Since education deals with people, not things, it is probably more accurate to say that there are only two basic approaches to the problem, one which represents a deliberate decision to rely on the thoughtful and experienced judgment of the evaluator and one which recognizes that no process so eminently human as education can ever be calibrated independent of human judgment but which seeks every device that emphasizes the gathering of data which stands independent of the attitudes, assumptions and feelings of both the teacher being evaluated and the evaluator.

The vast majority of evaluation systems that have been used in schools for the past generation have been essentially subjective. An examination of forms gathered from whatever source will show them to be characterized by evaluative criteria drawn from classroom atmosphere and appearance, teacher personality ("enthusiasm"), preferred methodologies ("individualization of instruction"), and peer and institutional relationships ("accepts responsibility for building improvement"). Evaluation forms in such a system are usually prepackaged and the evaluator is merely called on to render an Olympian judgement indicating the degree to which the teacher has achieved each designated characteristic — whether in "outstanding" or "satisfactory" fashion, or whether the teacher "needs improvement" or has been "unsatisfactory." In general, the teacher's only involvement in such a system is appropriate exultation over and effusive appreciation for a kindly judgment by the evaluator or anger or despair over the possibility of job termination that an "unsatisfactory" rating might forbode. Worst of all can be the frenzied uncertainty over what the evaluator is looking for caused by any rating in between the two extremes.

Teachers have long deprecated the whimsical nature of such systems, but since procedures were generally imposed only on probationary teachers and the teacher shortage prevented too many people from being hurt by them, teacher complaints were largely confined to the faculty room. It is hardly likely that teachers of great experience, now that evaluations will likely include tenured personnel, will willingly accept these subjective judgments, especially from evaluators who have spent less time in the classroom than the individual being judged or from evaluators who do not possess a background in the subject matter taught by the secondary teacher being scrutinized.

A system that minimizes the importance of the evaluator's perceptions, assumptions, and biases appears to have more usefulness for the years ahead. Such a system can differ in other important respects from the traditional methodology. It can emphasize gathering and analyzing data about student learning and teacher behavior which is verifiable by the teacher, the evaluator, or any third party (for example, the superintendent) who might be called on to intercede in the evaluation process. It also may be designed in such a way that the areas of teacher performance to be scrutinized can be mutually determined by both the teacher and the evaluator. In fact the Board of Education, and the community those people represent, can also have indirect but important input into decisions about what will be evaluated by setting district goals and objectives for each teacher to work on in the classroom.

The instrumentation for such a system can be nothing more complex than a blank piece of paper. For example, a column can be created within which the teacher and evaluator identify certain "task areas" that will be the objects of evaluation for the year. A set of four, five, or six problems enthusiastically and thoroughly worked on by the teacher will undoubtedly produce more real improvement than a laundry list of tasks which the teacher attempts to work on in scattergun fashion.

One useful way to create a list from which task areas might be identified would be, as Redfern has suggested,[3] to write a job description which would apply to teachers at all levels. Such a description would be broken down into the general categories of service rendered by teachers. For example, such a

1. George B. Redfern, *How to Evaluate Teaching: A Performance Objectives Approach,* School Management Institute, 1972.

2. Arthur Rice, Jr., "Tenure Strengthens Quality Teaching," *Michigan School Board Journal,* January, 1973, p. 16.

3. George B. Redfern, *op. cit.*

listing would include the following areas: instruction, teacher-student relationships, teacher-parent relationships, curriculum development, building improvement activities, and administrative responsibilities (e.g., record keeping).

In the next column on this blank sheet the teacher and evaluator can select one or two specific performance objectives to be achieved in the task areas selected. (We repeat and re-emphasize that it is *not* necessary to choose a performance objective from every task area within the whole range of responsibilities assigned to each teacher.) For example, the teacher and administrator might decide, through whatever information-gathering device available to them, that parents want more information about student progress in the teacher's class. The "task area" in need of improvement and therefore evaluation is in the broad category of parent-teacher relationships. The specific performance objective to be listed in the next column would be something that might read "improving parent understanding of pupil progress."

The third column on this blank sheet would then ask the teacher for a brief description of the "process" to be used in accomplishing this objective. This column is important because both the teacher and the evaluator will want to gather data which monitors the process to be sure it is working effectively. It would be foolhardy to determine important objectives and effective means to measure whether these objectives had been achieved only to discover that a year had been wasted because something went wrong with the process. For this example, the process selected might be to "send a folder of student papers home every other week, the folder to be signed by the parent."

The final column on this sheet of paper might be headed "Achievement Criteria." Here would be stated the results to be achieved. They should be stated in such a manner that both the teacher and the evaluator can conclude without argument whether or not the objectives had been met. Again a simple example may illustrate the point: The criteria selected by teacher and evaluator might be that "eighty percent (80%) of the parents will indicate through a survey sheet that the bi-weekly folder helped keep them better informed about the progress of their child."

It also becomes evident at this point that even a system as objective as this one has an important, perhaps crucial, subjective element. Teachers will not achieve all objectives. Ultimately someone will have to make a somewhat subjective judgment about whether the failure is attributable to the effectiveness of the process designated or the lack of skill of the teacher in implementing the process. Frequent and careful data gathering during the year should enable a supervisor to assist the teacher in finetuning the process being used. (It might be preferable if this supervisor were *not* the evaluator.) If this happens all should be able to agree whether a failure to achieve objectives is inherent in the methodology or in the teacher's performance. In any case problems should only arise if a decision is being made about job termination. In the vast majority of situations both the teacher and evaluator will have a common goal when objectives are not achieved, to try another way to reach the identified goal if it is truly an important one.

Another example in more graphic form might clearly illustrate the simplicity of the system:

Task Area	Performance Objective	Process	Achievement Criteria
Instruction	To individualize instruction in mathematics	1. Evaluate learning levels of CTBS scores, EPC diagnostic test and/or teacher made inventory 2. Organize class initially in two instructional groups 3. Move to individualized program	By March all children will be working in materials at their functional level

Will all teachers embrace an objectives-based system such as the one described? Not likely. Some will insist that their credential and experience are *de facto* evidence of competence. They will view any attempt to review their efforts as unwarranted interference. Happily, few teachers take such an uncooperative view. Most teachers, like everyone else, desire feedback about the quality of their work and this system provides ample opportunity to give teachers deserved praise.

Other teachers may question whether it is yet possible to define measurable objectives, particularly in the instructional area, for their most important goals since these goals involve changing attitudes and few reliable methods are available for measuring attitude change. Attitudes are based on information, however, real or presumed, and the acquisition of information can be measured.

Perhaps the single biggest hurdle to be overcome in implementing such a system is the general unfamiliarity most teachers and administrators have with such a system. In-service education, probably for administrators first and then administrators and teachers, is crucial, especially in developing skills for defining and writing good objectives.

Teacher evaluation will not lead us to educational Utopia. It likewise will not provide universally superior teaching. As Irving Kristol has pointed out, ". . .any scheme of education that needs excellent teachers to be successful is doomed at the outset. Excellence is always in short supply, and we have not the faintest idea how one goes about producing more of it. An institution — any institution: business corporation, post office, or school — survives and functions adequately when it is solidly based on routine competence. With that base secured, one may reasonably aspire to add a dash of excellence."[4]

It is to be expected however that a well considered and carefully implemented teacher evaluation program will enable a school system to raise a few notches its general level of competence.

4. Irving Kristol, "Lag Found in Tempo of Reform," New York *Times* Annual Education Supplement, January 8, 1963, p. 1.

Student Evaluation of Teachers

June E. Thompson

Systematic evaluation of teachers and counselors by high school students was virtually non-existent before the increase in student activism during the late Sixties. Because of student interest in participation in the evaluation of faculty performance, student groups throughout the country began formulating procedures through which they might assess the competence of their instructors.

Collegiate Models Unsatisfactory

Initial high school programs were modeled after those used on the college level. Unfortunately, such programs were often poorly designed, lacked validity, and evoked fear and resentment within faculties. The value of this approach was further limited by the lack of flexibility in course selection available in most high schools.

Confronted by staff resistance to the collegiate model of student evaluation, high school leaders have been challenged to develop programs which meet the unique needs of secondary schools. In general, they have found teachers and counselors receptive to projects which seek to provide helpful information to staff in a non-threatening manner. In a number of schools, faculties have enthusiastically endorsed programs in which individual data are returned only to the evaluatee and participation is voluntary.

When requested to participate in student evaluation programs, staff members often question the value and validity of this process. However, there is considerable support in the literature

NASSP BULLETIN, Oct. 1974, pp. 25-30.

for student assessment of professional performance. In an article published by Rammers in the 1930s, it was reported that reliable judgments of instructors' classroom traits could be obtained from both high school and college students.[1]

A report from the University of Michigan Committee on Student Evaluation of Courses stated that "students have a unique perspective from which any teacher can benefit, and often a perspective as valid as those applied by instructors and administrators."[2]

Further, it stated that a student is capable of evaluating his own classroom experience and that he can provide guidelines by which the teacher may be able to determine the relevance and usefulness of the subject matter, the reading material assigned and the classwork expected of him. "The results of a carefully conceived and administered student opinion program can help to provide some reliable basis for developing standards of good teaching."[3] Furthermore, the criteria by which students judge their teachers remain relatively stable. A teacher well rated five years ago will likely receive the same rating from students this year.[4]

In 1967, researchers at Colorado State's School of Education sought to determine if student sex, age, major, level of education, grade point average, or course grades previously received from an instructor had any bearing on student ratings of that individual. Findings were based on statistical analysis of data collected on 87 instructors from 4,285 student scales. It was concluded that student ratings of instructors were not substantially related to these items.[5]

Data from several high school studies have been analyzed by the author to determine if responses have been significantly affected by student characteristics, including: sex, year in school, grade point average, expected course grade, hours spent studying, and absenteeism. No significant relationship has been found between these items and student rating of faculty performance.

---

[1]Anal and Magoon Purchit, "The Validity of Student-Run Course Evaluations," University of Delaware, 1970, p. 3.

[2]"The University of Michigan Report of the Committee on Student Evaluation of Courses," Ann Arbor, 1968, p. 3.

[3]Ibid.

[4]Ibid.

[5]Nicholas F. Rayder, "College Ratings of Instructors," ERS Circular, 1970, p. 9.

Teacher and administrative support for the concept of student evaluation of staff is a vital element in developing a successful program. Student or adult leaders who wish to implement this process should review thoroughly the literature concerning the value and validity of assessment by students. Subsequently, they should present their findings to the faculty, propose general procedures to be used, and seek the staff's endorsement. Once the project has been sanctioned, a steering committee should be formed with representation from both students and faculty. This body should formulate specific objectives for the study, outline procedures, develop a timeline, and delineate individual responsibilities.

Suggested Procedures

The committee should address itself to key questions regarding the process to be used:

Should faculty members be asked to participate on a voluntary basis or should the administration be asked to mandate the evaluation?

Should personal results be released only to individual teachers and counselors or should results be published to facilitate student selection of teachers and counselors?

What student and teacher background factors should be studied in relation to student responses?

How many times a year and at what point(s) should the study be conducted?

Should departmental data be made available to administrators to provide a basis for identifying inservice training needs?

What computer facilities are available for processing data?

What programmer services can be secured?

What are the estimated costs of the study and how will it be financed?

Questionnaires used by other schools should be reviewed prior to selection of a tentative set of questions, and the preliminary draft should be submitted to the faculty for suggested revisions. It is advisable to select a class or classes in which the questionnaire can be pre-tested to determine whether any items are ambiguous or whether instructions are unclear.

If possible, space should be provided for individual teachers or departments to ask questions not applicable to the total faculty. These items can be read to students at the beginning of the survey and responses can be processed by the computer along with the standardized questions.

After final revisions have been made, the questionnaire should be re-submitted to the faculty with a form on which they may indicate their willingness to participate. It would be helpful for teachers to indicate which classes they wish to involve in the evaluation and the number of students enrolled in each, in order to facilitate preparation of packets.

It is advisable for the steering committee to arrange for computer and programmer services as early as possible. By reviewing the questionnaire, a programmer can often suggest changes in format which will expedite the processing of data.

Substantial efforts should be devoted to the orientation of the student body prior to the survey. Through school publications, displays, and announcements, the objectives and procedures of the study can be outlined. Students should be informed of the intended use of results and how to secure the data that will be made available to them. Teachers and counselors can also increase student receptivity to the project by discussing their personal desires for student feedback.

Packets of materials, including questionnaires, answer sheets, and instructions should be prepared in advance for each participating class, with extra packets available for those teachers who choose to become involved at the last minute. Each envelope should be labeled with the teacher's name, class period, and number of students. Code numbers assigned to the teacher, class, and department might also be written on the envelope to facilitate data processing.

It is suggested that packets of materials be hand delivered to staff members on the day they are scheduled to administer the survey. If possible the evaluation should be conducted over a period of several weeks to prevent "questionnaire fatigue" on the part of the student body.

Teachers should be cautioned against closely observing students while they are responding to the survey, and they should avoid handling completed questionnaires. Students within each class can be assigned responsibility for returning data to a central location before the end of each class period. To avoid misplacing responses, it is advisable for members of the steering committee to check off each envelope as it is returned and to seek missing materials immediately.

Format of Results

It is suggested that a program be written which will generate a question-by-question tally of student responses for each teacher and counselor. Staff members should receive a breakdown of the number and percentage of student responses in each category, i.e. *always, often, sometimes, seldom* and *never.* In addition, teachers should be able to compare the responses of each of their classes on every question.

Tables can be prepared for each teacher and counselor, enabling them to compare their own individual results on each question with those received by their department. Total faculty results broken down question-by-question may also be used by individuals as a basis for comparison.

It is also useful to generate a question-by-question analysis broken down by department and the total faculty. Such information can serve as a stimulus for discussion and change within departments and help identify focal points for future inservice programs.

Individual teacher and counselor data should be returned with a brief explanation of the format and suggestions for interpretation of results. In addition, it is helpful for members of the steering committee to designate a time and place at which they will be available to answer individual questions.

It is possible to determine the validity of the study by analyzing tables which relate student background factors such as year in school and grade-point-average to student responses. Other helpful information might be gained by relating selected teacher background characteristics to overall student responses.

Teachers and counselors should be encouraged to spend considerable time studying the survey results both individually and in their department meetings. Considerable attention should be given to the percentage of responses in the "does not apply" category.

Individuals and departments should study results to determine if student perceptions of irrelevant aspects of performance are consistent with faculty viewpoints. For instance, a large percentage of students may regard the question of teacher availability for conferences as not applicable to a given department, while members of that department see this as a significant responsibility.

Inconsistent perceptions held by students and staff of appropriate faculty roles may often be identified through the process of staff evaluation and provide the impetus for fruitful class discussion. The resulting communication between students and teachers may correct misconceptions held by both groups.

At the conclusion of the study, the steering committee should prepare a summary report of procedures used, problems experienced, and general conclusions. This analysis should be made available to all participants and used as a basis for the development of future evaluation programs.

While one of the primary objectives of student evaluation programs is to provide information to teachers and counselors that will help them improve their professional performance, data are not yet available to indicate to what degree this is being achieved in participating schools. The author is currently studying the results of several high school surveys to determine what changes, if any, are occurring in student ratings of faculty performance.

Conclusion

It seems reasonable to assume that increased awareness of weaknesses perceived by students will stimulate improvement in some areas by individual teachers and counselors. For instance, low ratings on being available for conferences or having a fair grading policy may be the result of poor communication and may increase significantly once students are better informed.

However, in other aspects of performance, faculty members may need professional help to achieve desired improvement. To meet such needs, inservice education programs should be cooperatively developed by teachers, counselors, and administrators.

Improvement of professional performance can best be achieved in a non-threatening atmosphere in which faculty members work with administrators to assess objectively their strengths and weaknesses. The evaluation of staff by students should be recognized as providing a unique and vital perspective of faculty performance. It should be studied along with assessments made by colleagues and administrators in an effort to improve the instructional programs of all secondary schools.

Evaluation of Administrative Performance By a School's Teaching Staff

William L. Gaslin

A principal is responsible for his school's programs, it is true, but his effectiveness is inextricably bound to, and influenced by, the effectiveness of his assistant principals. The evaluation model proposed in this article, therefore, is a scheme for the evaluation of the principal and his assistants as an administrative team.

Formative and Summative Evaluations

The model is predicated on two defensible premises: 1) The evaluation of any school principal and/or administrative team is of most value to those being evaluated when it is *formative* rather than *summative* in design. An evaluation is called *formative* if it is designed to simply provide data to decision makers to aid in improving programs or performance. *Summative* evaluation refers to using data to judge the success or failure of a program or performance. Dissemination of evaluation results in a formative design is usually restricted to the individuals most closely affected by the particular program under consideration. Summative evalua-

NASSP BULLETIN, Dec. 1974, pp. 74-81.

tion results are usually disseminated to a much wider audience. 2) The most effective formative evaluation results a high school principal and/or administrative team can receive come from the teaching staff.

The first premise ensures that the major goal of any evaluation of administrative performance must be to improve that performance in the variety of roles which members of the administrative team might play in instructional leadership and building management. The second premise assumes that any evaluation of an individual or a group's performance must be done by those most affected by any decisions made or leadership exerted.

Why should an administrative team allow staff evaluation of its performance? First, any attempt to measure staff perceptions of administrative performance provides the administrative team with readings on staff feelings and, if the evaluation is conducted repeatedly, how these feelings change over time. Second, by submitting to an evaluation by the teaching staff, the administrative team establishes credibility with the teachers, public, and superiors within the district administrative hierarchy. It is a demonstration of confidence by members of the administrative team in their own ability as instructional leaders and/or building managers. Third, if the evaluation is well-conceived, thoughtfully conducted, and conscientiously accepted it should result in improvement of administrative performance. Depending on specific situations, the evaluation can also provide those being evaluated with specific information on staff expectations of the administration.

What are some of the areas with which the evaluation should be concerned? Probably the most important area is teachers' perceptions of the quality of their relationships with the principal and other members of the administrative team. This includes measurement of the level of trust the teachers hold toward members of the administrative team and their perceptions of each administrator's openness, ability as a leader, and general effectiveness in a wide variety of situations.

A second goal of the evaluation of administrative performance is to measure teacher perceptions of the extent and quality of the administrators' contact with students. Since teachers are in a strategic position to judge how administrative actions are received by children, their perceptions can provide useful information. Much information regarding students' feelings about school-related issues is "overheard in the halls" by teachers.

177

A third consideration in the staff evaluation of administrative performance is the area of interpersonal relationships and mutual support among members of the administrative team. Do the teachers perceive the principal as leader of the team? Do the members of the team complement each others' strengths and weaknesses? How does the principal relate to his assistants? How does he work with department heads or lead teachers? Are divergent philosophies allowed among team members or do the principal and his assistants think alike on most major issues?

A fourth area for formative evaluation is the role of the principal as the instructional leader of the school. (Depending on the particular orientation of the assistant principals, they may also be evaluated in terms of roles in instructional leadership.) Do the teachers have confidence in the principal as instructional leader? To what extent do teachers feel the principal and/or assistant princpals influence curricular design? To what extent do the teachers feel they have input into curricular decisions?

The evaluation must provide data on teacher perceptions of the principal and/or administrative team in the area of building management. Are teachers satisfied with administrative performance with respect to encouraging and maintaining positive student behavior, mechanical procedures of attendance reporting and recordkeeping, enforcing school rules and regulations, ensuring that maintenance occurs when needed, and providing for the general aesthetic appeal of the school plant?

This list of components of the formative evaluation of the administrative team by a school's teaching staff is not exhaustive; it is not intended to be exhaustive. Strictly local concerns would undoubtedly call for addition or deletion of categories. Moreover, certain aspects of administrative performance are not obvious or important to teachers and should be evaluated by the school district's administrative hierarchy above the building level. This would include such activities as filing reports, fulfilling the requests of superiors, and adhering to school board regulations.

Who conducts the evaluation? To make the formative evaluation of administrative performance as objective as possible, it should, if feasible and practical, be conducted by a third party directly connected to neither the teaching staff nor the administration. Honest data collection and objective reporting of results are crucial to the endeavor. The evaluation can be used for no purpose other than the improvement of administrative performance. A formative evaluation must never be used as a threat, intimidation, or recrimination.

Who might be the impartial third party? Several possibilities exist, depending on the size of the school system and the particular evaluation model selected. If the school district has a research and evaluation department, an impartial evaluator is probably available. An administrator or lead teacher (or both) from a neighboring school are possible candidates. If sufficient funds are available, an outside evaluator could be hired for the singular purpose of conducting the evaluation of administration performance. An important consideration must be made: The evaluation must be conducted by an agency (or individual) with no *a priori* conceptions of the performance of the administrative team, no motive other than designing the evaluation to present the most accurate picture of faculty feelings possible.

Who should be the audience (consumers) of the evaluation results? The principal and his administrative team are the primary consumers of the results of the evaluation. Any dissemination of the evaluation report should be done only with the consent of the team. The evaluation report should probably not be circulated to the general public because of the nature of formative evaluation and the misconceptions that can result when reported information is taken out of context. Release of such an evaluation report gives the process an aura of being summative, which it is not. Formative evaluation results, by definition, are intended for improvement of existing structures (programs, individual practices or performance of tasks) and nothing else.

A distinct advantage of formative evaluation over summative evaluation is that the former allows for great objectivity with no threats implied toward those being evaluated.

First Step Is the Request

The initial step in the formative evaluation of a school administrative team is the request by the team for the evaluation to take place. Almost certainly, the request should come from those being evaluated—the members of the administrative team. An evaluation cannot by definition be formative without the consent of the evaluated. Thus, unless the evaluation is conducted with the endorsement of the administrative team, its credibility, success, and overall impact cannot be maximized. Without this endorsement those who would implement any changes which the evaluation suggests could resist to the point of rendering the results useless.

Prior to beginning the process of designing the evaluation of administrative performance, a complete plan for use of the results must be detailed. This process serves the following purposes:

1) It helps establish the credibility of the evaluation effort and the legitimacy of the request.

2) It allows determination of a timetable for completing the evaluation process.

3) It helps ensure that the evaluation report will do more than merely gather dust on several office shelves.

This is a crucial inclusion in an evaluation plan and must be completed at the time the decision is made to conduct the evaluation and before any further activities are contemplated.

Needs-Assessment/Category-Definition

After the decision has been made to conduct a formative evaluation of a school administration, the next step involves both teachers and members of the administrative team meeting separately with the evaluator to determine which specific aspects of administrative performance are to be examined. The following considerations are made in arriving at the definition of categories:

1) Are there any particular well-known needs of the school which are results of administrative performance?

2) Is the evaluation to be comprehensive?

3) What categories are of primary interest to the administrative team?

4) Are there particular categories of administrative performance which show special need of evaluation?

5) Are there special points of emphasis suggested by expert thinking on the important aspects of administrative performance?

There is no objection to including as categories for evaluation certain areas which may be of interest to teachers but not to administrators. Similarly, areas of interest to administrators may be examined even if those areas do not seem important to teachers. One crucial consideration must be taken into account when designing the evaluation: No category of administrative performance must be included which threatens the acceptance of the final results by the administrative team. This consideration will undoubtedly influence the thrust of the evaluation and could result in the collection of more or less data than either the administrative team or the teachers desire. However, such a consideration

180

will ensure that the final formative evaluation report will have legitimacy with respect to the administrative team.

As the evaluation is defined, its categories must also be considered in light of the needs of the organization. The important consideration is the following: What are the glaring organizational deficiencies? What specific changes in administrative behavior might help minimize these deficiencies?

Constructing the Instrument

Whether the evaluation is to be conducted by questionnaire, personal interview or some other means, the instrumentation must be constructed with utmost care and cognizance of the school situation. The instrument must allow for ease of administering and it must be of sufficient length to adequately cover the categories previously agreed upon. It must also be short enough so as not to be revulsive to the respondent.

The following are some components of the useful and practical evaluation instrument:

1) Adequate coverage of commonly accepted desirable administrative practices such as leadership, use of authority, and problem-solving.

2) The questionnaire must not reflect biases of the evaluator, members of the administrative team or teachers.

3) The items should reflect the needs of the organization.

4) Items must be clearly stated to remove any ambiguity in interpretation.

5) The items should yield results which are easily interpretable in reporting the study.

6) The instrument must be valid and reliable.

7) The instrument must not militate against the principle of confidentiality or responses by individual teachers.

The completed instrument must be approved by both teachers and administrators with respect to content and wording of items. Modifications will almost certainly be suggested by both groups. The evaluator must produce a final instrument compatible with the needs of the primary evaluators (teachers) and those being evaluated (administrative team). This is an arduous task, at best. Several drafts of the instrument will undoubtedly be constructed, each successive one modified according to reactions of the teachers and administrative team.

STAFF EVALUATION OF ADMINISTRATIVE PERFORMANCE

The administrative team (principal and assistant principal) of this school has requested that its performance be evaluated by the teaching staff. The results of this evaluation will be presented to the administrative team via oral and written reports by the evaluator. All individual staff members' questionnaires will remain anonymous. Please answer *all* questions.

Part I. **Background Questions:** Circle the appropriate response.

1. How many years have you taught at this school?   1   2-3   4-10   more than 10

2. At what grade level do you do the majority of your teaching?   7-8   9-12   even split

3. Have you ever been a department chairperson or faculty council member at this school?   yes   no

4. Rate the present state of faculty morale at this school.   low   average   high

DIRECTIONS: (Parts II-VI) For each of the following statements, circle the response which most accurately describes your feelings about the school administrative team.

> "1" means "strongly agree"
> "2" means "agree"
> "3" means "neutral"
> "4" means "disagree"
> "5" means "strongly disagree"
> "6" means "no opinion"

Part II. **Administration and Teachers**

5. The administrators play favorites with some teachers.	1	2	3	4	5	6
6. Teachers usually know where they stand with the members of the administrative team.	1	2	3	4	5	6
7. The administration is generally aware of faculty problems.	1	2	3	4	5	6
8. My opinion on important school matters is seldom sought by the school administration.	1	2	3	4	5	6
9. Faculty members have little input to matters of use of the school budget.	1	2	3	4	5	6
10. The administration is unable to objectively evaluate teaching styles different from their own.	1	2	3	4	5	6
11. The administration is out to get me.	1	2	3	4	5	6
12. The administration usually considers staff feelings when making program decisions affecting staff.	1	2	3	4	5	6
13. The administration is not direct in dealing with staff requests.	1	2	3	4	5	6
14. The administrative team usually stands by teachers in personnel matters such as personal leave, seniority questions, etc.	1	2	3	4	5	6
15. Teachers have little input to school staffing decisions.	1	2	3	4	5	6
16. The administration actively promotes high faculty morale.	1	2	3	4	5	6
17. The members of the administrative team are willing to "counsel" a staff member when the staff member's performance suggests that such an action be taken.	1	2	3	4	5	6
18. The administration is actively involved in seeing that good teaching takes place at this school.	1	2	3	4	5	6
19. The administration implements important changes in the school without consulting the faculty.	1	2	3	4	5	6
20. The current administrative team is capable of evaluating my success as a teacher.	1	2	3	4	5	6
21. I am comfortable conferring with the assistant principal working with my grade level.	1	2	3	4	5	6
22. The administration openly recognizes successful performance of staff members.	1	2	3	4	5	6
23. The administrative team does not effectively communicate school policy to teachers.	1	2	3	4	5	6
24. The members of the administrative team are accessible to all teachers.	1	2	3	4	5	6
25. The administrative team supports staff members in dealings with the public.	1	2	3	4	5	6
26. The administration generally mistrusts staff members' motivations.	1	2	3	4	5	6
27. I don't feel at ease when talking with members of the administrative team.	1	2	3	4	5	6
28. The administrative team encourages teacher independence.	1	2	3	4	5	6

Part III. **Administration and Students**

29. Students do not respect the school administration.   1   2   3   4   5   6
30. The administrative team has good contact with students.   1   2   3   4   5   6
31. The administrative team deals fairly with student problems.   1   2   3   4   5   6
32. The current administration does little to create a comfortable atmosphere for students.   1   2   3   4   5   6
33. The administrative team deals effectively with student discipline problems.   1   2   3   4   5   6
34. The administrative team actively involves itself in promoting satisfactory progress of students in classes.   1   2   3   4   5   6
35. The administration effectively communicates school policy to students.   1   2   3   4   5   6
36. The administrative team has done a poor job of improving student attendance.   1   2   3   4   5   6

Part IV. **Administration and Parents**

37. The administrative team seems to want to work with advisory groups. (Faculty council, PTA, department chairmen, etc.)   1   2   3   4   5   6
38. Parents generally support the school administration.   1   2   3   4   5   6
39. More effort should be made to gain parental input into running the school.   1   2   3   4   5   6

Part V. **Administration as a Team**

40. The administrators generally share a common philosophy of how a school should be operated.   1   2   3   4   5   6
41. I feel that the school has a weak administrative team.   1   2   3   4   5   6
42. The members of the administrative team have good rapport amongst themselves.   1   2   3   4   5   6
43. The administrators do not seem to support each other as individuals.   1   2   3   4   5   6

Part VI. **Administration and Running the School**

44. I am generally satisfied with the job the school administration is doing.   1   2   3   4   5   6
45. This school is run efficiently.   1   2   3   4   5   6
46. The teacher/administrator report lines have enhanced communication between faculty and administration.   1   2   3   4   5   6
47. The administrative team is interested in promoting the autonomy of individual departments.   1   2   3   4   5   6
48. The administrators retain their composure under pressure.   1   2   3   4   5   6
49. I usually trust the judgment of members of the administrative team.   1   2   3   4   5   6
50. The administrators are able to react well in crisis situations.   1   2   3   4   5   6
51. The administration seldom assumes a leadership role in curriculum and program development.   1   2   3   4   5   6
52. My department has been treated unfairly by the school administration in recent staffing decisions.   1   2   3   4   5   6
53. The administrative team actively works to improve racial relations at this school.   1   2   3   4   5   6
54. The administrative team has not improved communication at this school.   1   2   3   4   5   6

Part VII. **General**

55. Discuss any strengths or weaknesses of the administration which you feel are important.

56. In your opinion, what single change in the actions of the administrative team would make your feelings as a staff member more positive.

57. Make any comments about the administrative team which you feel are germane to this evaluation.

The final instrument should include open-ended items that allow respondents to verbalize concerns which might not have been allowed in a strictly forced-choice format. Such items might include the following:

1) What are the most prominent strengths of the administrative team?
2) What are the most prominent weaknesses of the administrative team?
3) What single change in administrative behavior would most enhance your feelings as a staff member?
4) Make any comments about the administrative team which you feel are germane to this evaluation.

Without commenting at length on advantages or disadvantages of certain kinds of instrumentation with varying types of responses required, it can be said that to avoid most ambiguity and allow for the greatest ease of responding, the forced-choice format minimizes the problems. A useful-item format is to have the respondent react to certain statements about administrative performance. The following two examples illustrate the format:

• Faculty members have little input into school staffing decisions.

Strongly Agree   Agree   Neutral   Disagree   Strongly Disagree   No Opinion

• I trust the judgment of the principal.

Strongly Agree   Agree   Neutral   Disagree   Strongly Disagree   No Opinion

The respondent selects one of the six choices. Of course, the respondent has a seventh choice in no-response.

Reporting the Results of the Evaluation

Although constructing the instrument is a negotiation process requiring some diplomatic behavior on the part of the evaluator, no task in the process of formative evaluation is more delicate than the reporting of the results. The compiler/writer/reporter must consider the following:

1) All individual responses must be confidential.
2) The report must be clearly and concisely written with only trends substantiated by data included in the discussions. The evaluator must resist the temptation to generalize from isolated bits of data representing strictly isolated and/or minority viewpoints.
3) The report must not reflect biases of the evaluator.
4) The report must be based solely on data obtained through the evaluation and not on other extraneous information.
5) The report must be presented to the administrative team prior to distribution to any other group.

The important point to consider in writing the evaluation report is the following: Does the report accurately reflect faculty sentiment in relation to the pre-determined categories of the evaluation?

The formative evaluation of an administrative team places primary responsibility for implementation of suggested changes on the administrative team. It would be a rare evaluation which did not suggest changes in administrative behavior. But the needed changes must be supported by hard data and must be endorsed by the administrative team. Extensive discussions by administrative team members must follow reporting of results. The critical point is that no matter how well designed or accurately reported an evaluation happens to be, it will produce no noticeable effect on the organization unless there is a sincere willingness on the part of the administrative team to study the results and make appropriate changes.

Advantages and Disadvantages

What are the major disadvantages of the proposed model? Its weaknesses include the following:

1) The design of the evaluation is a slow process requiring much time of teachers and administrators.
2) Forced-choice questionnaires force respondents to react to only certain stimuli in a prescribed manner.
3) The model outlined in this paper attempts to evaluate a "team" and places little emphasis on individual performance. It is difficult to ascertain whether a respondent was reacting to individuals or to the team.

What are the major advantages of the proposed model? The strengths include the following:

1) The evaluation will be objective since it is conducted by a neutral individual.
2) The evaluation instrument is situation specific. That is, it reflects organizational needs at a given point in time.
3) The model has prior acceptance by all parties concerned with its outcomes.
4) The model is minimally threatening to those being evaluated.
5) The model will not reflect on individuals, but on overall performance of the administrative team.
6) Use of the results are planned before the evaluation is conducted. This fact goes far in ensuring that appropriate action will be taken to implement behavioral changes suggested by the evaluation.

The question of teacher evaluation in negotiations

By MYRON LIEBERMAN

Teacher evaluation is one of the most troublesome issues in collective negotiations. Understandably, teacher organizations are constantly seeking to expand contractual protections for teachers. At the same time, administrators and supervisors are becoming more concerned about their eroding authority to discipline or discharge teachers, and such authority is often related to teacher evaluation. If teacher evaluations do not meet all of the contractual obligations of the administration, the administration's authority to take action against a teacher may be successfully challenged.

A recent Michigan arbitration case dramatically illustrates these points. The case involved a probationary teacher who was not rehired after three negative evaluations. The collective agreement in effect at the time included the following clauses:

"Prior to March 15 of each year, the Principal shall submit a recommendation to the Superintendent regarding the employment of all teachers. Should this recommendation include dismissal or additional probationary status it shall state fully and completely the reasons therefor and a copy shall be sent to the teacher. The teacher may submit a counter report in writing to the Superintendent within five days if he chooses to do so." Article XV, Section E.

"No teacher shall be disciplined, reprimanded, reduced in basic salary schedule or deprived of any professional advantage without just cause. Any such discipline, reprimand, or adverse evaluation of teacher performance asserted by the Board or any representative thereof resulting in reduction in rank and/or compensation, shall be subject to the grievance procedure hereinafter set forth . . . All information forming the basis for the disciplinary action will be made available to the teacher." Article XVI, Section E.

The teacher, whom we shall designate Miss B, was first evaluated in November and then in January by her principal. The evaluations, although negative, were specific and included recommendations for improvement. The third evaluation was conducted on March 10 and was followed by a conference on March 12 between Miss B and the principal. During the conference, Miss B learned that the principal would not recommend her reemployment. She did not receive a written copy of the evaluation until the afternoon of that day and did not sign it.

On the same day, March 12, the principal sent the superintendent a long detailed memorandum explaining his recommendation that Miss B not be rehired. On March 25, ten days after the date required by the contract, Miss B received a letter from the board, informing her that the board had voted unanimously not to offer her a contract for 1971-72. The letter quoted the principal's memorandum verbatim to explain the reasons for this decision. In other words, Miss B saw the principal's evaluation and his adverse recommendation prior to March 15 but did not see the board's detailed memorandum justifying her nonrenewal until March 25. This memorandum included some points covered by the three evaluations prior to March 15 and others not discussed or implicit in the principal's evaluations.

It should also be noted that Miss B prepared a report on March 17, attempting to rebut each of the three evaluation reports prior to March 15. Miss B also stated at this time, "I must receive a list of specified reasons for the recommendation that I no longer be employed . . . When this list is forthcoming, I shall sub-

SCHOOL MANAGEMENT, Apr. 1972, pp. 15-16.

mit a rebuttal of those specific reasons."

To summarize, Miss B did not receive a copy of the board's reasons until after the board had acted upon the principal's recommendations. The teacher did have an opportunity to respond to the principal's evaluations, but the principal's recommendations to the board included some items and inferences which were not on the evaluation forms. Since these recommendations were relied upon by the board, and the board acted upon them prior to deciding against renewing the contract, the teacher filed a grievance.

Claims and counterclaims

In its argument, the board contended that a refusal to reemploy a probationary teacher should not be construed as a disciplinary action or deprivation of professional advantage. The arbitrator cited a number of cases to show that this issue had divided courts and arbitrators, but as a matter of law and policy, he supported the view that refusal to rehire constituted a deprivation of "professional advantage." In other words, you can't refuse to rehire a probationary teacher and then claim he hasn't lost any professional advantage. Since Article XVI, Section E, specified that the board could not deprive a teacher of any "professional advantage without just cause," the board had to show just cause.

The gut issue in the case, therefore, was whether the board had complied with the contractual requirements concerning notice to the teacher. The arbitrator ruled that this had not been done. True, the teacher knew about the negative evaluations by the principal, but these did not meet the contractual requirements. The teacher was entitled to know the board's reasons prior to the time the board took action on them. Otherwise, the teacher would be denied her contractual rights to rebut the reasons while the matter was still open. The arbitrator gave little weight to the possibility that the teacher would have a fair opportunity to rebut the reasons after the board had refused to rehire; at this stage, the board would

have developed a vested interest in upholding its prior negative judgement, hence its objectivity was suspect. For this reason, the arbitrator ordered reemployment of Miss B with back pay as a result of the board's refusal to reemploy her.

What the decision means

There are several significant points about this case. One is that the arbitrator did not challenge the competence of the principal's evaluations. The problem was due to the fact that the board's reasons, which must be distinguished from the principal's, were not communicated to the teacher by the contractual deadline. Although based upon the principal's memorandum to the superintendent, the board's reasons differed in some important respects from the reasons communicated to the teacher by the principal prior to March 15.

What if the principal's recommendation to the superintendent about Miss B had relied upon precisely the same points he had made to Miss B prior to March 15? In other words, suppose the board had given as its reasons the evaluation report made available to Miss B prior to March 15, instead of a separate memorandum which Miss B did not see until after March 15. The arbitrator would probably have upheld the grievance, although it would have been a closer case. Unless and until the board adopts a set of reasons recommended by a subordinate, the reasons remain those of the subordinate, not the board. Realistically, a teacher might adopt a very different approach with the board than with the subordinate of the board, even though both are citing the same reasons. For example, an effort to discredit a reason cited by the board might involve data concerning the principal which would be omitted from efforts to discredit the same evaluation at the principal's level.

The practical implications of the case under discussion seem to be clear. Administrators must make sure that the substance of their observations and evaluations will support the recommendations they make. Secondly, they must scrupulously observe the procedural requirements spelled out in the collective agreement before taking action adverse to teachers. Thirdly, boards must recognize that the reasons for a personnel action recommended by a subordinate are not those of the board unless and until the board officially adopts them. Such adoption, however, cannot be used to deprive teachers of their rights to know the board's reasons by a specified date. Of course, the board might have avoided the problem altogether by different contract language, but any language on the issue is likely to be interpreted very rigorously by arbitrators.

In the instant case, the failure to fulfill the procedural requirement was the fatal weakness in the administration's position. To avoid such setbacks, administrators should systematically review teacher evaluations with the principals and supervisors. Such review should aim at ensuring that evaluations are comprehensive and are completed in time to fulfill all contractual deadlines. Fulfilling both the substantive and procedural requirements pertaining to teacher evaluation is an essential ingredient of effective contract administration.

INTERACTION ANALYSIS AND INSERVICE TRAINING

Ned A. Flanders

WHAT IS INTERACTION ANALYSIS?

INTERACTION analysis is a system for observing and coding the verbal interchange between a teacher and his pupils. The assumption is made that teaching behavior and pupil responses are expressed primarily through the spoken word as a series of verbal events which occur one after another. These events are identified, coded so as to preserve sequence, and tabulated systematically in order to represent a sample of the spontaneous teacher influence.

The most important criterion which any coding system must meet before it can be considered satisfactory is that a trained person can decode the data in order to reconstruct those aspects of the original behavior which were encoded, even though he was not present at the observation. A part of this article will describe inferences which can be made from a blind analysis of coded data.

Interaction analysis has been used to study spontaneous teaching behavior and it has also been used in projects which attempt to help teachers modify their behavior. In the first instance there may be a long period of time between observations and the analysis of the data. The data can be punched on IBM cards as they are collected over a period of several months, but a computer program to tabulate and analyze the data may be used only after all the observations have been completed. On the other hand, when interaction analysis data are collected in order to provide a teacher with information about his own behavior as a part of preservice or inservice training, then it may be advantageous to code directly into a desired tabulation form so that interpretations can be made at the earliest moment after the teaching episode is completed. This article will be more concerned with the procedures of interaction analysis which can be used during preservice and inservice training, and less concerned with applications in more basic research projects.

JOURNAL OF EXPERIMENTAL EDUCATION,

Fall, 1968, pp. 126-133.

A possible goal of an inservice training program might be to discover whether the spontaneous patterns of verbal communication which are observed are, or are not, consistent with the intentions of the teacher. In such a program, the assumption is made that modifying behavior in order to make it more consistent with intent will, in most instances, result in an improvement. The model toward which behavior is modified is created by the teacher attempting to change.

An inservice training program can also be designed in which all participating teachers attempt to make similar modifications, for example, developing more skill in making full use of the ideas which are expressed by pupils during classroom discourse. Here the model could be justified from the results of research which made use of interaction analysis, but special care would be necessary in designing activities which would help teachers accept and understand the desirability of such modifications. In brief, the value orientation would be that the quality of classroom instruction is improved when the ideas expressed by pupils are more adequately recognized, clarified, used in some step of a logical analysis, thus giving the pupils a more active part in the learning activities.

In nearly all applications of interaction analysis it is desirable to collect other kinds of data such as pupil attitudes, pupil achievement, and perceptions of the teaching situation held by the teacher and the pupils. These additional data permit the development of theory and explanation.

The resources of such a program, as with all inservice activities, require money in order to obtain time, space, and assistance for those who are participating. A number of steps can be anticipated: (a) Prospective observers and participating teachers must be trained to use the technique. This usually requires 6 to 12 hours under the direction of a qualified observer. (b) Personal, self-development goals must be clarified by the participating teachers. (c) Each teacher-observer team must set up comparison situations involving a planned change of behavior and two or more observations should be scheduled so that evidence of change can be assessed. (d) Plans to collect other types of information must be completed. (e) Social-skill training sessions, based on interaction analysis categories, are often helpful, especially when they are incorporated in the observation training. Such training often helps teachers set personal goals for changing their behavior. (f) Plans will be necessary to provide incentives for teachers and to maintain the momentum of the program, once it is started. (g) Care must be taken to insure freedom from threat, to make sure that the voluntary aspects of participation are genuine, and to avoid superimposing the program as an excessive demand on teachers who may already be too busy.

OBSERVATION PROCEDURES AND
MATRIX INTERPRETATION

Given ten categories, shown in Table 1, all verbal statements are classified at least once every 3 seconds by a trained observer. The events are coded by using the arabic numbers from one to ten which are written down in such a way as to preserve the original sequence. The data can then be tabulated in a table of ten rows and ten columns which is called a matrix.

Such a series is entered into a matrix two at a time. The first number of each pair indicates the row of the matrix, the second the column. The first pair consists of the first two numbers. The second pair consists of the second and third numbers, and thus overlaps the first pair. All tallies enter the matrix as a series of overlapping pairs.

With one tally approximately every 3 seconds, there are one hundred tallies for 5 minutes, 1,200 tallies per hour; therefore, 20 minutes, or about four hundred tallies, provide a matrix with sufficient data for a number of inferences about verbal communication.

In a sustained observation of a teacher covering six to eight 1-hour visits, it is necessary to tabulate separate matrices for different types of classroom activities. Each matrix should represent either a single episode of class activity or any number of homogeneous episodes that are combined. We use five activity categories for junior high school academic subjects; they are: routine procedures, discussion of new material, discussion to evaluate student performance or products of learning, general discussion, and the supervision of seatwork or group activities. Different activity categories may be useful for a self-contained elementary-school classroom. In any case, the purpose of tabulating the data in several different matrices, instead of in just one total matrix, is determined by the purposes of observation and the range of expected classroom activities.

In the case of the inservice training of teachers, data are tabulated into separate matrices in such a way as not to mask the comparison to be made. To illustrate, suppose the comparison is between two samples of teaching behavior, one before and one after several weeks of social skill training. Keeping the data in homogeneous activity matrices will help to avoid false conclusions. For example, a decrease, increase, or no change in certain categories, when the two matrices are compared, may be due to the differences in the learning activities observed, rather than due to change in teaching behavior which resulted from inservice training. Grouping the data to. represent homogeneous learning activities helps to avoid such confusion.

TABLE 1   CATEGORIES OF INTERACTION ANALYSIS

Teacher Talk and Student Talk

TEACHER TALK

Response

1. * Accepts feeling: accepts and clarifies the feeling tone of the students in a non-threatening manner. Feelings may be positive or negative. Predicting or recalling feelings are included.

2. * Praises or encourages: praises or encourages student action or behavior. Jokes that release tension, but at the expense of another individual; nodding head, or saying "um hm?" or "go on" are included.

3. * Accepts or uses ideas of students: clarifying, building, or developing ideas suggested by a student. As teacher brings more of his own ideas into play, shift to category five.

4. * Asks questions: asking a question about content or procedure with the intent that a student answer.

Initiation

5. * Lecturing: giving facts or opinions about content or procedures; expressing his own ideas, asking rhetorical questions.

6. * Giving directions: directions, commands, or orders to which a student is expected to comply.

7. * Criticizing or justifying authority: statements intended to change student behavior from non-acceptable to acceptable pattern; bawling someone out; stating why the teacher is doing what he is doing; extreme self-reference.

STUDENT TALK

Response

8. * Student talk — response: talk by students in response to teacher. Teacher initiates the contact or solicits student statement.

Initiation

9. * Student talk — initiation: talk by students which they initiate. If "calling on" student is only to indicate who may talk next, observer must decide whether student wanted to talk. If he did, use this category.

10. * Silence or confusion: pauses, short periods of silence and periods of confusion in which communication cannot be understood by the observer.

---

*There is NO scale implied by these numbers. Each number is classificatory; it designates a particular kind of communication event. To write these numbers down during observation is to enumerate, not to judge a position on a scale.

A tabulated matrix divides into special areas for interpretations that are shown in Table 2. Particular questions can be answered by comparing tallies within and between these areas. Here are some examples.

Areas A (1+2+3+4), B(5+6+7), C(8+9), and D(10) can be used to find the percent time the teacher talks, the pupils talk, and time spent in pauses, silence, and confusion. Comparisons between Areas A and B provide information about the relative balance between initiating and responding within teacher talk. Initiating teacher talk is more directive, tends to support the use of teacher authority, and restricts pupil participation. Responsive teacher talk is more indirect, tends to share authority, and expands pupil participation.

Area E is a block of nine cells that indicates the continued use of acceptance and praise, constructive reaction to pupil feeling, and clarifying, accepting, and developing pupil ideas, as well as transitions among these three categories while the teacher is talking. In any inservice training program devoted to increasing the teacher's attention to ideas expressed by pupils, before and after comparisons would require an analysis of these nine cells. In fact, an inservice training program which attempted to teach more subtle differences in the teacher's reaction to pupil ideas might require subdividing Category 3 in order to note the presence and absence of various types of Category 3 statements. For example, 3-1 -- merely repeats to show that the pupil ideas were heard; 3-2 -- reacts to specific pupil ideas, but only in terms of the teacher's perceptions of these ideas; 3-3 -- reacts to specific pupil ideas, but reactions incorporate the perceptions of one or more pupils; and 3-4 -- stimulate a reaction to a pupil's ideas by asking questions so that other pupils react. In effect, Category 3 is expanded into four categories for a special purpose. This would result in a 13 x 13 matrix instead of a 10 x 10 matrix.

Area F is a block of four cells that indicates the continued use of directions and criticism and transitions between these two categories. The two transition cells are particularly reliable indicators of discipline problems. Shifting from directions to criticism is tallied in the 6-7 cell, and indicates that expected compliance is judged unsatisfactory by the teacher. Shifting from criticism back to directions, the 7-6 cell, indicates a return to more directions after criticism.

Areas G_1 and G_2 are particularly interesting because they isolate the immediate response of the teacher at the moment students stop talking. One aspect of teacher flexibility can be discovered by comparing the balance of indirect and direct statements shown in G_1 and G_2 with those found in Areas

193

TABLE 2

AREAS OF MATRIX ANALYSIS

CATEGORY	CLASSIFICATION	CATE-GORY	1	2	3	4	5	6	7	8	9	10	TOTAL
ACCEPTS FEELING	RESPONSE	1			Area E								
PRAISE	RESPONSE	2											
STUDENT IDEA	RESPONSE	3											
ASKS QUESTIONS		4				"Content Cross"			Area F		Area H		
LECTURES	INITIATION	5											
GIVES DIRECTIONS	INITIATION	6											
CRITICISM		7											
STUDENT RESPONSE		8			Area G₁			Area G₂		Area I			
STUDENT INITIATION		9											
SILENCE		10											
Total			Area A			?(s)		Area B		Area C		Area D	
			Response					Initiation		Student Talk		Si-lence	

194

A and B. The difference between superficial, short, perfunctory praise or clarification, and praise or clarification that is more carefully developed is easily seen by comparing the tallies in Area G_1 with those in E, particularly the 2-2 and 3-3 cells.

Area H indicates the types of teacher statements that trigger student participation. Responses to the teacher are found in column 8; statements initiated by the student in column 9. As one might expect, there is usually a heavy loading of tallies in the 4-8 cell. High frequencies in this cell and the 8-4 cell, but not in the 8-8 cell, often indicate rapid drill.

Area I indicates sustained student participation. These may be lengthy statements by a few students, or student-to student communication.

So-called "steady state" cells fall on the diagonal from cell 1-1 to 10-10. Tallies here indicate that the speaker persists in a particular communication category for longer than 3 seconds. All other cells are transition cells moving from one category to another.

Outlined in the center of Table 2 by dash lines is the content cross. The total number of tallies in this area, compared with tallies not in this area, gives a very crude indication of the content orientation of the class activity.

In addition to making use of the areas just described, the following procedure can be followed to interpret a matrix.

First, locate the single cell within the ten rows and columns which has the highest frequency. The pair of events, represented by the cell, is the most frequently occurring and can be used as a starting point in reconstructing the interaction.

Second, from this highest frequency cell, you start forward or backward, in terms of sequence, to begin a sequence diagram. The row of any cell indicates the most likely third event, that is, the event which is most likely to follow, given an original pair of events designed by the highest frequency cell. The column, on the other hand, indicates which event most probably preceeded the pair of events in question. The flow of events is properly represented when the eye scans the matrix in a clockwise rotation. Should the highest frequency fall into a transition cell, not a steady state cell, the row or column of either number in the pair can be studied to retrace or advance the sequence of events.

An example of matrix interpretation will be shown later in this article. Skill in matrix interpretation, however, is not likely to develop from

195

reading this article, which serves only to propose guidelines. For that matter, skill in observation cannot develop from reading about how it is done. All aspects of interaction analysis require practice in order to develop skill. It is the opposite of a spectator sport.

FEEDBACK AND CONSULTATION WITH TEACHERS

The purpose of feedback is to provide a teacher with information about his verbal statements which permits a comparison with some standard or model of what should have happened. Without purposive comparisons which are planned in advance of the observation, the reactions of the person receiving the information may be reduced to incidental speculations or points of interest that happen to be noticed.

To be useful as a model or standard, one's intentions must be specified in terms of frequencies to be found in the cells of the matrix. Thus, if a teacher wishes to practice providing more extended praise, he will expect to find an increase in the 2-2 cell of the matrix, one situation compared to another. If a teacher decides he would like to stimulate more pupil talk in which ideas are initiated by pupils, he might study column 9 in the matrix to see what events trigger these pupil statements. In a program of inservice training in which all teachers attempt to increase the utilization of ideas expressed by pupils, attention will be directed to column 3 and row 3 of the matrix.

Most inservice training programs can achieve some success in bringing selected concepts and value orientations to the attention of teachers, these are matters of awareness. Evidence that such awareness has been implemented through overt behavior requires an objective assessment of spontaneous teaching behavior.

The assessment of the spontaneous behavior must be reasonably objective in order to be reliable. Unfortunately, interaction analysis is not free of bias and error, probably about one out of every ten classifications of an experienced observer is incorrect. Interaction analysis data can be and probably are more objective, when dealt with in summary form, compared with most other procedures for making judgments about spontaneous teaching behavior. Judgments about events which occur within time segments of only a few seconds and which must be repeated again and again tend to become more consistent with practice. Furthermore, noting the presence or absence of a short event is not a procedure which lends itself as easily to distortion and bias.

No matter how objective, reliable, and valid an assessment procedure, the results will be distorted if the behavior itself is distorted. Unfortunately, merely anticipating observation might cause non-representative behavior to appear, not to mention the observation experience itself. Below are some policies and suggestions which we have found helpful in reducing the tendency of a teacher to put on an act while being observed.

First, an observer should be in the classroom only when invited by the teacher.

Second, the invitation should be based on a plan of inquiry which was developed by the teacher and observer prior to any classroom visits. Observation should produce information which is relevant to some problem or question which is considered important to both participants. Thus, a teacher participating in an inservice training program which proposes to improve the way pupil ideas are handled during classroom discussion may be curious about this aspect of interaction before and after training. Such a question might involve creating two similar lesson plans in which a teacher would be confronted with opportunities to react to pupil ideas. One lesson would be observed before training and the second lesson after training. The plan could be embellished to provide greater insights by collecting additional data. For example, predictions about pupil perceptions, teacher perceptions, pupil attitudes and similar phenomena could be made, one lesson compared with the other. Then, instead of merely counting the incidence of constructive teacher reactions to ideas expressed by pupils, certain theories about the consequences of such teacher behavior might be investigated.

Third, the status and power difference between the observer and the teacher should be a minimum. Another teacher who is a best friend might make the most appropriate observer, providing skill in observation is present.

Fourth, the conference to provide feedback should follow a logical plan of inquiry. All the relevant data should be at hand and referred to in terms of questions to be answered and not in terms of idle curiosity. It often helps to have two or more matrices, since this facilitates the making of comparisons out of which theoretical explanation grows. A single matrix more often stimulates opinions about what is "good" and "bad," illustrated by the question, "Do you think the lesson was satisfactory?" Such questions place the observer in an awkward position, since he must express a general judgement. In this position he cannot be an equal partner in the inquiry process. On the other hand, when a hypothesis about behavior is being investigated and professional competence of the teacher is not in the foreground, the analysis of data is more systematic and unwanted defensive distractions are less likely to occur.

Fifth, the entire procedure including planning, execution, and analysis usually works more smoothly when the teacher, as well as the observer, has had approximately equal experience in observation. For example, setting up hypotheses, designing two comparable lesson plans, and knowing where to look in a matrix for the proper information are phases of the experience which should be shared by two partners who are equally competent. When the observer is more experienced and competent, the teacher defers and becomes the dependent member of the team. Both members of the team should have had previous experience in both teaching and observation.

ILLUSTRATIONS OF PRACTICAL PROCEDURES

For purposes of illustration, let us assume that the goal of inservice training is to increase the teacher's skill in making use of ideas expressed by pupils. In an article as short as this one, only four aspects of such an inservice training program will be mentioned. First, some initial performance data provides a before training performance pattern for which subsequent observation data can be compared. Second, skill training procedures can be closely correlated to observation procedures. Third, data in addition to interaction analysis are helpful in deciding whether or not a change in behavior is an improvement. And fourth, more advanced training designs and more complex data collection procedures will be necessary to push progress beyond the initial results. Each of these four topics will be discussed in turn.

INITIAL PERFORMANCE DATA

Initial performance data might be in the form of a short observation during a class discussion. Table 3 shows a matrix of a teacher which will now be interpreted to show how the observer and teacher make an initial diagnosis before training. The same data, of course, can serve as a before training standard in order to determine whether change has occurred.

Since the total tallies equals 380, one can estimate that the matrix represents about 19 minutes of interaction (100 tallies = 5 minutes, 20 tallies = 1 minute).

A number of percentages and other ratios, which help to form an initial picture, can be found at the bottom rows of Table 3. For example, the teacher talked 58.7 percent, the pupils 39.2 percent, and silence and confusion was 2.1 percent. The teacher was fairly directive, that is he initiated more than he responded, as shown by an I/D = 0.77 (divide all tallies in categories 1 + 2 + 3 + 4 by 5 + 6 + 7 to obtain this ratio). The highest cell frequencies are

198

TABLE 3

OBSERVATION MATRIX

CATE-GORY	1	2	3	4	5	6	7	8	9	10	Total
1	-	-	-	-	-	-	-	-	-	-	-
2	-	1	1	1	2	-	-	1	5	-	11
3	-	-	5	1	4	-	-	-	-	-	10
4	-	-	-	23	2	1	-	42	3	5	76
5	-	2	1	22	80	1	2	3	3	3	117
6	-	-	-	1	-	-	1	3	-	-	5
7	-	-	-	-	2	1	1	-	-	-	4
8	-	5	-	22	19	-	-	45	7	-	98
9	-	3	3	3	7	-	-	3	32	-	51
10	-	-	-	3	1	2	-	1	1	-	8
Total	-	11	10	76	117	5	4	98	51	8	380
%	-	2.9	2.6	20.0	30.8	1.3	1.1	25.8	13.4	2.1	100.
of	25.5				33.2			39.2		2.1	
Total	Teacher Total: 58.7							Student Total		Si-lence	

I/D = 0.77   Content Cross = 70.8%

I/D $_{s.s.}$ = 1.38   Steady State = 49 %

found in the steady state diagonal cells, such as the 5-5, the 8-8, and the 9-9 cells. This suggests that the teacher and pupils were able to continue a particular mode of expression once it started. Higher frequencies in these steady state cells indicate that the tempo of exchange was slower, for example, than might occur in a drill period. All silences were 3 seconds or less (note no tallies in the 10-10 cell) and most pauses followed teacher questions (N = 5 in the 4-10 cell) and teacher lecture (N = 3 in the 5-10 cell) rather than pupil statements. In six of these eight transitions, it was the teacher who broke the pause by talking (note that N = 1 in the 10-8 and 10-9 cells). This analysis of silence supports the interpretation that the teacher tended to initiate and did not permit a pupil more than 3 seconds to respond.

The matrix is sometimes more easily understood when it is translated into a flow pattern illustrated in Figure 1. In this diagram the most frequently occurring steady state cells are shown as rectangles and the size of the rectangle indicates the relative frequency of the pair. Transitions among these cells are indicated by arrows and the thickness of the

199

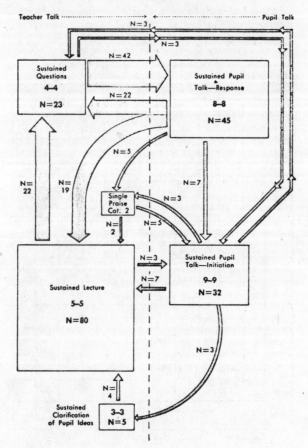

Figure 1: Initial Flow Pattern Before Training

arrow is roughly proportional to the frequency of these transitions. Anyone can learn to draw such a pattern flow diagram from a tabulated matrix. Begin with the highest frequency cell, in this case the 5-5 cell with eighty tallies. Proceed across the same row to find out the next most likely occurring events and inspect columns to identify the most likely preceding events. The arrows in Table 3 illustrate the clockwise direction of the flow. Thus in both the matrix and in Figure 1, begin with the 5-5 cell, sustained lecturing. The next most likely event is that the teacher will ask a question. Next, pupils are most likely to respond to this question, see category 8. There are two events of almost equal probability following pupil response talk, one is that the teacher will ask another question and the other is that the teacher will lecture. The four transitions shown by the heavy arrows in Figure 1 account for most of the interaction: these are, 5-4, 4-8, 8-4, and 8-5. Other transitions do occur, but the transitions just listed and their associated steady state cells account for 285 tallies or about 75 percent of the entire observation.

Many things could be said about this pattern of interaction, but by far the most certain inference is that in the event that this teacher increased his use of category 3, it could be clearly seen in the matrix. The use of category 3, especially the 3-3 cell, is below average for a classroom teacher. After training along these lines a second matrix and flow pattern diagram could be made as a comparison with this initial performance.

SPECIFIC SOCIAL SKILL TRAINING EXERCISES

Specific social skill training exercises can be conducted which are closely correlated with interaction analysis. A training skill exercise might involve three or four people who take turns providing certain patterns of verbal statements while responding spontaneously to the statements of others in the group. The person being trained is designated as the actor, one other person is the observer, and the rest are reactors or foils who provide spontaneity. Different assignments are given to the actor which he then carries out by interacting with his foils. The observer keeps a record of the communication bv. coding within the ten categories. The assignment can be given in terms of the categories, for example, the actor is asked to produce a 4-8-4-8-4-8-4-8, etc., sequence. An actor might be asked to choose a topic and produce any sequence which is relevant to teaching and is related to the goals of the training.

The activity of a training exercise follows a model in which an actor attempts a particular pattern, his foils provide a spontaneous setting, and the observer keeps a coded record of what happens. Some training episodes may last only a few minutes, others are longer. Each episode is followed by a discussion of the performance and ways that it can be improved. While this kind of activity can easily degenerate into superficial play acting, especially when first attempted, it is also true that serious and interested participants can use this technique to practice producing certain patterns of behavior under increasing difficult circumstances and make progress in the self control of spontaneous behavior.

Learning how to make full use of the ideas expressed by pupils is a goal to which spontaneous skill training exercises can easily be adapted. It is possible to gain practice in listening carefully, in listing ideas expressed by another person, in summarizing ideas which have just been expressed, in building questions on ideas expressed by others, and to teach pupils to initiate their own steps in problem solving by showing a pupil how his ideas are related to a problem.

Skill practice sessions become more realistic when they are closely related to classroom practice sessions. After one or two initial observations an

201

observer and teacher may discuss the **relationships** between the teacher's intention and the patterns which appear on several matrices. Skill practice sessions are then designed to emphasize a personal goal of the teacher based on discrepancies revealed by the matrix. If the training activities are custom built to the needs of the teacher, and if he sees them as relevant to his own professional development, then he is more likely to approach the training sessions with serious intent and a sense of optimism concerning personal development. It also helps when classroom patterns begin to change in a desired direction as a result of skill practice sessions.

Usually, the assignments of actor, foil, and observer are rotated during skill practice sessions. In this way a teacher not only becomes familiar with the coding system of interaction analysis, he also obtains some degree of observer proficiency. He also learns to accept and develop the perceptions that others have of his behavior.

The primary purpose of these training episodes is to practice producing certain patterns of statements, to translate concepts about teaching into spontaneous behavior patterns, to learn how to assess such patterns, and to discuss how these various patterns appear in classroom teaching. Many variations of training exercises can be directed toward these goals making them useful for inservice training.

DECIDING WHEN A CHANGE IS AN IMPROVEMENT

Deciding when a change is an improvement usually requires data in addition to interaction analysis. For example, merely giving a teacher instructions to "go in there and produce more threes," much like a football coach, is quite likely to increase the incidence of category three. This change may take place, however, without any insight into the teaching process and may possibly be seen as either inappropriate or not realistic by the pupils.

Utilizing the ideas expressed by pupils during classroom discourse involves several pedagogically sound principles. One such principle is that this kind of teacher behavior stimulates the perception among pupils that each pupil is free to express his ideas. Simple paper and pencil reaction sheets, to be filled out by pupils old enough to read and write, can be used to assess pupil perceptions immediately following a practice session in which the teacher tries to accept and clarify pupil ideas. When both the observer's records and the pupil's average perceptions from a paper and pencil instrument indicate greater expression and use of pupil ideas, then the additional evidence provides greater confidence that the change is an improvement.

Another pedagogical principle is that a pupil learns to cluster ideas because they are similar and then abstract the cluster with an appropriate label through directed practice in expressing his ideas. A second observer can keep an inventory of separate ideas expressed by pupils, he can note instances in which the pupils, instead of the teacher, noticed a cluster, and finally, he can record whether the teacher or the pupils supplied an appropriate label to a given cluster. This additional evidence also helps to show whether a change in teacher behavior is, or is not, an improvement.

PUSHING TRAINING BEYOND SUPERFICIAL CHANGE

Pushing training beyond superficial change usually requires special category systems of interaction analysis. For example, the division of category 3, mentioned earlier, can provide a record of different kinds of teacher reactions to the ideas expressed by pupils. A similar expansion of categories 8 and 9 will show variations in the different kinds of pupil statements. Often the expansion of teacher talk categories can provide more intricate and difficult social skill training assignments. Working back and forth between more elaborate category systems and more complex spontaneous social skill training assignments helps a teacher understand principles of pedagogy in terms of his own behavior. Unless a teacher can act out his insights about teaching, these insights are of little use for the improvement of instruction.

SUMMARY

The use of interaction analysis in an inservice training program places an emphasis on the analysis of spontaneous verbal behavior. This emphasis helps to translate ideas about teaching into classroom application.

For those who would like to try classifying verbal statements, but are inexperienced, a number of references are listed at the end of this article which include suggestions for beginning.

REFERENCES

Flanders, N. A. Intent, action and feedback: A preparation for teaching. Journal of Teacher Education, 1963, 14, 251-260.

Flanders, N. A. The role of the teacher in the classroom. Minneapolis, Minnesota: Amidon, 1963.

Flanders, N. A. Interaction analysis in the classroom: A manual for observers. (Rev. ed.) School of Education, University of Michigan, 1965.

Flanders, N. A. Teacher influence, pupil attitudes, and achievement. Cooperative Research Monograph No. 12, U. S. Office Of Education, OE-25040. Washington, D. C.: U. S. Government Printing Office, 1965.

CHAPTER VII

Professional Negotiations

The title "Professional Negotiations" may be the last
remnant of the concept of a unified profession in education
that exists in the literature about collective bargaining
in education. The era of the united profession (administrators and teachers working as colleagues toward united educational goals) in education is largely a pattern of the
past. Professional negotiations are a theory of the present
and the name of the game is negotiations. The demands of
education associations and unions are more similar than dis-
similar and the management procedures and techniques. School
boards by state statutes are accountable for the education
of youth. What's needed is a rectification of the statutes
so that all parties to negotiations are accountable.

What are the rules for collective bargaining and how
do you succeed? Which situations are and are not negotiable?
Are there key time saving, money saving suggestions for successful collective bargaining? Success in negotiating with
the superintendent of schools and the school principal is
a must. The personnel manager must be aware of the appre-
hensions concerning the attitudes of parties involved in
contract negotiations.

Chapter VII is designed to present practitioners answers
to the problems stated above. The articles were chosen with
the practicing personnel administrator in mind and may aid
the administrator as he prepares for negotiations and lives
with the contract.

Negotiations and Accountability

Charles R. Hough

During the last decade, many changes in the educational process have occurred, not the least of which has been the use of negotiations.

The process of negotiations is not new. What is new, however, is that formal negotiations have now become an integral part of American education. Whether the resulting changes in attitudes and actions between the elected school boards and the professional staffs will be for the advantage or disadvantage of the general public remains an open question. It may even be debatable whether an adversary relationship—that is, "You are on one side and I on another, and the two sides are of necessity in opposition"—has existed in the past between school boards on the one hand and the various school staffs on the other. However, it can safely be said that, with the enactment of state laws with respect to staff negotiations in schools, an adversary relationship has been created and does, in fact, exist.

What Are the Complications?

When the legislature says to an elected board, which already has certain legal charges assigned to it, that it must now conduct the public business of education through a formalized negotiations process, complications immediately arise. Included in these

---

NASSP BULLETIN, Dec. 1971, pp. 1-7.

is the question of accountability. Accountability, a word currently fashionable in educational circles, is long overdue, and with negotiations, formalized by legislative act, accountability will assume increasing importance. A board can always be made to account for its actions, but to what degree will the public's interest be promoted and protected?

By law, a school board is charged with certain legal responsibilities. It must see that the children within its district's geographical boundaries are provided access to an education, always within the financial and legal limitations imposed by its community and state. It must provide as a basic minimum a building, a staff, supplies, and transportation wherever walking is not practicable. Because the school board is conducting the public's business with the public's money, it must protect the public's rights. Its primary obligations, therefore, are two-fold: 1) to provide the student with the best facilities, staff, and materials that available money will buy and 2) to spend the taxpayers' (public's) money with the greatest possible efficiency and wisdom and thereby, ideally, to provide the kind of education that is for the best good of the individual student and the community.

For many years the school board has been able to perform its functions with varying degrees of success and frustration, but with the advent of negotiations laws, it has been placed in a much more exposed position. Just as in the case of recent labor negotiations trends, the question is being asked increasingly, "Who protects the public interest in negotiations?" In the case of the school system, the general voting public holds its elected board accountable. The citizenry assumes the board is responsible for its actions and decisions and, if it feels the board has not properly performed, influence and pressure may be applied or, if feelings are strong, board members may be voted out of office.

To Whom Are Teachers Accountable?

To provide the means to an education, the school board must hire a professional staff who will actually conduct and promote the process of education. And it is this very staff that has become the largest and most powerful group with which a board must negotiate—the teacher organization. Many words are written and spoken about the aims of these organizations, but it seems that much of the conflict that has arisen has been over economic

206

issues: salaries, health benefits, insurance benefits, length of the working day, preparation time. All issues relating to the welfare of the teachers themselves seem to bring disagreement. These areas of disagreement, while of benefit to the particular group of people within the organization, should their objective be achieved, may not be resolved in a way that is of the most benefit to the general public.

Strikes have occurred with increasing frequency during the last several years. In many instances, these strikes have been contrary to the policy established by law in the particular states involved: that is, a law exists forbidding strikes by public employees. At other times settlement of the issues has resulted in agreements that meant disproportionate gains for the teacher group without increased responsibilities and, thus, were not in the public interest. The negotiators for a teacher organization are working only for the interests of its membership—and possibly a national affiliate—at the negotiating table. Thus, a vital question here is, "To whom is the organization and the membership accountable?" Who can call upon these groups to explain their conduct and, if not satisfied with the explanation, "throw the rascals out!"?

When various legislatures enacted negotiations laws, they said in effect that power to conduct the public business of education must be shared. But the legislatures did not indicate *how* a teacher organization was to be held accountable. Therefore, although there is organizational accountability to its membership, there is no such accountability to the citizenry as a whole. With school board accountability to the public established by statute but little or none applying to the teacher organization, negotiations can become quite difficult.

While teachers and other staff groups negotiate with school boards within a formal, collective bargaining structure with its safeguards through the application of state laws, there is another informal type of negotiating process that is being used that is potentially quite dangerous when the accountability yardstick is applied.

Rise and Growth of Other Groups

There is more interest in education today on the part of the general public than ever before and, as a result, certain citizen groups have come into being. Some groups are appointed, some seem to just materialize, and some enjoy an elected status. Most serve in an advisory capacity to the elected board. Because these groups were not generally formed as a result of state law, but only because of public pressure and/or a wish on the part of the school board to involve more citizens in educational planning and to have a closer relationship with its community, the formalized collective bargaining process of negotiations may not apply. Yet there will, in fact, exist an informal type of negotiating, wherein accountability is rather dubious.

To whom is a particular citizens' group accountable? Theoretically, if it is an elected group, it is responsible to its electors, and, if appointed, to the appointing body, but the school board is the one the state legislature holds responsible for the proper and complete fulfillment of the duties given to it by law. These informal groups, while not given any legal power, do possess power in practice. This power can result in limitations imposed upon the board; i.e., suppose such a citizens' group were seriously opposed to a policy change which the board felt would be in the best interests of students. It is the prerogative of the board to make such a decision, but the practical politics of the situation may be such that the decision would become very difficult to carry out. Or, again, a board may be pressured into giving such groups a large measure of control in the hiring of administrative personnel within their own area, only to find that, through lack of experience and knowledge of education requirements, such appointments may not be in the public interest. Such a group, then, can force a school board into a position of making informal agreements (that may subsequently be formalized) that are very hard to change even though the result is a negative one for the district as a whole.

Students and Accountability

Another group that is increasingly becoming a part of the decision-making process is students. To whom are the students accountable? Yet, this group is exerting more and more influence in such ways as student senates, as members sitting on citizens' advisory councils, and as student advisory groups to boards of education. While such student groups may not have de jure power (that derived from a legal body), they do have it in a de facto sense. The trend appears to be increasing; and school boards, in answering to their public, may be hard pressed to explain some of their actions, for (trite as it may appear) it is still the man who pays the bill who makes the final policy decisions through the exercise of his right of franchise. Does a school board have a right to divide its authority in this way, when it is the only one of these groups who can be held legally responsible?

Still another area in discussing accountability that must be considered is the responsibility of operating the schools on a day-to-day basis. This responsibility, of course, rests with the boards' appointed administrative staff—the superintendent and his operating assistants, including the building principals. These administrative officers are held accountable by the board for the performance of their duties. Not only is accountability directly traceable through a line relationship to the superintendent and the board, but the public also feels many times that the principal is accountable to the local citizens for what occurs within a particular school.

The principal charged with the implementation of both board policy and a negotiated agreement often finds himself in a rather difficult position. He is charged with putting into effect negotiated items that may interfere with the efficient operation of the school. Therefore, the principal, if he is to have the responsibility for carrying out a negotiated agreement, and especially one in which the implication of accountability to the local citizens is included, should be a part of the management team. This team should be responsible for developing the school board's and administration's position which is to be negotiated with the teachers' group or other organizations.

Build Accountability Into System

I may have given the impression in this article that I am opposed to the negotiating process. On the contrary—the negotiating process with its necessary adversary relationship is an excellent way of establishing boundaries and an operational mode in which school boards, administrative staffs, and teaching staffs can operate. As long as there is in effect a system of checks and balances and as long as all parties are in an equally accountable position, the system is good. But unless and until that occurs, the system cannot operate without trouble.

Generally, in their negotiations statutes, the legislatures have failed to provide these necessary safeguards for the public interest. Therefore, it is to be expected that the conflicts will increase, becoming more acute and insoluble, until public pressure will demand that corrective action be taken by the legislatures.

What can be done when the positions in the bargaining process reach an impasse? The strike and lockout is one drastic way to try to force a compromise position. Strikes by public employees are not legal everywhere, and it is questionable whether a strike by a school employee group or a lockout by a school board would be very well received by the public as being for the public good. In considering accountability, perhaps groups contemplating such action should consider their accountability to the students. Is it one of the aims of education to teach solutions of problems by communication and compromise or by power struggles that usually result in at least some harm to all participants?

As long as both parties in such a conflict situation are essentially reasonable and of good will, two other ways of solving problems are open to them. The first is that of binding arbitration, requiring an agreement of both groups to submit to such a process. This method does not allow the adversaries any compromise but simply rules in favor of one party or the other. The alternate method of coming to an agreement from an impasse would be through a mediation service. In such a less formal process, "face" can be saved, a compromise effected, and differences solved without rancor. And, although mediation is in itself not binding upon both parties, real and moral pressure can be applied. Who wants to place himself or his organization in the position of refusing to accept a solution that appears fair and reasonable to his fellow citizens and taxpayers?

If accountability is indeed the name of the game, then some new factors must be introduced into negotiation laws and processes to take care of those situations in which compromise appears to be impossible. Negotiation laws try to rebalance a power structure. In a successful process of negotiations, balance is inherent. No one party must have the power to stop the process of education. The school board is presently accountable to the public by statute and must of necessity be more careful in its negotiations. Employee groups are not accountable by law and, therefore, have a more usable power of work stoppage. There must be a formalized process of rectifying differences resulting from the adversary relationship created by the statutory negotiations requirements. All parties to the negotiations process must be accountable in the same formalized, statutory way. The public's interest must be protected.

How to play the Comparison Game in collective bargaining

By Myron Lieberman

THIS is about the Comparison Game in collective bargaining. Here are the game's two basic rules:

1. The most important influence on the nature of the terms that will be contained in your bargained contract is what others are getting in theirs.

2. The closer — literally — other settlements are to your school district, the more they will influence the settlement your own district reaches. Teacher bargaining in St. Paul, for example, is affected more by teacher bargaining in Minneapolis (or vice versa) than by teacher bargaining in New York or San Diego. In fact, geographical closeness can be more influential than professional closeness —

AMERICAN SCHOOL BOARD JOURNAL,

May 1975, pp. 43-45.

a cost-of-living increase granted to firefighters in St. Louis will have more influence on teacher bargaining in St. Louis than will a cost-of-living increase won by teachers in Seattle.

These, as I mentioned, are the basic rules of the Comparison Game, and it is important that they be understood. Start by recognizing that bargaining is a political as well as an economic process. A school board that pays more than do nearby boards for the same school supplies and equipment faces severe criticism for waste and extravagance. Teachers, of course, are not standardized as precisely as chalk or desks or projectors, but it is difficult, nevertheless, to demonstrate meaningful differences in staff effectiveness between school districts. Clearly, the taxpayers rarely distinguish one district staff from another on this basis. For this reason, a school board that pays teachers (or other employes) substantially more than the going rate in the area is risking political retaliation. Minor differences usually are ignored or can be safely explained away — major differences cannot be so easily rationalized and certainly will not be ignored.

The same political process is at work on the teacher side. Naturally, every teacher negotiator would like to win as much as possible from the employer school board. In most cases, however, the concern of the teacher negotiator is not so much with achieving a victory as it is with avoiding a defeat — a settlement that is visibly inferior to other settlements in the immediate area. Comparisons are thus the keys to the politics of bargaining.

In order to get as much as possible from the board, the teacher negotiator tries to show how disadvantaged his constituents are. When agreement is reached, however, the negotiator must try to portray it as a victory for his side — which means emphasizing how the teachers he represents have fared better than their counterparts in nearby districts. This is not always easy to do. A good negotiator frequently has to tell his adversaries what a rotten deal they are offering — and walk into the next room to tell his principals what a terrific one it is.

In bargaining, each side emphasizes comparisons that can be expected to strengthen its respective case. If the salary schedule in District A has lower maximums than in District B, the teacher negotiator will stress the injustice done to deserving teachers at the top of the schedule. But he'll say nothing about the fewer steps required to achieve the maximum, or the fact that the teachers at maximum in District A received more on their way up the schedule than did their counterparts in District B.

Of course, school board negotiators follow the same strategy. Thus, District A's board negotiators are likely to propose increasing the number of steps to reach maximum, on the grounds that this aspect of the schedule is too generous (again, in comparison with nearby districts). The same board negotiators, however, can be expected to de-emphasize the lower maximum, the very point stressed by the teachers.

In the early days of teacher bargaining (let's say in the late 1960s), teachers often cited data on what doctors, lawyers, and dentists were making. Naive as this was, some teacher negotiators really believed a particular school board would or could deviate drastically from its neighbors, or from national patterns, by paying teachers at levels comparable to the fee-taking professions. Fortunately, most of this rhetoric has been abandoned, or is recognized for the rhetoric it is.

The search for advantageous comparisons extends beyond individual items to entire settlements and patterns of settlements. Suppose your school district has the third lowest salary schedule in a metropolitan area that includes 20 districts. To raise your standing, you offer a settlement that is more generous, percentagewise, than that of your neighboring districts. The offer is accepted.

Next time around, though, you find that you can't quite keep up with neighboring districts so you try to emphasize the fact that you provided the most generous percentage increase *last time*. Expect this argument normally to fall on deaf ears. The teacher negotiator will be stressing the need to maintain your *comparative* position. "We rank tenth," he'll say, "and your offer will drop us to the lowest quartile in the area. My teachers will never accept such a lousy settlement."

And so it goes — on both sides.

If a school board can maintain a favorable comparative position even with an unfavorable percentage increase, it will stress the after-settlement position; the teachers will stress the unfavorable comparison relating to the percentage of increase. In other words, no matter what you do, the teacher negotiator can always find a basis for alleging that your teachers are disadvantaged vis-a-vis their neighbors. If you pay the highest salaries in the area, the need to maintain that position by comparable percentage increases will be stressed by the teacher negotiator. If you pay the lowest salaries, the need to improve your position will be emphasized.

No earthshaking strategic conclusions follow from this, but some suggestions may be helpful. In the first place, most school districts — and most teacher organizations — are necessarily pattern followers, not pattern makers. What would be acceptable to one side for an early settlement is almost invariably unacceptable to the other. Early settlements involve the risk that subsequent ones may be less advantageous to both sides — a practical impossibility in most cases.

In most districts, a lot of time can — and will — be wasted in trying to get a settlement before the time is ripe, *i.e.*, before a basis for comparison materializes.

In the second place, it pays to pay attention to the basis for comparisons, even though union negotiators will always try to shift the basis next time to justify a better offer. If you settle on the basis of comparative data which are not likely to work in the union's favor in the future, emphasize the comparison in such a way that you can use it advantageously next time. Example: Suppose the teachers want dental insurance in spite of the fact that no district in your area provides it. If you agree to provide individual dental insurance, other districts also will do so, and you soon will have lost your competitive edge. Without doubt, the union will try next time to get family coverage so that you "maintain your leadership." It may be perfectly appropriate for you to move in front on a particular item, but exact a price for this — such as explicit acceptance on the part of the teachers that you will remain behind on other items. In other words, *don't negotiate particular items on which your school district lags behind other districts in isolation from those on which your district looks good* (if you are behind on everything, of course, you have a problem).

It seldom is feasible to include in the agreement itself any mechanism for resolving the comparison problem. Some school districts have negotiated clauses which specify that the salary schedule shall be a certain rank in the district's geographical area, but such clauses are of dubious legality and practicality. Aside from the fact that they constitute a delegation of authority to set salaries, they tend to ignore the need to compare settlements as a whole.

As fringe benefits consume an increasingly larger share of settlement costs, there is a growing need for management to compare total packages instead of individual items. If you know how your district's total salary and welfare package compares to those of others, you can be less concerned about comparisons of individual items in the package. The amount devoted to a particular item, such as sabbatical leave, can be considered chiefly in terms of the preferences of your teachers as to how they want funds for their welfare to be allocated. From a management point of view, it need not be of great concern that you pay more than your neighbors for insurance benefits if your over-all personnel costs are less. One persistent management problem, however, is the primitive state of comparing total packages. Perhaps if our professors of educa-tional administration ever wake up from their somnolent state, there will be some progress on this problem — but don't count on it.

The importance of comparisons is reflected in regional strategy. The state teacher organizations — or any unit serving an area — try to bring in the best settlement first. This isn't good for management, which hopes that contracts favorable to management will be negotiated first.

The upshot is for the parties to wait — and then to reach agreement en masse as deadlines approach. Inasmuch as interdistrict differences are not all that great, there might as well be regional bargaining in most areas. This has lots of appeal to teacher organizations, which cannot service a large number of small districts on an individual basis. It may also appeal to management, on the grounds that the costs of district autonomy in bargaining is not worth the minor differences in the agreements reached. Of course, if this point of view is accepted, settlements will be made on a regional basis and the comparison game will then be played between regions instead of school districts. ☐

How to speed up the process of collective bargaining with your teachers

By Myron Lieberman

Collective Bargaining with teachers does not (repeat: *not*) have to be the endless, fatiguing, directionless affair it has become in too many school districts.

Take that as a demonstrable given; then ask yourself: Why, when neither school boards nor, increasingly, teachers want protracted bargaining, do no moves seem afoot to speed up the process? My own experience in this field prompts me to conclude that too often neither side in the bargaining — but especially the school board side — understands the usefulness of certain procedures and the significance of certain factors that can minimize time required to reach an agreement. In this article, we'll look at some of these procedures and factors.

It's easy to cite a score or more of circumstances that can and do affect the time required for bargaining — the size of the district, the sophistication of the parties, the history of bargaining in the district, the timing of the negotiations, the state aid situation, the economic environment, and many more. Some of these variables plainly are subject to control by school boards (for example, whether the board's chief negotiator is a knowledgeable professional usually is within the scope of board control).

Another set of factors, while not subject to unilateral control by the school board, nevertheless can have considerable effect on the amount of time devoted to bargaining. To illustrate: Experienced teacher bargainers are as fully aware as school boards should be of the futility of starting in, say, November to bargain terms of a

AMERICAN SCHOOL BOARD JOURNAL,

June 1975, pp. 35-37.

contract that won't take effect until the following July or September. Boards and unions alike know that in the late fall there is no immediate pressure to settle and no patterns to follow. Furthermore, the fact that so much time is available encourages long laundry lists of demands, many of which would never be made, let along bargained, if bargaining were confined to a month or less before the current agreement expires.

A third set of factors, such as the general economic environment, is not subject to board control or influence. Controversy may arise over how to interpret or weigh these elements — the cost of living is a good example — but no way exists for a board to change any of the circumstances.

In my personal experience, time required for bargaining has ranged from a low of two meetings (in a 50-teacher district in Connecticut) to six months of protracted meetings (in a 600-teacher district in a suburb of New York City). The latter required approximately 20 meetings with two different organizations (in a representation election, a rival union dislodged the union that originally had been recognized by the board as bargaining agent).

An enormous amount of board and staff time also was required *away* from the table, largely because the board at an earlier date had foolishly recognized one teacher union without adequate proof that it was the choice of a majority of teachers. After I'd been employed as chief negotiator, I learned of the board's previous action — it had improperly recognized the union it deemed easier to deal with. Although I recommended that nego-

tiations be suspended pending a definitive resolution of the representation issue, the board refused to do so, believing (or hoping) that its earlier recognition would not be challenged. The upshot of this board decision was to ensure the victory of the union the board feared the more — and at least triple the time required to reach a viable agreement.

Presence or absence of an existing agreement is in itself, of course, an important consideration that bears upon the amount of time needed for bargaining. The process of reaching a first agreement, in fact, frequently requires a considerable interim merely for the parties to get to know each other. On the other hand, I've heard of cases in which the bargaining teams found each other's company pleasant to the extent that formal sessions almost developed into awaited social affairs where the business of bargaining became a virtual afterthought (don't count on that, though).

Even in renegotiating current agreements, the course of bargaining can vary enormously. A lot depends upon the range and language of the current agreement. If it is comprehensive and loosely worded, and being renegotiated long before any deadline is in sight, you can expect bargaining to drag on indefinitely. If, on the other hand, your existing agreement is tightly drafted and meets the basic needs of both parties, you probably won't need to do much more than renegotiate the economic package.

In the early days of collective bargaining, teacher teams often tried — sometimes successfully — to wear down management resistance. The parties worked all day at their regular tasks and negotiated until early morning, day after day. Administrators grumbled about teachers taking sick leave after negotiating until 3 a.m., but they seldom did anything about it. Such action might have seemed like a reprisal against the teachers.

Today, however, especially in states with bargaining laws, teacher bargainers are likely to be full-time field representatives of the union. Like their administrative counterparts, they are not paid by the hour. After negotiating several contracts a year for several years, their main concern becomes how to get the bargaining over with as quickly as possible, consistent with what the teachers will accept without serious dissatisfaction.

Some teacher bargainers are employed on a per-diem or per-session basis. The principal teacher union in New York state (a merged A.F.T.-N.E.A. organization), for example, employs 80 full-time and 25 part-time negotiators. Full-time representatives typically have responsibility for four contracts; part-time negotiators are paid $35 per session. Part-timers, consequently, may be motivated to drag out the bargaining — as may be board negotiators who are paid on a per-diem or hourly basis.

If the parties are afraid to settle until the annual question of state aid is resolved, it usually is futile to begin extensive bargaining — even on non-economic items whose resolution often is tied to economic considerations.

The best way to conserve time, it seems to me, is to use a combination of incentives. This might entail providing released time for bargaining during the school day for a small number of teacher representatives. If you grant released time, though, be sure your action is conditioned upon agreement by the union not to press for bargaining before it has a good chance of success, and also upon significant progress in bargaining during the school day. Frequently, the teacher union staff person welcomes such an arrangement since it helps him or her obviate the need to appear in several places during the same evening. In any event, don't provide released time until there is pressure on the union to bargain seriously, and don't commit yourself to sessions "on school time" without some appropriate concession from the other side.

A great deal of time at the bargaining table can be saved if the board insists that a consultation procedure involving teacher and board representatives is used during the year. If the parties are in regular communication, surprises (hence delay) can be averted. If teachers weren't concerned sufficiently within the year to raise an issue during consultation, board bargainers should not feel obligated to devote a great deal of time to that issue. Bargainers who are surprised are not prepared, and when they are not prepared, they tend to equivocate and delay. The same obligation to use the consultation procedure (and, consequently, avoid surprises) applies — without question — to the board, too.

Board negotiators also should avoid devoting excessive time to figuring out costs of union proposals that are not offered seriously nor with any genuine expectation that they will be taken thus. Suppose that teachers propose a salary schedule with a $14,000 minimum, going to $30,000 in eight steps; don't waste your time figuring out how much that proposal will cost. When demands are submitted you should require that their estimated costs be included. If teachers haven't developed such estimates, you usually are safe in assuming they are not especially serious about the demand. When bargaining gets serious, teachers typically have a good idea of what costs how much. In any case, not even the public relations value of estimating the expense of outrageous demands usually is worth your effort, at least at the beginning of bargaining. But if, as deadlines approach, teachers are holding out for excessive demands, you can and should be prepared to cite monetary appraisals of their proposals to the public. The point: Don't get sidetracked into estimating costs of proposals that are certain to be dropped or lowered.

Two other important points: (1) Avoid repetitious arguments at the bargaining table. (2) Once bargaining has started, don't allow the union to introduce additional demands at will.

If you have rejected a demand and explained your reasons, don't waste time listening to the same proposals and arguments, and don't repeat your position time after time. Make it clear that, unless something new has been added, you have stated your position on an item and are not about to rehash it. Be certain, of course, that your position has covered the item thoroughly and that you understand the union's position, but guard against getting worn down by sheer repetition.

If the union is offering a new proposal or a counterproposal, consider it carefully to determine whether it satisfies your objections, and ask whether the demands submitted represent the entire package. If the answer is negative, stop bargaining until you have the entire package. This should *not* be done in a way that encourages the submission of additional demands. Occasionally, you may find it advantageous to bargain on a late proposal — as distinguished from a counterproposal — but make sure the union understands that you are making an exception (if you've overlooked a demand of your own, this is the time to introduce it). Remember that when the union is allowed to introduce additional demands at will, you'll be severely disadvantaged in bringing bargaining to a conclusion.

If there is good communication during the year, agreements should be consummated in four to six weeks (two to three sessions per week) of serious bargaining on both sides — and even more quickly if released time for bargaining is provided during the school day. Allowing long periods to elapse between meetings usually is a bad idea because still more time will be used in trying to return the parties' thoughts to where they were when the previous bargaining was suspended. Three consecutive days near the expiration of an agreement are worth 10 to 20 days six months before expiration. Furthermore, preparation interims away from the table are extremely important in conserving time *at* the table — but this is not true if you have to repeat the preparation process because too long a period has elapsed between preparation and bargaining.

The central consideration, then, becomes one of assigning a proper value to time and accurately identifying the factors that waste or conserve it in the bargaining process. If you do not respect and value your own time, do not expect your adversaries to, either. They will conclude, and rightly so, that it isn't worth much. □

A MANAGEMENT TEAM
An Approach to Negotiations

By LEIGHTON WILKLOW and HENRY VERSNICK

WITH THE INTRODUCTION of laws providing for negotiations between Boards of Education and their employees, there have been many predictions concerning the ultimate role of administrators in the process. Some see the administrator becoming an adversary of the Board in collective bargaining, while others suggest that administrators should consider themselves "master teachers" and belong to teacher negotiating groups.

In Pleasantville, New York, we have rejected the notion that administrators must oppose the Board and yet have recognized that to be effective, certain conditions are best expressed in writing. The result has been a new management team construct.

The Administrator's Dilemma

With teachers bargaining directly or indirectly with Boards, administrators from the superintendent to department heads have found themselves in an "outside" position within the educational system. Teachers' contracts have often been consummated without the involvement of administrators who must implement them. In order to get into the "decision flow," the administrator could:

(1) *Do nothing (and hope)*. The hope in this case was that Boards would by experience come to appreciate the worth of management and would, therefore, eventually make an effort to accommodate administrators in a sort of unilateral or corporate fashion.

In practice the hope has not come true. Boards faced with the power base of the teachers and silent administrators have willingly or unwillingly curbed the role of the administrator. This approach, therefore, has been just about universally rejected.

(2) *Join the teachers in negotiating*. Not accustomed to negotiations and with little help from State organizations, many administrators took the position that it was better to join teachers then fight them. One could do this by considering oneself a "master teacher."

This made for strange bedfellows, indeed. Here we find the administrator supporting a group which came into being to further teacher welfare, not the welfare of administrators. Not really understanding the role of the administrator, teachers could not be expected to go to the limit to support the needs of administrators.

History, in its short span regarding negotiations, shows that the longer a bargain-

THE CLEARING HOUSE, Sept. 1972, pp. 8-11.

ing law exists, the more frequently one observes the break-up of the teacher/management marriage . . . witness the experience of Michigan and Connecticut in particular.

Administrators soon came to realize that they could not be effective when they were "contract-tied" to the people they supervise and that their small numbers were overridden on key conflict issues. They also eventually realized that joining the teachers put them in an uncontrollable adversary role with the Board. In some instances, administrators were just plain thrown out by the teachers or defined out by Boards.

(3) *Form administrative negotiating units.* Another alternative was to form negotiating units of administrators and go it alone with the Board. This had the advantage of being released from the teachers, but the distinct disadvantage of being an adversary of the Board. Small numbers diluted the effect of the so-called "power base" and the use of professional negotiators. The smaller the school district, the more ineffective the group. Because of the nature of the group, the relationship of administrators to the superintendent of schools became at best a guarded one.

To increase numbers, regional groups of administrators, perhaps on a county basis, for example, have been proposed. When and if this occurs, the individual administrator's negotiating unit will become subject to the manipulations of the larger group and individual units will lose all flexibility of action. Thus, the adversary position of management will become even more solidified and institutionalized.

(4) *Strive for a new role.* We submit that there is a fourth choice for administrators to form a new alliance with the Board and the superintendent and thereby reject the adversary role or the "benevolent despot" approach while at the same time providing conditions which will secure the welfare of administrators.

We call this a management team approach to negotiations.

The Management Team Approach

The Pleasantville Management Team approach has evolved by the mutual understanding of all parties that management must support Board policy and that to be effective, management members must be protected by written doctrine. This latter idea is the heart of the Pleasantville model and is the major innovation of the construct.

Too often, the superintendent (and Boards) have wished for the management team approach but have been unwilling to safeguard the rights of both in writing. Consequent inconsistencies in the application of policy to members then caused distrust and administrators abandoned the idea in favor of negotiations for discrete safeguards.

Definition and Non-Adversary Role

In Pleasantville, the management team has been defined in Board policy. The functional part of the policy statement follows with commentary:

The Board of Education considers all those who have an effective role in the recruitment or release of teachers to be part of a management team. The management team shall be headed by the Superintendent who shall convene meetings to discuss district policies, administrative procedures and such other business as shall be brought to his attention or which he deems appropriate.

(a) The Board of Education recognizes each principal as the chief educational leader in his school, responsible in his school for matters pertaining to the organization and administration of the building and the program, for matters pertaining to all phases of the instruction program, for matters pertaining to the direction of personnel and for matters pertaining to school management, all in harmony with the standards and goals for the schools and the district as directed by and in cooperation with the superintendent of schools.

(b) The Board of Education realizes that in order to discharge the responsibilities incumbent upon him, the principal must have commensurate primary authority in his building. To this end it is expected that the actions of each principal must conform to established, written policies of the Board. In those areas where no published policy exists the principal is empowered to act according to the dictates of his professional judgment.

The recognition of the superintendent as head of the management team is not only natural but ends his adversary role with the rest of the team.

The definitions found in (a) and (b) are designed to show the Board's confidence in the building principal and, therefore, aid him in effectively carrying out his duties.

The management team shall meet with the Board occasionally to review overall operations of the district and conditions affecting the management team. The management team shall, however, have no relationship to any formal negotiating unit.

To operate effectively, the Board and/or the superintendent and the Management Team should meet frequently in various combinations depending on the nature of the topic.

The last sentence further defines the nonadversary role of the Management Team.

In the event a member or members of the management team are unable to resolve a problem, a committee of one Board member, one management team member, and the superintendent shall investigate the circumstances and make a recommendation for solution. If the solution proposed does not settle the matter, the full Board and the full management team shall meet to resolve the matter. In the process of resolving the matter, the advice of outside management consultants may be employed.

There can be and are disagreements in the best of families. This paragraph attempts to set forth ways to resolve intramural conflicts in a rational way even if an outside management consultant is necessary in the end.

Benefit Considerations

Management team members shall be employed on an annual basis with benefits consistent with those granted to the superintendent of schools and/or with regard to retirement consistent with state-wide practices. Building administrators shall generally take their vacation during the summer.

All members of the management team shall be save harmless by the Board for legal services due to libel, slander or other damages incurred in exercising their duties.

These two paragraphs are the "safeguards" for the management team members expressed in terms which rely on trust rather than on a listing of "rights." To be management by definition is not to be "labor" and, therefore, specificity is avoided by generally referring to fringe benefits enjoyed by the superintendent as head of the management team.

The Board of Education in recognition of the role of the management team shall compensate members in accordance with their differing managerial functions which were defined as minimums in Board policy on June 29, 1970.

The ultimate question under the heading of compensation is obviously one of salary. It must be conceded that basically most school boards and their superintendents base their salaries for administrators on some ratio or proportion of the teachers' salary schedule. Even if the ratio is not a direct one, at least the average board member keeps one eye on what is happening to the district's teaching salary schedule. This position therefore maintains, if not a formal tie to the bargaining process of the teachers, an informal subservient reinforcement of the role of the administrators to the collective agreement.

Generally, it can be said that the only "real free agent" is the superintendent of schools. Normally, his contract is individually derived, unhampered either by the various agreements in force in the district or the minimum legal ratios set in some states.

The Pleasantville Board took cognizance of this inconsistency in the management team concept by divorcing the members

223

defined as part of the team from the negotiated teachers' salary schedule.

. . . salaries for members of the management team shall be derived by applying administrative percentages to prevailing salaries of chief school officers of K-12 districts as reported in the annual survey for Westchester County, New York.

A management salary committee consisting of the Board's budget committee, the superintendent of schools, and one management team member shall review the salary schedule annually, based on the annual survey.

Role Definitions

The remainder of the Board's policy statement on the management team defines the role of each team member, including participation in the creation of new policy, new positions, and the recruitment, selection, and appointment of personnel to the faculty and management team. Caution was exercised in devising statements of definition which would not unduly restrict situations of fluidity and thereby institutionalize the vertical or horizontal flow of decision-making powers.

Contrary to some who theorize that because of a "new era of public bargaining," middle management's role has been diminished, these redefined dimensions of the management team concept give to the team members and the Board a restructured role . . . one of dealing in the administrative process through a series of structured alternatives. These management structured alternatives have long been accepted as *modus operandi* in industrial relations. The management team concept developed in Pleasantville seeks to foster a firm base for new relationships with teachers and for furthering the district's educational goals.

Summary

While it is true that historically administrative personnel shared mutually definable roles with teachers because of a commonality of purpose, under the new parameters delineated by the collective bargaining process, sharp conflicts of interest arise from the primary administrative functions of hiring, assignment, evaluation, and retention of teachers. It is becoming more apparent that those districts that continue to isolate the members of management from the superintendent and the Board will begin experiencing a series of regressive frustrations in policy implementation. To effect any change without the full support of the management team is to negate the basic concepts which play a determinative role in the ultimate development of any program.

Ed. Note: Dr. Wilklow is now Chief School Officer in Barker, New York.

George W. Angell

GRIEVANCE PROCEDURES UNDER COLLECTIVE BARGAINING: BOON OR BURDEN?

A teacher in the final year of a probationary appointment was being considered for tenure. Disregarding the favorable recommendation of the academic department, the governing board, through its chief administrative officer, notified the incumbent of its intent not to reappoint. Through appropriate grievance procedures, the faculty union took the matter eventually to binding arbitration, claiming that the administration had acted "arbitrarily and capriciously" and demanding that tenure be granted. The board and the administration claimed "unrestricted right" and responsibility to separate nontenured faculty members when necessary to "protect the long-term interests" of the institution. In rebuttal, the union stated that, in accordance with terms of the negotiated contract, a nontenured faculty member may only be separated for reasons of 1) moral turpitude or 2) unsatisfactory teaching. Claiming that the board had neither made nor given proof of either charge, the union demanded that the arbitrator award tenure.

The arbitrator decided in favor of the board on the ground that the contract stated the board was not required to give reasons for separation of a teacher prior to tenure. The arbitrator reasoned that the burden of both charge and proof lay with the nontenured grievant. In other words, to establish a claim, the grievant must charge the board with a specific act of discrimination that is proscribed either by contract or by law. Since the contract did proscribe the denial of academic freedom, the griev-

ant *might* have charged the board with violating academic freedom by refusing reappointment to one who taught political beliefs contrary to the desires of the board. Because no such charge was made, the arbitrator needed only to decide whether the board had acted within procedures prescribed by the contract.

In another tenure case taken to arbitration in the same state, the teacher was awarded tenure based on the charge and evidence that the administration failed to follow procedures specified by the contract. In the absence of contractual due process, the arbitrator decided, the incumbent must be awarded tenure.

In one case, then, the administrator's decision was upheld by contractual grievance procedures and in another it was denied. Each decision provides insights into the limitations of employee and employer rights under new rules of collective bargaining. Each decision by the arbitrator was final and binding and each award was based on the terms of the specific contract rather than on common law as shaped by past court decisions. Had a court handled either case prior to a negotiated contract, the results might have been different. In the first case, a court might well have ordered the board to provide reasons and evidence for nonreappointment in order to determine whether any type of discrimination had in fact taken place. In the second case, a court would probably not substitute its professional judgment for that of the board, since it has no legal authority to do so. Had a court found the board guilty of not providing due process, it would more than likely have ordered the board to reopen the case, follow due process, and then make its decision.

The important impact of collective bargaining on the operation of schools and colleges, then, is that a negotiated contract has the effect of law and that future issues between faculty and administration will be settled more and more on the basis of an arbitrator's ruling, using the contract as the primary legal relationship between employee and employer. For the administrator in the first case the important fact was that the faculty agreed to a contract that gave the board the right to dismiss nontenured faculty without giving reasons. In favor of the faculty member in the second case was the fact that the board agreed to a contract which did not limit the role of the arbitrator to determining only the existence or nonexistence of due process. Had the contract so limited the arbitrator (as many contracts do) he would have been forced to remand the case to the board with an order to follow due process, thus leaving the board with final disposal of the case.

It is just such cases as these that raise serious questions of jurisdiction and priority among the various laws that govern employer-employee relations in schools and colleges. Labor laws, civil service laws, and education laws all affect these relationships and there are very few benchmark decisions helpful in clarifying which law takes precedence in a particular situation. Clearly, administrators and teachers must be especially careful about the words and phrases included in their negotiated contracts. Special attention must be given to the grievance procedures because they provide the means by which a faculty union attempts to enforce each provision of the contract. Without grievance procedures the contract would be meaningless.

PHI DELTA KAPPAN, Apr. 1972,

pp. 501-505.

The impact of grievance procedures on administration and faculty has been studied in New York State community colleges. The study, summarized here, was based on interviews with administrators and faculty as well as careful review of contracts.*

Procedures Specified in Contracts

Only 22 of the 29 upstate New York community colleges and the City University of New York (whose contract governs the city community colleges) had formally negotiated contracts as of February, 1971. Twenty-two of the 23 contracts specified grievance procedures and all were included in this study. A few contracts specified two sets of procedures, one for contractual items, and one for noncontractual items. The most significant difference in procedures lay in the final step: For contractual items this step usually involved the employment of a neutral arbitrator whose expenses were shared equally by the faculty union and the employer; for noncontractual items, grievances were terminated at the level of the chief administrator or the trustees.

About one-third of the contracts made a distinction between "academic" and "nonacademic" matters for purposes of grievance. Decisions involving appointments, tenure, promotions, academic policy, etc., were often specified as being nondelegable powers of the trustees and thus not subject to binding arbitration by a neutral party. Other contracts included special clauses relative to management rights, usually designed to protect the trustees' right to exercise full powers authorized by law. Grievance procedures in those contracts usually applied only to procedural issues and/or nonacademic conditions of employment specified in the contracts. The right of the employer to restrict the use of grievance procedures remains a major point of contention, and there is no doubt that faculty unions will exercise every possible effort to extend jurisdiction into all of the presently restricted areas.

Informal aspects of grievance settlement. Most of the 22 contracts specified that every attempt should be made to settle each grievance at the informal level. Indeed, 13 actually specified that the aggrieved *must* try to settle the matter by discussing it with his super-

visor before putting the grievance into writing. At 10 of the 22 campuses, faculty and administration agreed that all grievances to date had been settled at the informal stages. Inquiry revealed over and over again that faculty and administration worked diligently to settle matters prior to formal written charges. Comments varied as to the reason. Faculty expressed in different ways the feeling that administrators "really" tried to settle problems "now that formal grievance procedures exist," and especially where binding arbitration was available. Other comments from both faculty and administrators indicated that a new businesslike approach to settlement of problems had evolved from the contractual agreement. "The contract tells you who's right and who isn't," said one college business officer who handled many complaints. "You might as well settle it early and save time," said a dean. "We know what we can grieve and what we can't," said a faculty member. "Why wash your dirty linen in public?" said another.

Regardless of reason, everyone seemed to agree that settlement at the informal stages was salutary. Several administrators, nevertheless, complained about a sharp increase in the number of complaints by faculty. More than one administrator felt that a few unhappy faculty could and do use grievances as an effective method for harassing administrators. Said one administrator, "Grievance procedures invite faculty to complain." Probably deans felt more keenly than anyone else the burden of grievance hearings. They are often specified as the first line of grievance mediation, fact-finding, and/or arbitration beyond the immediate supervisory level. Few feel equipped to handle quasi-legal hearings leading to complex decisions. Most deans felt "caught in the middle," for their decisions often impaired working relationships with colleagues. This problem was confirmed by faculty members who felt uneasy about appearing before "their" dean. These facts should be carefully considered in negotiating new grievance procedures, whether

*A more complete text may be obtained by writing PERB, 50 Wolf Road, Albany, N.Y. 12205.

"I think the optimum pupil-teacher ratio ought to be 20 to 1 . . . twenty teachers to one student!"

in colleges or in public schools. A "middle management" representative (e.g., dean or building principal) often loses rapport with his teachers because he is required to represent a "management" rather than a "human relations" point of view in conducting first-level grievance reviews.

Final stage in grievance procedures. At one campus the final decision is made by an all-college grievance board. At another, the county executive makes a binding decision. College trustees make the final decision at four of the campuses, although in two instances an outside fact finder's report must be obtained prior to decision. Fifteen of the 22 contracts established binding arbitration by a neutral party as the last step in grievance settlement. In all but two contracts costs of professional arbiters, fact finders, and mediators were to be shared equally by the college and the faculty union. In the two exceptions the contract failed to specify who would pay the costs. At four colleges the contract specified that the decision would be made by a three-man arbitration panel, the trustees choosing one member, the faculty union choosing a second, and the two chosen members agreeing on a third. When the first two could not agree on a third member, the problem was usually resolved by asking the American Arbitration Association to appoint a neutral. Two contracts specified that nonunion members of the faculty were not to have the privilege of arbitration, a form of discrimination that has not yet been challenged in court under the New York State Taylor Law.

Types of Grievances

Although innumerable complaints had been made by faculty during the first two years of living under a negotiated contract, only 27 were reported as reaching the formal written stages of grievance. These grievances may be classified roughly into two categories: those occurring as a result of rather trivial detail being included in the contract and those that challenge the administration's interpretation of broadly stated agreements.

The first category accounted for 12 of the 27 formal grievances and included such items as these:

—The administration must consider at least one faculty member as a candidate for each administrative vacancy.

—The administration must consult

"I was displaced by a little old lady with a piece of chalk."

union officers about appointment of every nonteaching staff member.

—The administration must consult union officers about any reorganization of personnel on campus, no matter how little it may affect faculty interests.

—The size of a class shall not exceed a specific number of students.

—The teaching load of a faculty member shall not exceed a specific number of contact hours.

—Specified parking space for each faculty member.

—Specified clerical services for each faculty member.

—Specified bulletin board space for each faculty member.

Whenever such items are included in the contract, the administration can be certain of innumerable complaints which seldom go to formal grievance. "The faculty can kill you with complaints and threats of grievance," said one president. "I sometimes feel like an errand boy for faculty," said a dean. Even faculty union officers were beginning to be wary of such detail in contracts, since they often were asked to carry faculty complaints to the administration. "Details like that offer complainers the perfect opportunity to nag you day after day," said one union officer.

The alternative to detail is the broadly framed agreement on principle that depends on good will and sound judgment on the part of both parties. An

example of such an agreement is. "Teaching loads and class size will be kept within reasonable limits. Problems related to these matters may be placed on the agenda of the biweekly meetings between association officers and the president." This statement permits faculty members to make complaints, but the complaints go to union officers, who then have a chance to sift out the valid from the biased and proceed accordingly. A union that complains publicly about trivia may soon lose its momentum and credibility in the eyes of its own membership. A wise union officer can often get many details ironed out by going directly to the business officer with details about bulletin boards, parking space, cleaning services, clerical service, telephones, etc. Business officers are usually matter-of-fact in resolving valid complaints. In such cases the union may serve an important function in removing non-academic detail from the desks of department chairmen and deans. In a few instances a dean or chairman may resent being bypassed by the union and thus deserves the detail which accrues.

There are two important aspects of the broadly written agreement: 1) Discretionary authority remains with the administration, and 2) there is provision for regular meetings at which the union may represent the needs of its membership on a systematic basis throughout the year. The optimism most frequently expressed by faculty was in regard to the increased communication between faculty and administration. The complaints most frequently expressed related to the administration's lack of understanding of faculty problems. Faculty members obviously wanted to work with effective administrators, and they knew that to be effective, administrators must have the power to exercise discretion and that discretion must be tempered with understanding. Thus a broadly written agreement that recognizes not only the duty of administration to make decisions but also the duty of faculty to provide information is likely to promote harmonious relationships in the long run.

Too many broadly written agreements fail to provide regularly scheduled meetings by which teachers may submit information in a manner that satisfies them and produces salutary change. When such channels are lacking or ineffective, formal grievances are likely to raise the following types of questions:

"The swift and equitable handling of grievances is perhaps the most important factor in securing harmonious and cooperative relationships between employer and professional employees in educational institutions. Grievance procedures, therefore, should be carefully prepared in each contract."

—Should nonteaching professional staff receive pay for evening work?

—Should a part-time lecturer be given a full-time appointment when such a position is open? When he teaches more than six hours?

—Is the time between semesters considered working time or vacation?

—How much credit toward a full teaching load should a teacher receive for supervising a two-hour laboratory?

—Does the administration have the right to abolish a job? Under what circumstances?

—Is the administration required to give reasons for not reappointing a faculty member? When? In what manner?

—Did the administration fail to reappoint a person active in the union because of his union activities?

—Does the contract require the administration to accept the judgment of a faculty committee regarding promotions?

—Does a cost-of-living salary raise include or exclude the annual increment?

—Does the faculty have all of the rights it had prior to the negotiated contract, or only those mentioned in the contract?

Obviously, any faculty union intent upon pleasing individual members may press grievances of the types listed, regardless of the manner in which the contract is written. However, when the contract is written broadly to permit administrative discretion and provide regular consultation, the union is more likely to press only those few unresolved grievances which will be popularly supported or even demanded by its membership. Without popular support for grievance, the union is not only likely to lose the case but lose face, which it cannot afford.

Recommendations

After the review of procedures, contractual cases, and comments by faculty and administrators, certain thoughts emerge as being worthy of consideration:

—Administrators should accept faculty unions and include them as a resource for strengthening the operation of their college or school.

—Regular meetings between top administration and top union officers should be planned on a cooperative basis to identify and resolve issues amicably.

—An informal stage of grievance hearings should be strongly encouraged by both the administration and the union. Such hearings can increase the responsibility and willingness of both parties to resolve issues cooperatively without resort to formal arbitration, which gives a neutral the authority to overrule either or both parties.

—The number of grievance settlements at the informal stage is increased when swift and public resolution by a neutral party is available.

—The number of enervating personality conflicts leading to formal grievance is often reduced when public settlement by neutrals is assured.

—Separation of responsibilities for conflict settlement and program development may be one of the most important advances in college and school administration during the decade of the seventies. In the public domain the powers of arrest, seizure, trial, and penalty have long been separated from responsibility for program development. Academic deans or building principals primarily responsible for program development should probably not be responsible, except at an informal stage, for resolving personality conflicts, disciplining faculty, holding formal hearings, and meting out penalties. The two responsibilities are often incompatible and may destroy the effectiveness of administrators not possessing the juridical wisdom of Solomon. In addition, the matter of time becomes a controlling factor. An educational administrator sooner or later may become either an educational leader or an excellent contract administrator, but seldom both.

—More grievances will be processed, justice will be increased, and time will be saved when the total procedure is not too long. (Some contracts specified as many as seven steps in the grievance procedure.)

—There should be at least three stages: the informal, the full review with intramural neutrals at no cost, and the opportunity for appeal to extramural neutrals at reasonable cost. A hearing with neutrals at no cost assures minimal due process without discrimination as to ability to pay. The opportunity for appeal is also an essential right of the individual, but to provide it without cost is to encourage the bypassing of early grievance stages without reasonable attempt at settlement. A recommended procedure for handling grievances, therefore, is in three stages.*

The Informal Stage. At this point a faculty member should be given the opportunity to talk with his departmental chairman or the administrator directly concerned, in an attempt to resolve the issue as quickly as possible. Should the individual prefer, the union representative may also talk with the chairman, either with the faculty member present or alone. In some cases the individual and/or the union representative may request the next level of administration, ordinarily the dean or a building principal, to review the case privately for an informal and quick resolution. The administrator must be free of coercion in deciding how he wishes to use his time and in determining whether the case at hand is important to his particular work. The department chairman also has certain informal resources available. If he thinks the case will go to formal grievance, he should seek advice from other faculty members, preferably a departmental committee of not more than three people, selected in advance to advise the

---

*One recommended grievance procedure for teachers in public schools includes four steps. See Van Delinder and St. Germaine, "A Model Four-Stage Grievance Procedure," Today's Education, February, 1970.

chairman on all types of matters. Committee advice should be informal, without votes being taken, in order not to prejudice a later decision should it go to formal hearing. Committee discussion should attempt to bring out all factors from both sides, thus helping the chairman to make a reasoned decision.

Formal Review by Intramural Neutrals. One possible procedure would be a panel of neutrals, chaired by the institutional director of employee relations, available to hold formal hearings. The director should be a person respected for his objectivity and understanding of collegial governance. He may be a full-time or part-time employee selected by the chief administrator for his ability and skill in handling employee relations. Preferably, he will be a full-time employee; he may be the chief negotiator for the employer and therefore fully acquainted with the details and meaning of the contract. He could also be the chief administrator of the contract, meeting regularly with union officials and the chief administrator to resolve informal issues throughout the year. His primary interest must be the welfare of the institution as a whole and he must know the importance of good relations with the union. He should report directly to the chief administrator and not be beholden to any other academic officer. He should be instructed by the chief administrator to resolve all issues, if possible, in a just manner that minimizes the need for outside conciliation.

The first job of the director might well be to establish a permanent review panel of approximately 10 staff members, including five administrative and five teaching faculty.* When asked to review a grievance, the director would appoint a five-member hearing body, ordinarily selecting two panel members on advice from the union and two members on advice from the supervisor. The hearing should provide for briefs, rebuttal, and cross-examinations of witnesses by the panel only. The union may represent the aggrieved, but it may not utilize professional counsel or other "outside" help. The supervisor may

---

*Some unions feel that permitting their members to sit on a preliminary review board is unwise because it may prejudice a later decision by an appeals board. The same may be said, however, by the administrator. The answer lies in a firm determination to solve the institution's problems in a cooperative, harmonious manner within the institution – which is the stated purpose of most labor laws. The alternative is a sterile type of administrative review which leaves the union unrepresented, seldom satisfies the grievant, and almost never settles the issue.

request his dean (or principal) or other administrators to help prepare the "official position of the department chairman." The director should be required to prepare a majority opinion (without reference to individual opinions) and present it to the chief administrative officer within 10 days after the hearing and panel deliberations. The chief administrator should be required to render a decision within 10 days of receipt of the majority opinion. Presumably, the 10 days will provide minimal time necessary to consult with other administrators, advisory groups, and/or board members. The chief administrator should not be required to accept the decision of the panel and he may direct the panel to reconvene for further hearings. Board members should not interfere with this executive decision, since their role is legislative in character and they have already approved a contract which provides for a third-stage appeal. They do, on the other hand, have every duty to advise the chief administrator in critical cases, perhaps preventing unnecessary hard feelings and costs of stage three grievances.

Arbitration by Extramural Neutrals. Stages one and two should provide effective deterrents to requests for external arbitration. Sharing the cost equally between the union and the college provides an additional deterrent. The union will need the support of its membership to spend funds for arbitration. The cost usually involves paying the arbitrator and counsel. If the parent union provides counsel free, it too will probably review the issues to determine

"I learned a new word at school today . . . S-T-R-I-K-E!"

feasibility of entering the case. Final arbitration should be conducted completely by outside neutrals. Advance agreement in the contract should identify the source of arbiters such as the American Arbitration Association, state or federal conciliation agencies, or other neutral bodies, in order to expedite action. In any case, the contract should be clear as to scope of arbitration* in order to avoid later litigation in civil courts. The arbitrator's decision should be accepted as final and in good grace. When the issue is excluded from arbitration, the third step provided should meet all requirements of due process, including hearings with professional counsel, and should leave the final decision to the governing board of the institution.

Common Law for Education

The swift and equitable handling of grievances is perhaps the most important factor in securing harmonious and cooperative relationships between employer and professional employees in educational institutions. Grievance procedures, therefore, should be carefully prepared in each contract, kept flexible through the early years, and constantly reviewed and strengthened in each succeeding contract. Properly conceived, grievance procedures can be a boon to both administrators and faculty whose common concern is progress based on justice and harmony. At first contact, grievances can appear to be time-consuming and discouraging to administrators. But the results should be worth the investment. Local grievance settlements, arbitrators' rulings, and court decisions will slowly but surely provide a new body of "common law" for education that not only protects the rights of the employees but encourages administrators to exercise managerial controls essential to efficiency and effectiveness in the expenditure of public funds. It is the lack of common law that underlies most current conflicts between teacher and employer. Without it, neither can hope to know the limits of his jurisdictional rights.

---

*For a comprehensive, detailed discussion and analysis of collective negotiations in the public sector, administrators and employers may obtain a copy of *Municipal Negotiations: From Differences to Agreement*, Handbook No. 5, Labor-Management Relations Service, 1612 K Street, NW, Washington, D.C. 20006. Grievance and arbitration procedures and suggestions on pp. 24-26 are helpful in dealing with scope of arbitration. □

Myron Lieberman

THE FUTURE OF
COLLECTIVE NEGOTIATIONS

In December, 1961, the United Federation of Teachers, Local 2 of the American Federation of Teachers, won the right to bargain for New York City's teachers. The UFT gained bargaining rights only after a long and bitter election contest, the first of many that dominated the teacher representation scene in the 1960's. At the time of the election, opinion was divided as to whether the UFT or the Teachers' Bargaining Organization (the National Education Association affiliate in New York City) would win the election. There was even greater disagreement over the significance of the election. At one extreme, some observers thought that the election outcome would mean very little one way or another. At the other extreme, it was asserted that the election outcome would have a catalytic effect upon teacher organizations in this country. Today, it appears that even the latter group largely underestimated the impact of the New York City experience and of teacher bargaining generally, not just upon teacher organizations but upon many other aspects of education as well.

In a field notoriously subject to bandwagons and exaggerated predictions of one sort or another, teacher bargaining or negotiating has drastically modified the institutional structure of education within a relatively short period of time. By 1971, approximately 70% of the nation's teachers were covered by collective agreements. Thus in less than a decade personnel administration has been forced away from its historic orientation toward individual contracts and from an approach which emphasized relations between administrators and individual teachers, totally ignoring teacher organizations. Teacher organizations now play a crucial role in formulating and implementing personnel policies affecting teachers. At the school level especially,

teacher organizations typically play a vital role in grievance procedures. The organizations are involved in defining grievances, setting the time limits for their initiation, determining the steps in the grievance procedure, identifying who can grieve, and setting the conditions of grievance arbitration.

Within teacher organizations themselves, sweeping changes have resulted from the advent of collective negotiations. The number of full-time professional staff members has increased at least tenfold. Significantly, a considerable proportion of the increase, especially in NEA affiliates, has been in local associations which previously lacked full-time staff. Collective negotiations thus reflect a basic shift away from a legislative approach to teacher welfare. Actually, the negotiations revolution has greatly strengthened the legislative and political capability of teacher organizations, but this greater capability is now exercised in conjunction with a much more effective representational capability at the local level.

Teacher organizations have changed in other significant ways. Administrators have left or have been excluded from NEA affiliates in enormous numbers, especially since the middle 1960's. In 1961, one could legitimately characterize the NEA as administrator-dominated; in 1971, such a criticism would be clearly unwarranted, although it might still apply to a few state and local affiliates not fully involved in collective negotiations. As a matter of fact, the proposed new constitution for the NEA would render anyone representing a school employer ineligible for NEA membership. Even the AFT has adopted more stringent provisions governing administrator and supervisor membership as a result of the collective negotiations movement.

The process of administrator exclusion and/or

PHI DELTA KAPPAN, Dec. 1971, pp. 214-216.

withdrawal from NEA and AFT has, therefore, brought about a realignment in administrator organizations. Although this realignment is still in process, it is clear that the upper echelons of administration are rapidly and unequivocally identifying themselves as management. At the same time, however, there is much ambivalence and uncertainty among middle management, especially principals and supervisors. Most organizations of middle management retain ties with the NEA and state associations, but there is no clear-cut resolution of the role of middle management in the negotiations picture. In some districts, middle management is becoming organized as an employee group, sometimes under the jurisdiction of the AFL-CIO. Some of the variations in the role of middle management are due to differences in state laws regulating collective negotiations in public education. It may be that unless and until federal legislation brings about a more consistent approach to their role, there will be no definitive resolution of the negotiations issues pertaining to principals and supervisors.

Collective negotiations have clearly resulted in a significant reorientation in the functions and budgetary priorities of teacher organizations. The need for full-time staff to negotiate and administer contracts has created enormous financial pressures upon the organizations at local, state, and national levels. The number of teachers paying dues and the amount of dues paid have increased substantially, but the pressure on services and programs not directly related to negotiations and teacher welfare is unremitting. In fact, there is a tendency for teacher organizations to divest themselves of some of the so-called professional functions and services they formerly provided.

The pervasive changes in teacher organizations have inevitably led to some fundamental changes in educational administration. School districts have been forced to establish new administrative positions or graft negotiating functions upon previously established positions. For the most part, educational administrators were unprepared for negotiation, and many are still not prepared for it. Resort to outside negotiators is still common and is likely to continue indefinitely.

Of all the significant consequences of collective negotiations, perhaps the one which has received the least attention thus far is the gain in the power of administrators and the corresponding decline in the power of school boards. This shift has gone unnoticed because so much attention has been devoted to the increased power of teacher organizations vis-à-vis boards and administrators. There is no doubt that such a shift has occurred. It is not generally recognized, however, that equally important shifts of power and authority have been taking place within as well as between the employer and employee sides. Negotiators for school boards must have the authority to negotiate. If they must first secure the approval of their boards for each individual concession, negotiations are practically impossible. Furthermore, the dynamics of negotiations require that negotiators be in a position to make a deal at the appropriate time — and this literally may be any time of the day or night, when it may be virtually impossible to have a board meeting. Thus boards of education have increasingly found it necessary to delegate more authority to their negotiating teams; the latter have been making more and more of the crucial decisions governing school personnel relationships. This is a basic change from the pre-negotiations era, when a board of education could consider terms and conditions of employment as individual issues, on a schedule unilaterally set by the board. It is also significant that teacher negotiating teams, which are increasingly dominated by full-time professional staff, are playing the same decisive role on the teacher side.

Perhaps the most important outcome of the negotiations movement will be the increased political effectiveness of teachers. Such an outcome, although highly paradoxical, is almost inevitable. In the pre-negotiations era, teacher organizations were politically ineffective. One major reason was the ideology that education is or ought to be a nonpartisan activity of government. Another was the absence of full-time activists at the local level. As previously pointed out, however, collective negotiations are bringing about an enormous increase in the number of full-time staff of teacher organizations. These staff members are rapidly providing the political clout which teacher organizations lacked in the past. Thus, although the negotiations movement is itself due to the prior overemphasis upon a legislative approach to teacher welfare, one of its most important consequences is a much more active and influential political role for teacher organizations.

Although all of the preceding consequences have yet to reach full maturity, they are clearly visible in developments to date. At this point, however, let us consider what are likely to be the major developments in the next decade. Like those previously discussed, some of these are already under way. In general, however, they can be considered the second generation of developments in the collective negotiations movement.

Without trying to list them in any particular order of importance, I suggest that the following developments will predominate in the 1970's.

1. The widespread acceptance of collective negotiations in higher education and in nonpublic schools.

2. A trend toward regional and statewide bargaining.

3. Greater scrutiny and public regulation of the internal affairs of teacher organizations.

4. An intensive effort to organize paraprofessionals in education.

5. Greater negotiating and legislative emphasis upon organizational security, especially agency shop clauses.

6. A major effort to enact federal legislation

regulating collective negotiations by state and local public employees.

7. A tendency to avoid substantial organizational expenditures for curriculum, teacher education, and other activities not central to negotiations, and a corresponding effort to have nonrepresentational services financed by the government.

8. The clarification and resolution of issues relating to elected and appointed personnel of teacher organizations; the trend will be toward the election of full-time policy-making officers and the appointment of those below the policy-making and political level.

9. A growing concern with performance contracting, voucher systems, and other institutional changes that appear likely to undermine traditional employment relationships in education.

10. Widespread internal as well as external conflict over organizational activity intended to protect teachers from racial or sexual discrimination.

It is also my belief that the NEA and the AFT will merge in the 1970's. It is already evident that the major factors impeding merger are not ideological but political – who gets what job, or what staff and allied interests (e.g., insurance companies and attorneys) will prevail after the merger. It also appears that the 1970's will see teacher leadership achieve unprecedented levels of political influence at all levels of government. This will happen concurrently with a greater emphasis upon better management in school districts generally.

One of the most important but least predictable matters is who will exercise the dominant leadership roles in the years ahead. In the AFT, it seems safe to say that the dominant figure is Albert Shanker, the president of the UFT; as a matter of fact, probably no other organization leader commands as much respect in both NEA and AFT as Shanker does. With or without a merger, he will unquestionably be one of the top teacher leaders of the 1970's.

Partly because it is a much larger organization, partly because no state or local affiliate in the NEA is as dominant as the UFT is in the AFT, and partly because of unresolved issues pertaining to the role of elected as distinguished from appointed officers, it is much more difficult to identify individuals who will play the critical leadership roles in the NEA in the 1970's. Top talent is certainly there among both elected and appointed officers, but the present NEA structure is not conducive to leadership accountability to the membership. If the NEA's new constitution successfully resolves this issue, some of the most important and exciting political contests of our time will be those to decide the national leadership of teacher organizations.

As our nation moves toward a new economic structure, it is essential that teachers be effectively organized if their needs and interests are to receive adequate consideration. In my view, and without endorsing any particular organizational position on specific issues, teachers are better organized and represented today than at any other time in the history of this country, and there is every reason to expect even higher levels of organizational representation and service in the 1970's. ☐

CHAPTER VIII

Salaries

The question of evaluation of teachers would not command the attention it receives and would not result in the fireworks often accompanying it were it not for one fact -- that often the determination of raises and salaries is based on the results of the evaluation. Obviously, where money is concerned, teachers are as directly concerned as anyone and as interested in furthering their individual salaries as the members of any other working group. The problem lies not in the fact that this self-interest exists, for this is only human and inevitable, but rather in the way in which it is dealt with in seeking to provide equitable salaries for worthy members of a profession.

Considerable debate swirls around the question of what constitutes "merit" on the part of teachers and how such merit can be identified and ultimately rewarded. McKenna presents a description for the incentive evaluation and salary related program. The success of his program is based primarily upon staff involvement.

Often overlooked in consideration of salaries is the presence of so-called "fringe benefits". These have grown to the point that they represent a significant financial consideration and therefore deserve attention as part of the salary structure. Several approaches to dealing with these difficult problems have been identified and deserve our attention as professional people seeking to conduct our school business in a professionally consistent way.

Parke B. Loren and Jeffrey M. Elliot

TEACHER SALARIES AND THE U.S. ECONOMY

Resolving the problems of school finance and teachers' salaries requires a glimpse into the future economy of the United States. Despite the current downturn, projections of economic growth in the U.S. over the next several decades anticipate a phenomenal expansion which can support extended educational programs and increased teacher salaries.

We are fully aware that altered economic conditions resulting from the energy crisis, ecological problems, and limitations of raw materials may have a modifying effect on the rate of U.S. economic growth. Furthermore, we realize that the economy of this country is affected significantly by the economic well-being of other nations. However, we believe that technological and scientific advances will reduce or counterbalance the adverse effects of current crises.

The January, 1975, issue of *Money* featured a discussion of future economic growth as projected by several leading forecasting firms. These forecasts suggest that the gross national product of the U.S., in constant dollars, will reach a growth rate somewhere between 2% and 6% by the end of 1975 and will continue at this level during 1976.

The April, 1974, *Survey of Current Business* reported that economic growth in total personal income (TPI) in the U.S., in constant 1967 dollars, rose from $313.5 billion in 1950 to $708.6 billion in 1970. The projected TPI for 1980 was $1,068.5 billion, and for 1990 was $1,517.2 billion. TPI will increase by 1990 to 2.14 times the 1970 purchasing power, according to this fore-

PHI DELTA KAPPAN, Apr. 1975,

pp. 546-547.

cast. These projections assume an economic growth rate of 4.2% annually between 1970 and 1980 and of slightly less than 4% annually between 1980 and 1990.

While we believe that this growth rate is attainable, a reduction in the rate of economic growth will not alter the heart of our proposal: Educational funding and teachers' salaries should be tied to some valid index of economic growth so that those concerned will be able to participate equitably in the fruits of economic growth. We suggest that economic growth in the United States during the next two or three decades will support the educational services required for the leisure-oriented, affluent, technology-based society which is currently emerging.

When these projected data are converted into per capita personal income (PCPI), we find a suitable justification for adequate salaries for teachers. The *Survey of Current Business* projects PCPI, again in constant 1967 dollars, of $4,780 in 1980 and $6,166 in 1990. Since the PCPI in this country was $3,188 in 1967, purchasing power should increase 49.94% from 1967 to 1980 and 93.41% from 1967 to 1990. Although a lower rate of economic growth would reduce these figures, we anticipate substantial economic growth prior to 1980 and 1990.

We believe that teachers' salaries should be tied to economic growth as reflected by changes in PCPI. We further propose that salary changes be determined by increases – or decreases – in the PCPI for the particular locale served by a school system. The average teacher salary in the United States in 1967 was $6,830. In 1971 the average salary had increased to $9,265 and by 1973 had reached $10,114. However, if the average salary had been bound to changes in the nation's PCPI, the average would have been $8,919 in 1971 and $10,599 in 1973. Note that our approach would have resulted in a reduction in the average salary in 1971 and an increase of $485 in 1973.

We offer the salary changes in the public schools of Dade County (Miami), Florida, as an example. In 1967 the average salary of Dade County teachers was $8,300. This average had increased to $10,435 in 1971 and to $11,886 in 1973. However, if these average salaries had been locked into the changes in PCPI in the United States, the average would have been $10,921 in 1971 and $12,881 in 1973. Furthermore, had the average salary been tied to the growth in PCPI in Florida, it would have been $11,933 in 1971 and $13,790 in 1973. Basing salary increases upon changes in the PCPI in the Miami, Florida, Standard Metropolitan Statistical Area would have resulted in an average salary of $12,074 for 1971. (Data for the Miami, Florida, SMSA for 1973 will not be available until May, 1975.)

If the average salary of U.S. teachers were bound to the nation's projected PCPI for 1980 and 1990, the $6,830 average for 1967 would increase, in constant 1967 dollars, to $10,240 in 1980 and to $13,209 by 1990. If the average salary of Dade County teachers were locked into the projected PCPI for the U.S. for 1980 and 1990, the $8,300 average for 1967 would increase, in constant 1967 dollars, to $12,445 in 1980 and $16,053 in 1990. However, if the average salary were tied to projections of PCPI in Florida, the average salary of Dade County teachers would increase, in constant 1967 dollars, to $13,200 in 1980 and to $16,995 in 1990. Naturally, adjustments for inflation would increase these salary figures.

We suggest that this approach to the determination of teachers' salaries would eliminate much of the friction which may adversely affect education. Since salaries in the private sector of the economy tend to change in concert with changes in the PCPI, the establishment of some fixed relationship between teacher salaries and the changes in the PCPI should provide some measure of fairness in the development of salary schedules. In such a system, educators would have to be prepared to accept the effects of possible downswings in the economy. However, such downswings would probably occur only in the event of pronounced economic dislocation which would affect the revenues of the school systems. Furthermore, these economic dislocations would also generate severe contractions in the private sector of the national economy.

Whatever the nation's economic future, educators must be prepared to play a central role in creating and preserving the stability of our society. Educators must become increasingly future-oriented in research, leadership, and service. Educational spending should be regarded as an investment in the future welfare of the nation — not as an expense to be avoided. We hope that educational leaders will accept this challenge. □

Merit Pay: Review and Rejection

MITZI MIDDLEBROOKS

$\mathcal{T}$HE idea of merit pay is of ancient origin and has long been the subject of study, debate, and controversy. Although most merit pay plans have been developed locally, several states, including New York, Delaware, and Florida, have passed laws in past years mandating such plans, only to repeal them later. Those local merit pay plans still in existence are based primarily on objective criterions such as the number of hours of education above the Bachelor's Degree a teacher has. Many merit plans in local school districts have actually been "demerit" plans where normal increments were withheld from teachers not deemed worthy.

The idea that merit pay is a widespread and accepted practice in business and industry for persons doing the same kind of work is a misconception. Efforts to apply the principle of merit pay to industry have led to almost as much difficulty and failure as similar efforts in education. An Esso study says that the *process* industries don't lend themselves to wage-incentive plans. Education *is* a process industry.

Before we delve any further into the pros and cons of merit pay, it is important that "merit pay" be defined. The NEA in 1956 defined it as: "Subjective, qualitative judgment of a teacher made administratively by one or more persons with or without the participation or the knowledge of the person rated, for purposes of determining salary."

The proponents of merit pay usually think in terms of certain basic premises. These are:

1. Superior teachers are important and should be rewarded.

2. If superior and poor teachers are paid alike, initiative will be killed and mediocrity will be encouraged.

3. Some teachers aren't good teachers and the public won't stand for paying them professional salaries.

Some accompanying assumptions are:

1. That it *is* possible to make a qualitative and comparative evaluation of teachers.

2. That someone in the administrative and supervisory staff *is able* to make this evaluation.

3. That merit pay will make

• • • • • • • • • • • • • • • • •

BOARDMAN, Feb. 1975, XXIX, pp. 10-14.

teachers try harder to be good teachers.

4. That school boards can't afford to pay professional salaries to all of the teaching staff.

Most teachers and administrators deny the validity of these assumptions. First, the key stumbling block to merit pay is the method of identifying the superior teacher. Educators don't believe that a qualitative evaluation is possible, at least not yet. An American Educational Research Association study found few outcomes that a superintendent can safely employ in rating teacher effectiveness. Merit pay ultimately depends on subjective judgments. No valid or reliable instrument has yet been developed for measuring teacher effectiveness or the total growth of students, which involves growth in values, ability to think, understanding of self, and other intangibles.

Those who have attempted to determine specific criterions for a merit system have found it difficult. In 1957, West Hartford, Connecticut, had in operation one of the more promising merit pay plans. It *did* have specific criterions. After 10 years' trial, West Hartford abandoned its plan. A survey proved that only *two* of the *16* criterions were being met. One major objection was that it *could not* be shown to have improved instruction. The same objection has been raised repeatedly to other merit plans. It just seems impossible to measure the qualities of superior teaching.

Secondly, studies have indicated that administrators and supervisors themselves resist merit schedules. These people feel that rating for the purpose of salary is an interference with their major function—to promote and improve instruction. Teachers are not opposed to the idea of evaluation. In fact, most teachers welcome it to help them recognize and correct their mistakes—an important tool for the improvement of instruction.

The TEPS (Teacher Education and Professional Standards) Committee at its 1974 conference asked educators at all levels to consider the evaluation procedure to determine the purposes for evaluation and the most effective means to be used. The consensus of all there was that evaluating for merit pay caused a breach between administrators and those evaluated. It was felt that it destroys the cooperative spirit which should exist between teachers and administrators.

Third, educators don't believe that a competitive merit schedule will actually buy more good teaching for a community. Merit-rating plans tend to create problems in teacher relationships and morale. Instead of teachers sharing ideas with each other, problems related to jealousy, fear, favoritism, undesirable competition, and insecurity appear. Merit programs tend to discourage creativity in teaching. Teachers tend to conform to preconceived ideas of some person or to a stereotyped criterion.

A merit system can have harmful effects on teaching because it undermines morale through denial of increments. Young teachers might be denied the privilege of being rated for merit increments.

Merit rating is no substitute for adequate facilities, good working conditions, decent salaries for all teachers, faculty team work, and effective supervisory services. The best guarantee of improving the quality of teaching is to be found in developing a professional climate in which continued growth in creativity and cooperativeness among teachers is guaranteed.

Merit rating is oppressive politically, because the persons who are directly affected by it are not the ones who originate it, put it into operation, and administer it. It inhibits cooperative discussion of salary matters between teacher groups and boards of education and thus reduces professionalism.

Alternatives

There are some alternatives to merit ratings:

1. Colleges should do a better screening job of prospective teacher candidates.

2. School boards need to be more selective when choosing teachers. This is certainly possible now since there seems to be an abundant supply of applicants for teaching positions.

3. More adequate supervision is needed in the schools. Supervisors now have more teachers to supervise than they can effectively handle. Principals need to take a closer look at probationary teachers and not have the attitude ''they will probably get better.'' If a supervising teacher of a student teacher indicates that the student teacher does not have the qualities of a good teacher, then the student's files should indicate such. Superintendents should consider the recommendations of principals that a teacher not be rehired.

4. Specialists and coordinators could be selected from among the better teachers.

5. School boards could pay additional compensation for those teachers who have an additional work load—sponsors of cheerleaders, student councils, and clubs.

6. Additional pay could be given in step lots for hours taken above the Master's Degree.

7. Some teachers could be employed for more than a nine-month school plan in such capacities as writing curriculum programs, conducting workshops, etc.

8. School boards could staff a school with ''master'' teachers and send teachers there who need help so that the better teachers could help the poorer teachers. □

JOHN F. SULLIVAN

The Future of Merit Pay for Teachers

Traditionally, the salaries of classroom teachers have been determined on the basis of only two criteria—level of formal education and years of teaching experience. The result is that teacher salary schedules tend to look like 30-cell matrixes, with years of teaching experience (e.g., 1-10) as rows and level of education (e.g., B.A., M.A., M.A.+30) as columns. Salaries increase with increasing levels of experience and/or education, and to determine a teacher's salary under such a system one has only to note where the years of experience and education

COMPENSATION REVIEW, Fourth Quarter, 1970, pp. 23-30.

intersect on the schedule. Once a year the entire schedule is increased to compensate for cost-of-living increases and, more recently, to ensure that teachers' salaries catch up with those paid to other professional groups.

Since no one would argue that teachers should be paid simply for living from year to year or for acquiring additional education, the logic implicit in such a system of salary administration is that a teacher's performance and worth to the school system increase with added years of experience or of formal education. Thus, the teacher's performance level or worth is inferred from the measurement of two "input" variables, education and experience.

This is basically comparable to performance appraisal and compensation in industry about ten years ago. At that time various personal and background characteristics of an employee (i.e., input variables) that were presumed to result in either good or poor job performance were measured and used as the basis for determining salary. Industry has learned, however, that job performance is the result of the interaction of a great many complex variables, some measurable, some not, and to relate pay to performance, performance (i.e., output) must be measured directly.

Focusing on the employee outputs is fast becoming one of the hallmarks of progressive managers and organizations, but so far this kind of thinking has had little, if any, impact on school systems. The teachers' organizations seem to be the most vociferous opponents of determining pay levels by direct, individual-by-individual evaluations of output, and continue to support the use of such criteria as levels of education and teaching experience. In the field of education, this is the merit pay controversy. The American Federation of Teachers (AFT) and National Education Association (NEA) present two major arguments against merit pay:

• No attention should be given to compensation programs utilizing individual performance evaluations until teachers' salaries, in general, are brought up to the levels found in other, comparable professional groups.

• A satisfactory way to measure a teacher's performance (output) has never been, and probably cannot be, developed.

The next section of this article will examine each of these arguments.

Upgrading Salaries The first of the two major arguments against merit pay contends that it will be hard to establish pay plans based on professional merit until teachers receive salaries competitive with those paid in other fields. However, many who take this position also believe that as salaries for teachers approach those of other professionals, merit pay plans will become common, because the tax-paying public will not consent to pay every teacher a high salary based simply on training and experience.

Actually, the data available regarding such prognostications indicate that teachers' salaries have been increasing rapidly and now approach the levels found in comparable, nonteaching professions, but that the number of merit pay plans is decreasing. In other words, it now appears that the tax-paying public may very well consent to pay every teacher a high salary based simply on training and experience.

In April 1969 a Bureau of Labor Statistics report showed that salaries of public school teachers in urban areas had increased faster between 1965 and 1967 than had the salaries of any other occupational group except city policemen and fire fighters. In one of its recent research publications the NEA estimated that during the 1969-70 school year the nationwide average salary for elementary school teachers was $8,311, and $8,835 for secondary school teachers. The information most relevant here, however, concerns the relationship between teachers' salaries and those paid to other professional groups. Figure 1 shows (a) the average annual salaries for the entry-level positions in metropolitan areas for various nonteaching, professional occupations (BLS figures) and (b) the average salary schedule minimum for elementary and secondary school teachers, in urban areas, with Bachelor's degree and no experience (NEA figures). Comparing these salary figures, however, would be misleading, because teachers work only about 80 percent as many days a year as do those in the other occupations shown:

Teachers		*Others*	
52 weeks x 5 days	260	52 weeks x 5 days	260
Minus summer vacation	210	Minus annual vacation	250
(10 weeks x 5 days)		(2 weeks x 5 days)	
Minus days off during	190	Minus holidays (10)	240
school year (20)			

Therefore, in Figure 1, the actual average salaries for the other occupations have been reduced by 20 percent, and this "adjusted" average annual salary is then shown as a percent of the average salary schedule minimum for urban area school systems. The inescapable conclusion is that classroom teachers' salaries have caught up with those paid in comparable, nonteaching professions, at least at the entry levels.

At the same time that this has been happening, the indications are that the frequency of merit pay plans has been decreasing. The NEA has reported that during the last 25 years, most of the largest cities in the United States have tried merit pay plans and discarded them. (Those cities included Washington, Philadelphia, Detroit, St. Louis, Pittsburgh, Atlanta, Buffalo, and Milwaukee.)

This movement away from merit pay plans for teachers is somewhat surpris-

Figure 1.

Average salaries for entry-level, metropolitan area positions in selected, nonteaching professions compared with the average salary schedule minimum for teachers in urban areas, 1969.*

Occupation	1969 Average annual salary	1969 Adjusted avg. annual salary	Adjusted salary as pct. of avg. salary schedule minimum—urban areas
Accountant	$8,040	$6,432	94%
Buyer	7,956.	6.365	93
Chemist	8,832	7,066	103
Engineer	9,672	7,738	113

* 1969-70 average salary schedule minimum, elementary and secondary classroom teachers, urban areas: $6,874

ing, for, as Keith Davis observed in *Human Relations at Work: The Dynamics of Organization Behavior:*

"The trend in the United States is toward somewhat more emphasis on merit for pay increases and other personnel actions. Merit is especially favored by persons with higher education and by persons in complex jobs permitting variations in quality of performance."

The reason for the discontinuance of merit pay plans heard most frequently is that no satisfactory way for evaluating teachers' performance has been developed—the second major argument against merit pay and perhaps the most cogent.

Evaluating Performance   The position of the NEA and the AFT is that one cannot accurately measure teaching performance, but the fact is that the performance of every teacher is evaluated—by the teacher himself, his students, his peers, and his organizational superiors. Unfortunately, however, these informal—and even some of the formal—evaluations of teachers nearly always focus on inputs and activities, rather than on outputs. Too often a teacher is thought of as "good" because he or she stays after the students have gone in order to work on lesson plans, or because he or she gets along well with other teachers, keeps the classroom neat, completes a course at a local college, and so forth. Not only are such evaluations likely to focus on inputs and activities, but they are also likely to be highly subjective. When they become part of a formalized system, administrators are asked to express judgments concerning teachers' loyalty, appearance, intelligence, personality, and so on. Naturally, everyone resists systems like this.

It is difficult to justify the subjective evaluation of the irrelevant, but it is even more difficult to justify basing salary decisions on such evaluations. Most of the current teacher compensation and appraisal methods have, therefore, turned to criteria that appear to be relevant and, what is probably more important, criteria that can be evaluated objectively—education and experience. Thus, they objectively evaluate that which should be relevant, but often is not. In essence, they have moved from cell 1 to cell 2 in the figure shown below.

Employee Performance Appraisal Programs

		Criteria Measures	
		Subjective	Objective
Performance Criteria	Irrelevant	1	2
	Relevant	3	4

What is needed now is a movement to cell 4.

This then, raises a key question: "What is relevant for the evaluation of a teacher's performance?" The answer to this question is that one must evaluate a teacher's output or the results that he or she attains. Since a teacher's job is to teach, there might be an attempt to measure the progress that students make under the guidance of various teachers. Many teachers informally evaluate each other on the basis of such outputs already. This writer is reminded of a conversation with a woman who taught second grade and who expressed a good deal of dissatisfaction with one of the first-grade teachers in the same school. When the writer asked why she thought the other a "poor" teacher he was informed that by the end of the first grade the average student was expected to meet some very specific standards in reading, printing, and arithmetic, and that students from the other first grades generally met these criteria while those who were taught by the "poor" teacher did not. Thus, it appears that relevant results that can be measured objectively already exist in many, if not most, school systems. These kinds of performance measures should become the basis for teacher evaluation plans.

The development of such plans and their incorporation into the salary-determination process will require cooperation among administrators, teachers, and the leaders of teachers' organizations. As in industry, however, the final responsibility for employee evaluation and compensation rests with management, in this case the school board members and the superintendent. The *cooperation* of other interested parties should be solicited, but not their *permission*.

To say that such evaluations can be developed and should be used as a basis for

ANALYZING TEACHER "ACCOUNTABILITY"

Writing in the *New York Post* (June 22, 1970), the paper's education editor, Bernard Bard, discussed the "objective criteria of professional accountability" specified in the New York City Board of Education contract with the United Federation of Teachers and an attempt to define those criteria:

Working out a formula for "teacher accountability"—making teachers answerable for the success or failure of their students—may be easier said than done. The complications in setting up a system of measuring teacher output were outlined by the Rand Corporation, the Santa Monica "think tank," in a report to the City University of New York for a conference on the subject it sponsored in June.

An accountability system can be developed, said Rand consultant Stephen M. Barro, but the problem of setting up measurement devices that are accepted as "objective" and "fair" by the teachers themselves is large.

At the outset, he said, "performance norms" would probably have to be confined to the teaching of reading and math in the early grades where standardized tests are already available. Before they could be extended to high schools, he said, it would have to be decided what are valid measurements of educational success or failure—dropout rates, college acceptance, absenteeism, vandalism, incidence of delinquency.

The biggest problem in setting up an accountability formula, Barro said, is how to separate the contributions (or lack of them) to the educational process of the members of what is essentially a school team.

"Who should be accountable for what?" he asked. "How much [have] teachers, principals, administrators, and others ... contributed to the measured results?" For the system to work, he said, "each participant in the educational process should be held responsible only for those educational outcomes that he can affect by his actions and decisions and only to the extent that he can affect them." In other words, according to Barro's thesis, care must be taken not to blame (or give credit to) one person for what is mainly the responsibility of another.

The only way the measurement of teachers can be scientifically acceptable, Barro said, is to make sure that they are being measured against other teachers "in similar circumstances." What Barro is saying, basically, is that a teacher in an impoverished area should have her class scores compared to those in another impoverished area, not to scores in a well-to-do suburb.

Before an accountability formula can be put into effect, says Barro, weight must be given to such variables as ethnicity, income level, and earlier school experience—factors over which the teacher has no control but which can affect pupil progress.

When it comes to applying an accountability formula to school brass, the problem becomes even stickier, says Barro. All other things being equal (teacher competence, pupil background, et cetera), he asks, are there "unexplained differences among schools that can be attributed to differences in the quality of school leadership and administration?" If so, he asks in effect, how do you go about it? The problem is that "when two or more persons work together to perform an educational task there is no statistical way of separating their effects."

pay determination is not to say the doing will be easy. It won't. Above everything else it will take courage for school board members and administrators to accept the primary responsibility for developing and implementing such evaluations, and it will take courage for the leaders of teachers' organizations to participate and urge their members to participate in the development and implementation of merit pay plans. Later on, it will certainly take courage for a principal to inform a teacher of unsatisfactory performance or of a below-average salary increase based on below-average performance.

It is much more comfortable to continue with the traditional teacher salary administration program in which everyone moves ahead at essentially the same rate every year, but this is equal treatment of unequals and, therefore, discouraging to the well-qualified and otherwise highly motivated teacher. If the traditional program appeals to anyone, it is certainly the marginal, the superannuated, and/or the poorly motivated performer, whom the traditional system protects. They are the lowest common denominator to which all of the other teachers' salaries are reduced, and the result is negative, rather than a stimulus to superior performance.

The Next Steps Once the evaluation plan has been adopted and implemented there are many alternatives for relating salary to performance. One, at least as an intermediate step, would include the retention of an education experience matrix, but with these provisions:

• Those teachers who were satisfactory or slightly below or above would move in the traditional way.

• Those who were marginal or less than satisfactory would not change their position in the matrix but would receive structure adjustments that would be considered cost-of-living increases.

• Those whose performance was unsatisfactory would not change their position in the matrix and would be excluded from structure adjustments. In today's inflationary economy these people would, in effect, suffer a reduction in purchasing power, just as the school system suffered from their unsatisfactory performance.

• Truly superior performers would be able to move forward at the rate of up to three steps per year to a ten-year maximum.

• There would be a super-maximum for each level of education (column) equal to 120 percent of the tenth-year salary for that educational level. Movement from the normal maximum to the super-maximum would be based on outstanding performance. To ensure that movement above the normal maximum would be reserved for truly outstanding performance, it might be advisable to specify that no more than 5 percent of the system's teachers could be above the normal maximum during any school year.

In such a salary administration program the salaries of a few outstanding and experienced teachers would approach and might even exceed the salaries of beginning principals, but is anything really wrong with this unconventional situation? Why should the teacher be forced to move into administration to make more money? Conversely, why should a new or a marginal principal be paid more than an outstanding teacher?

A few words of caution are in order at this point. First, not only the teachers, but also the entire employee population of the school system, including the superintendent, must be evaluated and compensated on the basis of results. It is particularly critical to do so at the principal level and above, and, in fact, the place to begin such a program is at the top of the school system's organization, preferably before including the teachers.

It should be recognized that school boards and administrators who attempt to develop and implement such systems will meet with resistance, as is sometimes the case in industry. Most of this resistance will come from the weakest of the present employees, who, of course, will feel threatened. On the other hand, the majority of the competent, the superior, and the truly professional employees will welcome the change. This group should be motivated to join and stay with school systems that relate pay to performance, whereas the incompetent will tend to avoid or to leave such school systems, perhaps the entire field of education—a move that is hardly to be deplored.

Allen W. Smith

HAVE COLLECTIVE NEGOTIATIONS INCREASED TEACHERS' SALARIES?

Probably the most important development in public education during the past decade has been the rapid expansion of collective negotiations (CN hereafter). In 1961 an American Federation of Teachers affiliate defeated a National Education Association affiliate in a representation election in New York City. The subsequent competition between the AFT and the NEA, along with various other factors, resulted in a very rapid expansion in CN in the nation's schools. In 1960 none of the states had statutes authorizing CN in public education. By 1969 at least 18 states had enacted such laws. A study I conducted revealed that in Indiana the number of school systems practicing CN increased from 30 in 1961 to 166 (over 65% of the total) in 1969.*

A major factor underlying the sudden emergence of teacher militancy in the sixties was the fact that teachers' salaries were continuing to lag behind those of many other groups. Teachers, in increasing numbers, were coming to the conclusion that CN offered the best hope for attaining higher salaries and improved working conditions. After a decade of experience with CN in public education, it is appropriate that we try to determine whether teachers' salaries have in fact been increased by the new approach.

It is impossible to establish a direct cause and effect relationship between CN and teachers' salaries. There are no control groups. Although there are still

many school systems that do not engage in CN, the movement may have had an indirect effect on salaries in these systems. It is a common practice in the private sector for nonunion employers to match or surpass salary increases of neighboring union employers in an effort to avoid union organization attempts. It is likely that many school boards also engage in this practice. In the Indiana study, several superintendents commented that they were forced to match the salary increases of neighboring school systems in order to hold their faculty. In short, if negotiations substantially raise salaries for some teachers, they also probably raise salaries to some degree for most teachers. The appropriate question, therefore, seems to be whether or not average teacher salaries have increased relative to the average earnings of other groups during the CN drive of the past decade.

The data in Tables 1 and 2 provide at least a partial answer to this question. In Table 1 the average annual salary of the total instructional staff in full-time public elementary and secondary day schools in the United States is compared with personal per-capita income for the nation for a period of years both before and after the beginning of the massive drive for collective negotiations. In Table 2 a similar comparison is made between instructional staff salaries and gross average annual earnings of production or nonsupervisory workers on private nonagricultural payrolls in the

United States. In both tables an index of relationship between the two measures presented is shown in the third column.

Since the beginning of the massive upsurge in organizing and bargaining activity is generally considered to coincide with the 1961-62 events in New York City, a break in Tables 1 and 2 is shown after the 1961-62 school year. Therefore the top half of each table represents a period before the acceleration in collective negotiations, and the bottom half represents a period in which CN was expanding at a rapid rate.

Although teachers' salaries have been increasing throughout the entire period, there is no evidence of a substantial acceleration in teacher salary gains to match the acceleration in CN activity of the past decade. In fact, as revealed by Table 1, the ratio of instructional salaries to per-capita income appears to have reached a peak of 2.54 in 1963-64, with a slight decline since that time. The ratio of 2.44 in 1970-71 is less than that of 1961-62, just before the acceleration in collective negotiations activity began. Thus instructional salaries have not been increasing relative to per-capita income in recent years.

Table 2 reveals a gradual but steady increase in instructional salaries relative to gross average earnings of private production or nonsupervisory workers in recent years. However, this trend begins before the acceleration in CN activity and does not appear to be substantially affected by the CN drive. In the 8-year period prior to the acceleration in CN, the ratio of instructional salaries to average earnings of private production or nonsupervisory workers

PHI DELTA KAPPAN, Dec. 1972,

pp. 268-270.

Table 1. Ratio of the Average Annual Salary of Public School Instructional Staff to Annual Per-Capita Personal Income in the United States

Year	Average Salary of Instructional Staff	Per-Capita Personal Income	Ratio of Instructional Staff Salaries to Per-Capita Personal Income
1951-52	$3,450	$1,652	2.09
1953-54	3,825	1,804	2.12
1955-56	4,156	1,876	2.22
1957-58	4,702	2,045	2.30
1959-60	5,174	2,161	2.39
1961-62	5,700	2,264	2.52
Beginning of Collective Negotiations Drive			
1963-64	6,240	2,455	2.54
1965-66	6,935	2,765	2.51
1967-68	7,630	3,162	2.41
1969-70	8,840	3,687	2.40
1970-71	9,570	3,920	2.44

Source: Per Capita Personal Income from *Survey of Current Business*, U.S. Department of Commerce (August, 1970, and April, 1972). Average Annual Salary of Instructional Staff from *Statistics of State School Systems*, U.S. Office of Education, 1957-58, 1961-62, and 1967-68 issues, and (for 1967-68 to 1970-71) from *Fall Statistics of Public Schools*, U.S. Office of Education.

rose from 1.15 to 1.33. During the next nine years it rose from 1.33 to 1.54. Thus, while this ratio has been steadily increasing, there is no strong evidence that the increase is due to CN activity.

In Table 3 the results of a Department of Labor study of the average pay increase for selected public employee occupations for the 5-year period ending 1969-70 is presented. The average annual percent increase in average teacher salaries is higher than that for federal classified employees. However, it is lower than that for policemen and firemen, who have also been engaging in collective bargaining in recent years.

There is, therefore, no strong evidence of an acceleration in teachers' salary gains relative to other groups as a result of CN. However, these findings do not necessarily lead to the conclusion that CN has had no effect on teachers' salaries. Supply and demand conditions in public education have changed drastically during the period of the CN movement. A nationwide shortage of public school teachers existed in this country from World War II until the end of the sixties. In June, 1970, the U.S. Office of Education reported that the nationwide teacher shortage was over. Since that time the nation has experienced a substantial surplus of teachers in many fields.

The teacher shortage must certainly have played a role in raising teachers'

salaries during the years prior to the CN movement. The CN drive took place during a time when teacher supply was gradually catching up with demand. Thus competitive pressures (due to the shortage of teachers) were being reduced at the same time that teacher

organizations were attempting to increase pressures for higher salaries through collective action. It is, therefore, impossible to determine the magnitude of the effect of CN on teachers' salaries. It is quite possible that had there been no CN drive during the sixties, salary gains would have decreased as the teacher shortage gradually disappeared. CN may have been responsible at least for sustaining the rate of increase in teachers' salaries. In other words, the increases in teachers' salaries taking place in recent years, during a period when teacher supply was gradually catching up with and surpassing teacher demand, might have been much smaller in the absence of CN. (We shall not discuss the equally feasible hypothesis that CN and its related militancy had something to do with growth of the teacher surplus.)

Then there is the question whether particular groups of teachers may have made substantial gains as a result of CN. There is little doubt that in school systems where salaries are substantially below the area average, pressures from a strong teacher organization can hasten improvement. Substantial gains by a small number of school systems would not substantially affect the national average.

Even if CN had no effect on teachers'

Table 2. Ratio of the Average Annual Salary of Public School Instructional Staff to Gross Average Annual Earnings of Production or Nonsupervisory Workers on Private Nonagricultural Payrolls in the United States

Year	Average Salary of Instructional Staff	Gross Average Earnings of Production or Nonsupervisory Workers on Private Nonagricultural Payrolls	Ratio of Instructional Staff Salaries to Average Annual Earnings of Production or Nonsupervisory Workers
1951-52	$3,450	$3,009	1.15
1953-54	3,825	3,316	1.15
1955-56	4,156	3,521	1.18
1957-58	4,702	3,813	1.23
1959-60	5,174	4,097	1.26
1961-62	5,700	4,295	1.33
Beginning of Collective Negotiations Drive			
1963-64	6,240	4,600	1.36
1965-66	6,935	4,943	1.40
1967-68	7,630	5,296	1.44
1969-70	8,840	5,960	1.48
1970-71	9,570	6,212	1.54

Source: Gross Average Annual Earnings of Production or Nonsupervisory Workers on Private Nonagricultural Payrolls in the United States from *Employment and Earnings*, U.S. Department of Labor, Bureau of Labor Statistics, April, 1972. Average Annual Salary of Instructional Staff from *Statistics of State School Systems*, U.S. Office of Education, 1957-58, 1961-62, and 1967-68 issues, and (for 1967-68 to 1970-71) from *Fall Statistics of Public Schools*, U.S. Office of Education.

salaries, there would still be considerable justification for their existence, since they cover many nonsalary areas. In the Indiana study it was found that a total of 74 additional issues, ranging from salary-related areas to curriculum and general school policy, had entered negotiations somewhere in the state. Issues such as class size, teacher assignment and reassignment procedures, teacher evaluation, nonteaching duties, and physical facilities may be of greater importance to teacher welfare in the long run than salary gains. Furthermore, CN is likely to be more successful in bringing about improvements in these areas in the long run than they will be in raising teachers' salaries. Improvements in working conditions are usually less costly to the taxpayers than are improved salaries.

In summary, although the evidence does not indicate that average teacher salaries for the nation have substantially increased relative to other groups in recent years, this does not mean that collective negotiations have had no effect on teachers' salaries. Since the CN drive took place during a period in which the teacher shortage was being eliminated, it may have been responsible for preventing a decline in teachers' salaries relative to other groups. Also, substantial gains may have been experienced by a small number of school systems without affecting the national

Table 3. Percent Increase in Average Pay for
Selected Public Employee Occupations:
Five-Year Period Ending in 1969-70

Occupation	Total	Average Annual Rate
Public School Teachers, Average Annual Salaries	38.2	6.7
Federal Classified Employees, Average Annual Salaries	34.1	6.0
Police Patrolmen and Firefighters:		
Minimum Annual Salary Scales	45.9	7.8
Police Patrolmen	46.9	8.0
Firefighters	44.3	7.6
Maximum Annual Salary Scales	44.1	7.6
Police Patrolmen	44.8	7.7
Firefighters	43.0	7.4

Source: U.S. Department of Labor, Bureau of Labor Statistics; News Release, November 30, 1970, No. 359.

"Well, our firm evaluated the goals of all the local teachers. Seems they all have the same goal . . . to find a summer job."

CHAPTER IX

Related Topics

Can organizations have goals apart from the people within them? In other words, are school systems really entities with goals of their own, seperate and apart in some way from the persons who inhabit them? School system objectives are often formally set, but these are not necessarily the real goals of the organization. The latter must be associated with the management, which in turn is composed of persons who live in a social as well as an educational environment.

School systems are organizations made up of administrators, teachers, and other personnel working as a team, striving to achieve mutually attainable, agreed upon goals. These goals can be achieved more readily when the environment in which people interact is sensitive to the needs of the individual. "Human nature" is the only raw material that manpower management has to work with to produce job competence and job satisfaction - the two "end products" vital to management processes. Doctor Blai lists ten musts he feels should be followed if we are to build sound human relations in our system.

This chapter attempts to give its reader some of the effective processes within an organization which promote a warm and accepting relationships and an environment where management uses delegation and where people feel they are making sound useful contributions to fulfilling the goals of the organization. Through effective participation within the organization, a desire to work through successful motivation and the avoidance of promoting incompetents each individual will achieve personal and social needs.

MBO:
What's in it for the individual?

Ethan A. Winning

M any organizations that have introduced management by objectives (MBO) have assumed that achievement of objectives per se is motivation for the individual—but this assumption lies behind the failure of many MBO programs. An awkward number of individuals still ask, "What's in this for me?" For that reason, this writer believes that achievement of objectives is not a motivator unless it is linked to a reward system.

The rationale of organizations adopting MBO is this: Achievement is a motivator; meeting objectives is achievement; therefore, meeting objectives is a motivator—something satisfying to a person. The problem lies with the defining of achievement and motivation. In their dictionary of psychological and psychoanalytical terms, English and English define achievement as "success in bringing an effort to the desired end." In this case, who is stating what the *desired* end is? Usually, it is the organization; even when the individual has a say in the definition of the goal, it is external to that person. And achievement has quite a different base from motivation, which English and English describe as "the general name for the fact that an organism's acts are partly determined in direction and strength by its own nature . . . and/or internal state." What is motivating to an individual is, then, determined by the individual. What is achievement to an individual is shaped by external forces—the supervisor, the

Reprinted by permission of the publisher from PERSONNEL, Mar/Apr. 1974 © 1974 by AMACOM, a division of American Management Associations.

organization, for example. And how does the individual know he has achieved? He may have a *sense* of achievement, but it is the external reward for attaining the desired end that overtly tells him that others recognize his achievement—an essential condition to his internal motivation.

In other words, MBO without tangible rewards is MBO in a vacuum. Rewards are tangible referents by which the individual can measure whether or not, and how much, he has achieved, grown, and been recognized. Motivation depends on how well an individual's needs are met. If achievement is one of those needs, the individual *may* be motivated by his own sense of achievement, but if his sense of achievement depends on confirmation by the rewards he receives for meeting objectives, then he will need the rewards, both as confirmation and as a device to measure how well he has achieved.

What is needed is a greater incentive for the individual to set and meet objectives, to be fully involved in MBO as a *process*. MBO is usually thought of as a *program*, and a program has both beginning and end. The fact that most MBO programs do have an end—die a natural death—may point to the underlying flaw in hypotheses companies have about MBO and what the individual will attain from them. The incentive should meet the individual's needs, the driving forces that propel (motivate) an employee toward a goal that is most often self-centered, rather than company-oriented.

Because motivation is internal, it is difficult to ascertain, but achievement is external to the individual, and achievement can be measured. MBO is a system for measuring achievement, or at least it can be. By itself, it may satisfy only the organization's needs. It may aid in planning. It may help in assessing productivity, costs, overhead, and so on. If it doesn't satisfy individuals' needs, however, in the long run MBO won't work for the organization, either. MBO with a reward system is a viable approach to meeting corporate needs *and* individual needs, to meeting the terms of the company-employee "psychological contract."

In an MBO/Rewards system, what rewards?

There are, of course, a number of different incentive or reward plans, the success of which is dependent on the type of organization involved. One of these incentive systems, piecework or commission, predates MBO by several decades. Another, the bonus, goes at least as far back as Bob Cratchit's Christmas turkey. Last, we have a percentage system; it may be a percentage of salary increase based on productivity, or a percentage based on sales, or profits.

The idea behind piecework was to get the employee to produce more by paying him in terms of the number of items he produced. It is still a common practice, especially in textile, electronics, and other assembly line industries. The commission, one step above piecework, is usually paid in sales areas, the salesman reaping a percentage of the sales he has generated. One step further is, of course, salary-plus-commission. These three (two-and-a-half?) systems have one common underpinning: The individual is rewarded, or paid, according to his own productivity.

Is the piecework or commission system a good one? To the extent that both have at times excluded other motivational factors, no. To the extent that both place the responsibility for productivity on the individual, yes. The individual sets his own pace and in doing so has set certain objectives within corporate standards to be met. Both systems are MBO approaches without being labeled as such.

The bonus is probably the oldest form of incentive system, and is currently particularly popular at upper-management levels. The bonus is based on an individual's present salary, his status in the organization, his productivity, or the company's profit picture. It is an incentive, but it loses much of its motivational impact because it is too far separated in time from performance, or it may be given across-the-board without regard for individual productivity.

Moreover, its impact is limited; it does not reach far enough down into the organization to affect the middle- or lower-level employee. Thus, the lower-level employee who gets no bonus feels that he is doing the "real" work, while upper-management reaps a percentage of the profits the employee has been instrumental in attaining. If such is the case, why should the lower-level employee write objectives and try to meet them? He may do it because he has been told to, but he will really want to write and meet objectives only if there is something in it for him, a tangible reward when the goal has been reached.

If the bonus is given once a year, then how does one sustain the momentum to reach the desired goal? Perhaps the bonus will have to be a large one, or perhaps it should be given out several times a year—for instance, at the end of every objectives-review period. If a bonus system is used, it should be related to objectives and based on productivity. For that matter, all incentives should be based on productivity, or value to the company. If bonuses are handed out across-the-board, they will satisfy only a few, and may actually demotivate those who feel that they have been more productive than others who are receiving the same reward.

Some of the defects of a bonus system may be avoided in a percentage system, which, all in all, is probably the most palatable and most productive when combined with MBO. The percentage of salary (perhaps with an upper limit of 25 percent and a lower limit of 5 percent) would be entirely an individual matter. The employee's performance, and only his performance, would be the basis for such a reward. His performance would be measured by how well he met the objectives that he was committed to and had contracted for with his supervisor. Since objectives can be set for anyone at any level in the organization, all employees could benefit from such a program. Moreover, since a manager is supposed to be in control of his organization and his subordinates' reaching or not reaching their objectives will reflect on his abilities, it is a fair system to use in both the evaluation of the manager's performance and his reward.

A percentage increase of salary can be seen as a type of bonus, but it is more specific and does not have some of the drawbacks of other bonus systems. It is related only to the individual's performance and on what he has agreed to attain, and the distance-in-time objection can be eliminated if it is tied to fairly short-term objectives, if, for example, objectives are set on a quarterly basis, and percentage increases are given (or not given) at those intervals.

The problems of an MBO/Rewards system

There is no question that there are negative aspects in all incentive systems, and they are complicated by problems inherent in MBO. The first question that comes up is that of the negative incentive, the reduction in salary or the loss of bonus because the employee hasn't met objectives. In theory, if an employee is to be rewarded for meeting objectives, then there should be a reduction or withdrawal of the reward for not meeting them. In practice, though, the theory should probably be "bent," so that there is always some percentage increase of salary, perhaps a cost of living increase. If an employee does meet objectives and gets a 20 percent salary increase, the employee who does not meet his objectives should receive a minimal increase at least for his effort to meet objectives.

There are some who would go so far as to give an individual a decrease in salary depending on the degree to which objectives were missed, and in an "entrepreneurial" context, this might be acceptable: If the individual had total control over his environment, the staffing, the budget, and the way the organization operated, like the self-employed businessman, he should expect to reap the profits, but he should also expect to take any loss, too. Setting objectives is a tricky business, however. Control of conditions is difficult enough at upper levels and sometimes nonexistent at lower ones. There, aside from external determinants of productivity—the market, raw materials, and the like—much of an individual's achievement may be contingent on that of others inside his company. If a reduction in salary were to be imposed, in part because of factors he could not control, the employee's reaction to MBO/Rewards would become evident in a number of ways: He would set easily attainable goals; he would argue that *no* objective can be counted on as being attainable in present-day circumstances; he would set objectives having due dates months past the times when they can be achieved; he might reduce the number of his objectives; or he might just plain balk.

Overcoming the drawbacks in an MBO/Rewards system

Assuming that an MBO/Rewards system is decided on, how can these problems be solved? First, as is customary in MBO, objectives are set by the supervisor and employee together, to reflect the unit or corporate objectives. Ultimately, it's the boss's responsibility to see that objectives are reasonable and feasible, with dates that are neither too far off or too close, and that the number of objectives is realistic.

Second, the number of objectives, their timing, and their rationale should all be open to later negotiation and adjustment. Since it is difficult to fix objectives because of the control factor, the objectives should be flexible; the MBO process should allow for the changing of objectives when circumstances change beyond the employee's control.

Third, if the reward for performance is assured, the employee will probably want to achieve more than easy objectives. Of course, the supervisor or manager should not accept objectives that are "too easy," but he should not agree to too-difficult objectives, either.

To sum up, the points made here are these:

• MBO without an incentive program is a system without sound foundation.

• The individual is self-centered and needs a reward in order to meet management's expectations of him.

• There are three types of incentive systems that may work along with MBO and make MBO a stronger tool.

• The positive aspects of MBO/Rewards outweigh the negative.

• The negative aspects of MBO/Rewards can be handled.

A crucial step in the MBO process is the discussion between supervisory and subordinate in setting objectives, a discussion that should include both the definition of responsibilities and a definition of expectations. Expectations are more than objectives. They are statements of desired behavior of both supervisor and subordinate. While the supervisor has expectations of the employee in terms of productivity and performance, the employee has expectations of the supervisor in terms of directon, support, training, and so on. If he is to achieve objectives that are aligned with corporate or unit goals, then he must be given the opportunity to explain what he needs from his supervisor in order to meet those goals. And the expectation of the company that he will meet those goals will be considerably more realistic if the employee himself has the expectation of a tangible reward if he does meet them. "What's there in it for me?" is a very human question.

Delegation: Key to Involvement

Marion E. Haynes

WHEN you pick up a business oriented periodical today, you will probably be exposed to someone's urgent appeal for employee involvement. Much of the meaning has been taken out of jobs, according to observers of the business scene. Employee talents, skills and abilities lie fallow due to the constraints of the bureaucracy. Involvement in decision making is often proposed as a means of increasing both productivity and employee satisfaction.

How can such involvement be achieved? One way is through delegation. Delegation, as a principle of management, is still not used to its maximum by many managers. Why do they hesitate to use this proven tool? Some simply believe that the work won't be properly done unless they do it themselves. Others who are, or at least feel they are, less competent than some members of their staff fear the consequences of being out-performed. While it is necessary to recognize that these attitudes exist, they represent only a small portion of the total problem. There are many more reasons.

A manager may enjoy doing a task to the extent that he is reluctant to let someone else

PERSONNEL JOURNAL, June 1974, pp. 454-456.

handle it. This is especially true when he is promoted within the same department so that he is now expected to manage work he formerly performed. Some managers do not delegate because they don't fully understand their roles. A manager's superior may expect him to know every detail of a project, thereby making it difficult for him to delegate. Or his staff may resist accepting more responsibility because of their own insecurities or lack of motivation. Many managers who endorse delegation in principle do not delegate because they mistakenly believe it is an all-or-nothing arrangement.

DEGREES OF DELEGATION

There are degrees of delegation ranging from fact-finding to decision-making. As manager, you decide which degree is appropriate by considering the nature of the task, the ability of the person doing the work, the amount of top management interest, and the time available for task completion. W. H. Nesbitt of Westinghouse Electric Corporation* is credited with detailing these degrees of delegation:

1. *Investigate and report back.* You make the decision and take appropriate action.
2. *Investigate and recommend action.* You evaluate the recommendation, make the decision, and take action.
3. *Investigate and advise of action you intend to take.* You evaluate the decision made by your staff member and approve or disapprove.
4. *Investigate and take action; advise of action taken.* Here you display faith in

---

* **Harvey Sherman, "How Much Should You Delegate," *Supervisory Management*, October 1966.**

your staff's ability but want to be kept advised of what's going on.
5. *Investigate and take action.* This is full delegation and displays complete faith in your staff's ability.

Full delegation should be your goal in the delegation process. It means the staff member has been given an area of decision making and his decisions are accepted. To reach this level you must be willing to give up a portion of your authority. You must support decisions after they have been made whether you feel they are the best ones or not. You must be willing to gamble that your staff can do a better job when left on their own than when closely supervised. To play it safe and avoid risk by not delegating, merely makes your staff an extension of yourself rather than separate, complete individuals.

HOW TO DELEGATE

Delegation must be both personal and individual. As such, it depends to a large extent on the relationship between you and each member of your staff. However, there are some general guidelines to follow:

— Delegate by results expected, not by the method to be used in performing the task.
— Set performance standards to measure accomplishment against results.
— Give the staff member all of the relevant information you have about the task.
— Delegate only to qualified members of your staff. (This may mean that you will have to train some of your staff in preparation for further delegation.)
— Establish controls that will alert you to exceptions to normal operations.

IDENTIFYING WORK TO BE DELEGATED

The first thing to do, if interested in delegating more work, is to analyze your own involvement in the work of your department. In this analysis you should categorize all of the work you now perform into three groups:

1. Work which can only be done by you, the manager.
2. Work which can be delegated as soon as someone is trained to do it.

261

3. Work which can be delegated immediately.

Work which only you can perform includes your leadership role and your duties as coordinator. Other duties in this category are those which you may not be authorized to delegate, such as personnel and cash disbursement decisions. As far as possible, you should delegate all of the routine work of your job. As manager, you should confine yourself as much as possible to the unique action — to doing things the first time.

When you have identified work which can be delegated, but which no one is trained to perform, you have identified training needs to be accomplished by you or other appropriate people. Start immediately to provide the necessary training to prepare someone to take over these duties. Then proceed to delegate by degrees until full delegation has been achieved.

Work you are now performing which can be delegated immediately should be assigned to staff members in accordance with the currently appropriate degree of delegation. Then, as you acquire confidence in your staff's abilities, you can increase the delegation until you have accomplished as near complete delegation as possible.

EFFECTS OF DELEGATION

One of the most marked effects of delegation is the feeling of importance it gives staff members. When you give someone a job to do and let him make his own decisions as to how it should be done, you make it plain that he is capable and important. If, on the other hand, you expect him to come to you for each decision, it is apparent that you have very little faith in his ability. Giving your staff the authority to make their own decisions gives them a vested interest in the results produced.

There is no greater motivating force than to put someone in charge of a portion of the department's work, give him the authority to make decisions which spell success or failure and then reward him in terms of his accomplishment. An employee working for a manager who delegates as much as possible has an excellent opportunity to learn. Since it is an accepted fact that people learn by doing, the best way to prepare for a position that requires decision making is to have delegated responsibility for making decisions. This training can be instrumental in helping a person grow within the organization.

As manager you also receive benefits from delegating. The most obvious benefit is the time that is freed for managing — more time for planning the future of your department, coordinating the efforts of your staff, developing new and better techniques to do the work, and establishing better relationships with those you deal with in your day-to-day contacts. When your staff is properly trained and performing the duties assigned, you will have a well managed, smooth operation. What better recommendation could you receive for a more responsible managerial position than that you are an excellent manager who motivates his staff to peak performance?

Transactional Interviewing
Or, Who Does What to Whom?

(Continued from page 453)

one of preventing such situations from occurring, or if they occur, of helping the interviewee extricate himself as gracefully as possible.

Most people bring to a situation a fairly well-defined set of expectations. If you, by your respect, support and active encouragement, can help a person gain insight into himself and provide you with insight into his behavior rationale, then you have become a fine interviewer. Increased awareness of, and sensitivity to, the vital role you play in every personal transaction will hopefully improve your effectiveness as an interviewer, and as a person.

Some Basics of
Sound Human Relations

Boris Blai, Jr.

I T is "old hat" to note that the efficient and economical use of manpower, money, methods, and materials, are the shared responsibilities of all members of management. However, to place these varied responsibilities in proper perspective, what does bear repeating is the fact that achieving fully effective utilization of manpower resources is a capstone responsibility inherent in *all* aspects of management.

In manpower management, the "raw material" dealt with is human nature; the "end products" sought are job competence and job satisfaction. Today, it is generally accepted that job competence and job satisfaction go "hand-in-hand." And no longer is it a matter of debate that sound human relations make a major contribution to job satisfaction. Therefore, it is not simply an idle exercise to assess how well the "end products" are achieved, but rather, a vital dimension of the management process.

Knowing the following principles of sound human relations and practicing them is undoubtedly the best guarantee for creating and maintaining a healthy and productive work atmosphere, one in which cordial, sincere, and

PERSONNEL JOURNAL, Aug. 1973, pp. 710.-713.

cooperative human relationships exist:

1. WE RESENT DOMINATION

Most of us merely laugh at ineptness in high places, but one thing we apparently refuse to put up with in those high places is anyone using authority to push us around. Traditionally, we side with the underdog. As a result of this feeling, American workers welcome leadership, but bitterly buck bossism!

Ordinarily there are two major reasons why people work diligently. One is *fear*, the other is *respect*. Some supervisors, through indifference or lack of knowledge, resort to domination in order to get the work done. This is a method fraught with built-in problems, because today's workers will put forth their best efforts only if they respect the boss, and believe him to be a reasonable, fair and sincere person.

Criticisms and tongue-lashings lead to production inefficiencies mainly because they create resentment or emotional upset. Constructive corrections, offered by the so-called "sandwich method"—consisting of prefacing the correction with a pleasant remark and following it with a word of encouragement—avoid these abrasive implications of domination. The best method for solving problems of domination is to avoid them, and they may best be avoided simply by being tolerant of others.

Speaking of tongue-lashings brings to mind the story that is told of a Quaker matron who, while driving along in heavy traffic, was brushed by a truck. The truck driver leaped from his cab and reviled her for a full two minutes. She listened patiently until he finished, then quietly said, "When thee gets back to thy kennel, I hope thy mother bites thee!"

2. WE ENJOY A GOOD SCRAP

Each of us feels that he is just as good as every other person. If an individual with whom we deal indicates in any way that he thinks he is better than we are, you can bet we are ready to argue, and if necessary, to show him otherwise. On the other hand, we do find it difficult to fight with those we like.

3. WE AGREE MORE READILY WITH THOSE WE LIKE PERSONALLY

It is neither good human relations nor good management practice to antagonize the very people with whom we work. Whenever anyone "negotiates" by implying that the other party has all the characteristics of a child born out of wedlock, the method is virtually guaranteed to raise hackles and blood-pressure, but neither job satisfaction nor job performance!

The only sensible way to get along with people is to try to know and understand them. Being impersonal is probably the cardinal sin in dealing with people. The story is told of one labor leader who is reported to have said: "I'm glad the employers I deal with are coldly formal, because if I really knew them, I might like them—and I don't!"

4. WE ARE SENTIMENTALISTS

Our home is the pleasantest; *our* school the best; *our* children the most accomplished; *our* ball team the scrappiest. It really doesn't matter to us that perhaps none of these thing we believe to be true is actually so. But just let someone try to puncture one of our pet sentimental fantasies and immediately he becomes an enemy!

It cannot be over-stressed: never, but never, take pot shots at someone else's castles in the air, and certainly, the very least of all, at those of fellow employees!

5. WE ALL WANT TO FEEL IMPORTANT

Recognition and considerate treatment as individuals are as desirable to many people as financial advantage; to many they are of even greater importance. What each of us wants is acceptance as a person, a fellow human being. Equally true is the fact that lack of personal recognition is certain to embitter people. For many, if not most individuals, the greatest possible cruelty is to be ignored entirely, or to be treated simply as one of an anonymous group without individual identity.

We all want to be more than just a number. We want to be recognized by name, and dealt with as a specific person, with meaningful aspirations and feelings and problems. We want our opinions to be asked for and considered: not necessarily accepted, but at least considered. None of us like to be talked down to, for we would rather give than receive advice. And that "we" includes just about all of us: journeyman employees, supervisors, and executives alike!

6. WE ALL WANT TO BE "IN THE KNOW"

Closely allied with our desire to feel important, is the wish (a very powerful one) to be fully informed about whatever concerns us. In the past, many supervisors, and management executives as well, have failed to develop adequate means for passing along information of direct concern to their employees. A sound rule to follow in this key area of communications is "never overestimate the worker's knowledge, nor underestimate his intelligence."

Experience—some of it bitter—has shown time and time again that if correct (accurate) information is not available to employees, guesses and rumors will automatically fill the gap. It is characteristic of most people that we tend to think and act in accordance with the extent of identification which we find between our personal interests and those of the organization.

As employees, and in one way or another virtually all of us are employees, we like to be "in the know" as to where we stand, individually. We like to feel that we are making progress and if we are not, we want to know why and where we have failed.

7. WE LIKE TO WIN OUT OVER OBSTACLES

Usually we place little value upon that

which we easily get. Surely paternalism toward employees leaves much to be desired in the practice of human relations. We all want to feel that we are justly entitled to everything that we receive. Appeasement is an ugly practice, which leads only to contempt and disrespect on the part of those who have been on the receiving end.

8. WE ARE ALL DIFFERENT

All machines are alike in that if accurately fabricated and properly cared for, they have about the same potential capacity. But human beings have neither the same potential, nor the same actual capacities. Among psychologists and other behavorial scientists, this is labeled as the principle of individual differences. Of course, this simply means what all of us recognize to be a fact: everyone is simply different from everyone else. Yet, though we know this, many of us are inclined to assume that every normal worker is motivated by the same aims, desires, and values as our own. Many years ago, Samuel Butler offered an observation that was more accurate. He stated that there were two great rules of life: the one, general; the other, particular. The first rule is that everyone can, in the end, get what he wants if he only tries. This he offered as the "general" rule. The "particular" rule which Butler noted, is that every individual is more or less an *exception* to the "general" rule!

9. WE ALL WANT FAIR PLAY

If employees, who are, after all, just a lot of people like you and me trying to get along in the world, are treated honestly and fairly, "healthy" human relations leading to job satisfaction and job competence are not that difficult to attain. When given a chance to thoroughly understand a situation, people aren't inherently unfair, nor are they particularly unreasonable.

10. WE SHOULD PROCEED GRADUALLY

Most people resent being rushed. It was some 600 years before men were willing to admit that there was any other way to take off a shirt than by pulling it over one's head (honestly, that's a fact.)

It is a virtual certainty that when anyone is too anxious to have his ideas accepted, he creates his own resistance by "rushing" people. Proper timing is always important in human relations matters. In fact, most people are pretty much like the fellow with a toothache who asked the dentist how much it would cost to have a tooth pulled. "Ten dollars" was the reply. "Ten dollars," he exclaimed, "Just for a few minutes work?" "Well," said the dentist, "If it will make you happier, I'll pull it slowly."

In summary, to create—or maintain—a satisfied and productive work force, there are ten musts to be followed in building sound human relations.

1. Speak to People. There is nothing so nice as a cheerful word of greeting.
2. Smile at People. It takes 72 muscles to frown—only 14 to smile.
3. Call People by Name. The sweetest music to anyone's ears is the sound of his own name.
4. Be friendly. If you would have friends —be friendly.
5. Be Sincerely Cordial. Speak and act as if it were a genuine pleasure.
6. Be Considerate of the Feeling of Others. Nobody likes to be rebuffed.
7. Be Thoughtful of the Opinion of Others. There are three sides to a controversy: yours—the other fellow's—and the "right" side.
8. Be Genuinely Interested in People. If you are willing to try, you can like anybody.
9. Be Generous with Praise—Cautious with Criticism. As they say—"You can catch more flies with honey than with vinegar."
10. Be Willing to Give Service. About all that *really* counts in life is what we do for others.

Peter's Principle and the proximity illusion

By Macon Wilbourn

The Peter Principle is passé. Sufficient time has elapsed to permit ingestion of Dr. Peter's unique contribution into the overall body of modern management thought. A tandem offering, *Peter's Prescriptions,* is currently a best seller, and the principle itself has become a colorful addition to management jargon. But what is to follow in the wake of this popular work?

Both academicians and the general public humorously debate the ramifications of *The Peter Principle* with benign dilettantism. The mainstream of management thought concurrently moves to embrace such resolute expanses as decision theory, systems, and organization development. *The Peter Principle* has, however, caused organization theorists as well as the individual within the organization to take a jaundiced look at the interworkings of the system. For this alone, Dr. Peter and Mr. Hull deserve lasting recognition.

Of perhaps even more importance in the long-run is the possibility of an exciting new dimension in organization theory scarcely tapped by *The Peter Principle.* This article is presented in the spirit of that new dimension.

Dr. Peter has stated that "... in a hierarchy every employee tends to rise to his level of incompetence." Logic dictates that through seniority privileges, luck, or outright merit itself, the individual would "tend" to rise in the organization. Concurrently, every individual has his personal level of incompetence — physical, mental, social, sexual, etc. — which may or may not be attained within a lifetime. Thus every employee "tends" to rise toward his level of incompetence.

Emphasis is placed on the verb "tends," with the implication that prudent individuals need not necessarily suffer the fate of becoming incompetent or of reaching what Dr. Peter calls "final placement." Accepting the "givens," the principle is logically valid, but it unfortunately denotes nothing more than an implicit truism with both humorous and somewhat disturbing connotations.

Stymied progression

According to Dr. Peter, a judgment of "incompetent" assures termination of the subject's advancement up the organizational hierarchy. Further progression is forever stymied. *Caveat lector!* This may be only the beginning. The superior himself may be an incompetent judge of the subordinate's performance, and probably graded him on

THE PERSONNEL ADMINISTRATOR, May/June 1973, pp. 15-16.

unrelated variables anyway.

Such incompetent appraisals — through professional or technical inability or insufficient data — may allow an individual to actually rise *above* his level of incompetence when rational standards are used as a gauge. The resulting dysfunctional effects on the organization, and the drag on society, may far surpass in magnitude what the casual student of *The Peter Principle* originally perceives.

Consider, for example, the aspiring executive who rises to a particular position of leadership in the organization. In such a position, he manages a large bureaucratic division in which he has neither the leadership ability, technical competence, nor problem-solving skill to perform effectively. Advancement to this position should conclude his organizational climb.

Meanwhile, the bureaucracy — with some competent members — muddles along clumsily solving problems and haphazardly bungling the job. Will the incompetent manager ever receive another promotion? Possibly. If his superior is an incapable judge of achievement, or if the wrong characteristics are considered, very possibly. If the superior *wants* to grant the promotion, rationalization frequently insures that he will.

To insure promotion above his level of incompetence, the executive must possess a certain characteristic. Statesmen might call it "political awareness," while marketing theoreticians would refer to it as "salesmanship." In the blue-collar vernacular the characteristic is known as "clout," but to Dr. Peter it is simply "pull."

With the above example illustrating a common form of promotion above incompetence, how may the problems resulting from pull be avoided? Obviously, the first step is that of recognition. This prefatory stage is precluded by a common but rarely discussed phenomenon which we shall henceforth refer to as the *proximity illusion.*

Faulty logic

The Proximity Illusion is nothing more than faulty logic resulting from close association. The reality of a situation becomes clouded by personal feelings and opinions concerning unrelated variables. A dog, for example, is faithful to an unpropitious master because of prior association. In politics, the old adage that "it is better to be disliked than to be unknown" derives from the proximity illusion — the idea being that it is easier to change the electorate's mind about a familiar candidate than to promote one who is unfamiliar.

Military officers recognize the career advantages implicit in a staff position under the observing eye of the commanding officer. Such close proximity insures being noticed — the prerequisite for all promotions. In any organization, those with favorable proximity to the superior are normally the first to be promoted.

The proximity illusion habitually induces the familiar "gut" feeling about an individual's ability. Gut feelings are usually just that; logic stems from higher places. And yet this faulty logic — resulting from the proximity illusion — is the basis for many promotions in the organization.

Selections are often justified on the basis of the selectee's prior experience. But experience *alone* is useless. Merely being associated

268

with a task, or occupying a management position throughout the duration of a particular project, guarantees nothing. To judge performance by such variables is to focus on the process, not upon the accomplishment of measurable objectives.

If organizations are to avoid promoting incompetents, the proximity illusion must be recognized and guarded against. Realistic performance standards must be carefully applied to accommodate specific tasks. The entire management process must be attuned to the accomplishment of specified objectives. And above all, the focus must always be on objectives and not on the mere *process* that is inherent in any task or function.   **end**

New perspectives on the will to work

By Frederick I. Herzberg

THE PROBLEM IS work motivation — all over the world. It's simply a matter of people not wanting to work. This is a very serious problem because we can no longer rely on our resources, we have to rely on our potentials.

Today we are seeing three managerial systems — three philosophies — that underline our organizations.

Taylorism

The first is scientific management — Taylorism. Under the Tayloristic concept, we have the idea that people are functions, not human beings.

This worked very successfully. Taylorism reduced everyone down to the lowest common denominator. It meant training costs and material costs were reduced. When Henry Ford set up the assembly line he had tremendous turnover, but he said if he could train them in two hours, he could pay them $5.00 a day. There was another bonus — he could get away with cheap management. He didn't need managers but rather checkers.

He gave managers titles rather than functions or responsibilities. The unions bought this method because it created a homogeneity in the constituency represented. It is much easier to represent a very homogeneous group than to represent people with differentials, so both management and labor profited. The unions could offer very simple, easily understood, numerically designated criteria for any differential — seniority.

This is very efficient. It was so efficient that two years ago we produced 10 million cars in the U.S. and called back 13 million.

When people say that they will not tolerate buying waste and junk, then Taylorism is no longer efficient. Taylorism is out as a managerial philosophy.

Ideologically-based

On the ideologically-based system — if we have common goals and beliefs and values, then the natural process would emerge to run an efficient, harmonious sort of nation. In some ways, this has been one of the most tragic busts of the 20th century. Certainly nationalized industry has its problems for motivation: Sweden nationalized the mines and had one

THE PERSONNEL ADMINISTRATOR, July/Aug. 1974, pp. 21-25.

of the biggest strikes in history. The decentralized system of Yugoslavia with its works council had major problems. The most magnificent of all that we know is Israel, an ideologically-based system; truly grandiose and successful in its application with only three percent of the population producing the greater part of the GNP particulary in agriculture. They've done this by clearing the farms with a very healthy youth with no drug problems. They provided all their growth with political and military leadership without violation of any humanistic principles, respecting human dignity and freedom.

What has happened there? If you go back to their beginnings, their people came from all over the world, from all walks of life. They came with three ideological goals: first, to create the Zionist state; second, to create a socialist society; and third, to create a Jewish farm proletariat population.

All were completely equal — the doctor, the lawyer, the shoe cobbler and the common laborer. The work assignments were the same; and they were all equal — equally ignorant. The doctor knew little about running the dairy herd and the orange grove. The communal family farms, over the years, were turned into factories of the field.

Let's see what happens. The Ph.D. in animal husbandry who should be running the dairy farm agreed to wash dishes and clean floors. The common laborer knew nothing about running the farm, and so on throughout the land. It is extremely important to remember as we get into the democratization techniques, there is one equality — an equality of ignorance — which is the reason most ideologically-based systems fail.

American system

The third system is the American system. We reverse the plan when we face a central problem by developing know-how. When it came to the handling of the management of people, we said that is not a value problem, that's a technological problem. So, we developed a human relations problem. We started with Dale Carnegie courses and escalated them up to sensitivity training, encounter therapy, transactional analysis and all the rest.

I'm afraid human relations technology is failing because it's become text book stuff. We have, therefore, said, "I am a function." People are no longer moved by an ideology or a slogan and people have learned very quickly that what we considered human relations has been merely manipulation.

What is being sought is a new ideological base for organizations. As I go around the world, I see several basic, important things taking place. The most fundamental is the change in the central existential question which has gone so rapidly from "What is the meaning of the past? The meaning of traditions? The meaning of death?" to "What is the meaning of the present? The future in life?" "What kind of life am I leading?" rather than "What kind of traditions can I call on?"

This has led to the end of the immigrant labor philosophy. Immigrant labor was essentially concerned about three things: propelled by security, hoping for some security and "my son, the doctor" routine — my children will make it. He performed "Mickey Mouse" work and he could care less what he did as long as it provided the three basic needs. He had, however, the psychological benefit of his ethnic, political, religious, social and family traditions.

Well, the kids come off the Lordstown jobs and those traditions no longer are meaningful. So they have no psychic income from work. That is the end of obligation. "If my life is important — the meaning of my life — rather than the meaning of my traditions becomes important — then I am no longer willing to diminish my life." Viet Nam brought the same response; no military traditions are important. It's the end of the military obligation of serving our country. The women's "lib" movement is what? "The end of obligation to diminish my life because of male traditions."

The blacks — the natural athletes — failing to recognize that they historically came up through the entertainment industry, end an obligation. This is the end of obligation, similarly, to the church for the rebel priest movement. In the Soviet, it is the end of the obligation to the tradition of communism for no society can get along without a set of mutual obligations because that's exactly what society is.

We have gone through a period since World War II when we deprived people from meaningful work, when it became an instrumental act in order to get a car, a house or a boat — leisure. And as we diminished the meaning of work and robbed it of some of its significance, then, of course, we tried to make it up outside of work. We couldn't make it up with tradition, so we tried with other aspects and overloaded leisure. We no longer enjoy leisure, we consume it.

We've overloaded interpersonal relationships. A wife is bored. The husband is bored with work. They overload each other. They seek more than they can get from each other. We've even overloaded sex. We've run out of perversions.

In this attempt to find a new managerial philosophy, there are a number of approaches that have taken place to get people activated — motivated to work.

When Zorba the Greek was asked if he had a wife, he answered, "A wife, children, a house, the whole catastrophe." Some organizations feel the same way about behavioral scientists — that they too have had the whole catastrophe. Managers are beginning to accept the basic theory behind job enrichment for an understanding of human behavior. The behavioral scientists have already jumped on the bandwagon offered on even but shallow understanding. The result is that job enrichment has come to represent many approaches intended to increase human satisfaction in performance at work. The original meaning, the installation of motivated factors into an individual job, are not diverted.

Four approaches

Now there are four approaches to job enrichment that I see. The first I call "orthodox job enrichment". Here is the usual hierarchy in which the workers do the job and the managers do the planning, the functioning and the motivating of people. In this orthodox plan, we try to bring the job module up, to give the worker a more longitudinal grasp of work — an enriched job module.

The second approach is the socio-technical systems. Lower organizational levels have received heavy applications of scientific management. These modern work processes made up of a cycle of interdependent component tasks are seen by social-technical theorists as not allowing worker interrelationships to develop. Consequently, the answers to worker dissatisfactions seem to be in the redevelopment of interdependent relationships within a work group. The social-technical approach (work through either inter-worker social relationships by establishing semi autonomous work groups) within a job, work rotation or enlargement provides more variety of tasks and gives individuals a larger picture of the whole concept.

The actual worker-task relationship is due to and is often determined by the technology involved. Thus, a social/technical approach attempts to compensate for the deficient worker-task relationships by suggesting that a worker can attain a sense of personal worth and achievement from the achievements of the group and the social relationships within that group.

We can call this the enriched group module.

The third contemporary approach to improve work is participative management. It is really an outgrowth of the human relations movement. The assumption is that the over-riding need of the worker is to be involved in decisions affecting his work. The primary need for personal involvement can be obtained through worker participation and will provide the commitment necessary to motivate him.

Thus, giving the worker more meaningful job content, the need is secondary to the legitimate need for being consulted and involved in aspects of decisions which affect him. Naturally, some decisions in which he participates will concern the job content and only in these cases can concrete job design changes fall out of participation. Most often, however, the manager is in effect saying to the subordinate, "If you don't have a responsible, meaningful job, I'll let you visit my job, but you'll have to return to your own."

Participation is sometimes held to be an alternative form of consultation. Instead of passing responsibility down the line and possibly losing control, the manager can consult his subordinates before making a decision. Involvement — making him feel part of the team — it all seems to be a matter of degree, after all. Participation in this sense of consultation is seen as a safe "half-way" house to job enrichment, improved production and to satisfying to parties concerned. For the difference between consultation and enrichment is a difference in kind. Counsultation does not give the subordinate a chance at achievement which he can recognize as his own. Participative management suddenly denies him the exercise of responsibility which would lead him to his own development.

The next approach is called industrial democracy, a European-based philosophy. Advocates contend that with most institutions operating in a democratic matter, the institution of work should similarly operate in a democratic manner. To maintain democracy at work, it is necessary to initiate programs where workers are represented in all the decision-making organizations within the organization. A major assumption is that when workers are given a representative voice in making a decision about operating the organization, they will be more committed to its democratically developed goals. At the individual job levels, no redesign or enrichment is included in the philosophy, but management does admit that some types of changes are needed and, in fact, says to the worker, "If you will visit me outside the hierarchy, we can discuss it."

The follow-up of these visits can be job redesign typically in the form of socio/technical groups. This approach may respect that work ought to be improved for the congruence of civil, social and work. But in actual practice, the management/worker consultation system has proved to be a complex and time-consuming method of attempting organizational improvement. While this approach has some merit for widening democratic institutions, its slow political involvement to job redesign relegates it to secondary consideration.

A fifth approach is encompassed around the term "organizational development" or "O.D.". Frankly, I am not sure what O.D. is, and many of its practitioners aren't sure either. O.D. views the lack of effectiveness in today's organizations as the result of inefficient human processes, communication, decision-making, collaboration for problem solving, conflict-management and others. O.D. consultants observe individuals, group process behavior, organizations and help managers support and diagnose behavior in effective ways. The change agent then attempts to educate individuals and groups in the use of effective behavior skills such as risk taking, interpersonal and open communication, feedback, owning up to one's behavior, participative leadership styles and confronting conflicts.

This is done in the various kinds of training programs and group meeting strategies. Typically, the change agent, models, the effective behavior, helps to establish behavior skills as group norms in the organization. Hopefully, these strategies will result in a reorientation of basic values to a more humanistic view of man. These changes, in turn, will facilitate organizational processes and better organizational performance.

Obviously, there are many variables involved in organizational processes, one of which is the behavioral skills of individuals. A program aimed in this direction is a valid need in many organizations. My only belief is that poor job designs are responsible not only for a majority of motivational problems in organizations, but for many of the interpersonal processing problems as well. If this is true, much organizational developing and consulting could be more correctly labeled as merely treating the symptoms of fractionated jobs.

But, even if one accepts the operational O.D. assumption that most organizational problems are those of interpersonal behavior, such behavior is very complex, often involving an ethical problem.

One of the things the kids taught us in the revolutions of the 60s before they copped out was the distinction between morality and ethics.

The revolution they created was the opening up of the pluralism of taste. "What kind of clothes do you wear?" "How do you fix your hair?" "What kind of women do you like?" "Men?"

Let's get back to ethics. The counter attack on the kids was preaching morality and everytime you preach morality, you do it at the expense of hiding behind ethical behavior. This is the Watergate. The administration preached morality and forgot ethics. And, most of the problems that I see in organizations that are using therapeutic process of O.D. or one or more of the processes is not a problem of personality — it's a problem of ethics.

What companies can use is a better course in ethics rather than in human relations training.

There are also problems in differential ability, problems in structural situations that create interpersonal problems and, finally, there is the problem of the lack of behavioral skills involved in the interaction. Ethics means human fairness. There is a certain ethical relationship between people that has nothing to do with skills. For example, if I leave my wallet in your presence and don't expect you to take money out, that is an ethical function. But, if I use the wallet to manipulate your trust, I have resorted to an interpersonal ruse that will lead you to develop a counter-skill to handle my manipulation.

O.D. approaches the ethical issue by its emphasis on humanistic values. It's very easy for people to learn and use behavioral skills in order to preserve poor ethics or values. Without ethics as the basis of behavioral skills, the result will be much higher levels of manipulation. Secondly, differentials of ability partly determine interpersonal relationships. People protect against their own incompetence.

For example, another person is an expert on a certain subject, and I am not. Our interaction is limited by our knowledge or lack of it. By the simple fact that I am not certain of the ability for certain forms of interactions, here my non-ability acts as a constraint on the interpersonal relationship.

Next, interpersonal problems arise by suggestion from the work structure attempts to change people's job behavior, apart from the job's content, have been in the main unsuccessful in the past. If a checker in a production process with a given skill needs to interact with production workers, nothing can actually change. The situation is one where the checker role is determined by the design of the two interacting jobs; it is not significantly affected by additional behavioral skills.

There are some situations where communications, risk-taking, and other behavioral skills are very important and I am not de-emphasizing the need for more legitimate work in these areas, but all behavioral skills may account for only a small percentage of the interpersonal problems in organizations today.

For organizations to overemphasize interpersonal process aspects at the expense of attending to job redesign — effective selection, placement, technical training — is unwise. It will not resolve in the desperate improvement needed today. All of these approaches have their own unique emphasis that is orthodox. All are subject to distortion and misuse. And each of these techniques is more relevant to some situations than to others. There is massive confusion existing today among these approaches. My research and study has led me to believe that orthodox job enrichment is the most promising of all the organizational improvement strategies. For many other consultants and managers emphasize one or more of the other approaches.

Hopefully, we will proceed without the expectations of panaceas and will learn to improve our management abilities. For the managers who are faced with the confusion of "What do I do?" "Who do I rely on to bring about needed organization changes?", I would like to recommend a new intervention — use the behavioral scientist. He knows about the organization's human resource problems in an intellectual sense. But, he hasn't seen the concrete change in jobs — he knows nothing of the history of the job.

When Zorba the Greek was asked where his practical wisdom came from, he always answered that, "A wise old Turk told me." There are many "wise old Turks" in companies that know the history of the numerous jobs concretely and visually and experiencially.

Many have come through the ranks and experienced the various levels of the organization. They know what boredom is — often the result of changes that have been made in the past in the name of efficiency. Behavioral scientists or a manager wishing to enrich a job can start by finding him and asking him, "What are some of the past changes of the job made in the name of efficiency that should be eliminated?"

The first test of job enrichment in an organization is to find "a wise Turk" — one that really knows the score. He's already on the payroll, and he'll quickly tell you: "Hell, that's the way we used to do it!" □